Bennett
AND THE
Pathfinders

Bennett
AND THE
Pathfinders

JOHN MAYNARD

ARMS AND
ARMOUR

Dedication

TO MY WIFE, MARGUERITE

for her enthusiasm which inspired me to write, her loving
encouragement which spurred me on, and her long hours of
typing whch made everything possible. I am deeply grateful for
her gentle tolerance of my obsession with British aviation!

Arms and Armour Press
An Imprint of the Cassell Group
Wellington House, 125 Strand, London WC2R 0BB

Distributed in the USA by Sterling Publishing Co. Inc.,
387 Park Avenue South, New York, NY 10016-8810.

Distributed in Australia by Capricorn Link (Australia) Pty. Ltd,
2/13 Carrington Road, Castle Hill, NSW 2154.

British Library Cataloguing-in-Publication Data:
a catalogue record for this book is available from the British Library

ISBN 1-85409-258-8

Designed and edited by DAG Publications Ltd.
Designed by David Gibbons; edited by Jonathan Falconer;
printed and bound in Great Britain.

CONTENTS

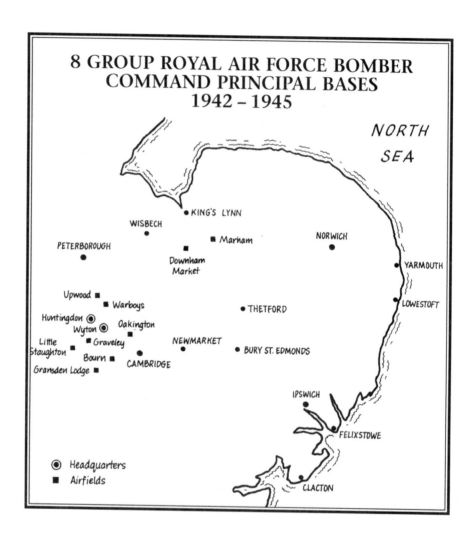

8 GROUP ROYAL AIR FORCE BOMBER COMMAND PRINCIPAL BASES 1942 – 1945

NORTH SEA

KING'S LYNN

WISBECH

PETERBOROUGH

Marham

Downham Market

NORWICH

YARMOUTH

Upwood

Warboys

Huntingdon

Wyton Oakington

Little Staughton

Graveley

Bourn

Gransden Lodge

CAMBRIDGE

NEWMARKET

THETFORD

LOWESTOFT

BURY ST. EDMONDS

IPSWICH

FELIXSTOWE

CLACTON

Headquarters

Airfields

ACKNOWLEDGEMENTS

I witnessed a little of the Luftwaffe's night blitz on Southampton in the winter of 1940 as a frightened nine-year-old, watching from my bedroom window in our home in the Hampshire countryside. I can still recall the flares and the hunting searchlights, the bursts of gunfire, and the strange tearing noise of exploding bombs. Most of all I remember the cloud base stained red by the burning city. Three years later, away at school, I lay awake listening to the nightly triumph of mighty engines as the aircraft of Bomber Command set out for Germany and the growing realisation of victory. At the time I had a simple unqualified admiration for their young and courageous crews and for all that they were doing and this emotion has, if anything, grown over the years. Also, I now recognised the dogged persistence and single-mindedness of those who directed the British bombing offensive and the ingenuity of engineers and scientists who provided the RAF with its awe-inspiring means of waging war. The defeat of Nazi Germany is the true measure of their signal achievement. When a measured chronicle of the 20th century is eventually written, Bomber Command will take its place in history alongside Nelson's fleet and the armies of Marlborough and of Wellington, as great victors in the cause of Britain and the good of mankind.

In the past 40 years I have met a great number of men who served as aircrew in Bomber Command. Now, of course, the survivors are old but all have retained a proud, confident serenity that seems to set them apart and touch them with a particular distinction. Their pride, I believe, comes from the memory of comrades and commanders, their confidence from having survived the unsurvivable, whilst their serenity is born of the utter justice and justification of all that they did.

My thanks are due to a score of people for their help to me in the researching and the writing of this book. In particular I single out Ly Bennett, Don Bennett's widow, whose reflections, help and interest made my task so much easier and enjoyable. Next I must thank that

7

irrepressible enthusiast Group Captain Hamish Mahaddie, who typically responded to all my requests for information, discussion, or introductions almost before I had made them! He took me with him to several events where Pathfinders were gathered and made sure that I met so many gentlemen with so much to tell. Most notable of all such occasions was the Pathfinder VE-Day reunion in the City of London which was, to me, an infinitely moving occasion. Hamish did all this for me despite the developing personal tragedy of his wife's last illness.

Air Vice-Marshal Michael Hedgeland read my draft and corrected many of my misunderstandings over the development of bombing radars. I owe a great debt to him and also to Alan Vial who flew as a Pathfinder and whose combination of praise and pungent comment on my manuscript was both helpful and tremendously encouraging! There were many others who contributed their thoughts, experiences and indeed their log books, to give added dimension to this heroic story of a man and the Force which will forever be associated with his name.

Finally, I owe a great debt to the Archive Staff of the RAF Museum, to the Bomber Command Association, and to the editor and staff of *Aeroplane Monthly*, all of whom were unstinting in their help, guidance and encouragement.

John Maynard
West Malling
January 1996

FOREWORD
by Group Captain Hamish Mahaddie
DSO, DFC, AFC & Bar, CzMC, CEng, FRAeS, RAF (Retd)

I have always considered myself something of an insider on matters concerning the establishment of the Pathfinders and relating to that force's great contribution to the success of Bomber Command's offensive against Germany. Don Bennett and I were of much the same age and I was privileged to serve him and to know him well for almost three years between 1942 and 1945. I am now fascinated to read the results of John Maynard's researches at the RAF Museum during which he has had access to Sir Arthur Harris's files and papers.

The early attacks led by the PFF gave, I remember, much pleasure to Don Bennett's critics. The Flensburg raid should never have been mounted, the weather was impossible and the whole operation was a waste of time. A little later I suppose I was as responsible as anyone with my crew for the mis-marking of Saarlouis instead of Saarbrücken and the subsequent bombing débâcle. We had illuminated a loop in the Rhine within which we thought the target conveniently lay, but unfortunately we picked the wrong loop! I am pleased to read that Bert Harris was fairly philosophical about the error, but my recollection of Bennett's inquiry at Oakington the next day was not so happy. I am sure that I was extremely lucky to remain a Pathfinder!

The author affirms that Don Bennett was above all a great professional. When one considers that at the time of his appointment to command PFF he was only 32 years old the full measure of his reputation and achievements becomes apparent. By 1942 he was already a veteran of more pioneering aviation and action against the enemy than most of us managed to pack into a full career. That is what gave him the edge over the other AOCs and we all suspected that he managed to keep his operational experience 'fresh'.

I cannot understand why he should have written to the C-in-C asking for permission to 'commentate' on a raid as Master Bomber, or to accompany other attacks to see how techniques were developing in practice. He must have known he would be refused, but he kept on flying his unmarked Beaufighter or Mosquito, vanishing into the night and turning up at subsequent debriefings remarkably well informed! I used to accompany him on more peaceful missions round the airfields in the headquarters Proctor and was always full of admiration for his ability to grasp and retain detail, and for the clarity of his thinking. He certainly had a chilling and abrasive side to his character and was infinitely demanding, but I must say that I have never understood his oft quoted prediction that PFF would end the war with 'only posthumous VCs'. That certainly is the way it turned out, but long ago I compiled a list of some 10 survivors who certainly deserved this high award.

I have always regretted that we did not have a public relations man in PFF, but Bennett would never appoint one, I suspect because he thought such a job frivolous. But Cochrane had a particularly good ex-journalist at his 5 Group headquarters who brought to life many of the exploits of his squadrons for study by post-war generations. I am sad about the lingering resentment amongst some wartime senior officers that the formation of PFF should have become essential to Bomber Command. Certainly a subtle pressure on Harris was maintained by some of them amongst all the other lobbying that the C-in-C had to tolerate! The transfer of one Mosquito and two Lancaster squadrons from PFF to 5 Group was a manifestation of the results of this pressure which spoke volumes on Cochrane's powers of persuasion, but did little or nothing for the war effort. A lesser man than Bennett would have found it too much to take such an insult. No 5 Group did not require the squadrons, it was indeed simply a case of Cochrane shouting loudest!

John Maynard has spent very many hours on his study of the correspondence between Portal, Harris, Bennett and others. I was amused that he found occasional reference to my so-called 'horse trading' or 'thieving' around the groups to get the best crews for pathfinding. The AOCs of 4 Group and the Royal Canadian Air Force 6 Group were very co-operative, but I must say that I got little help from the rest, at least at senior level. The SASOs, most of whom were ex-operating squadron commanders, were much more helpful and understanding! I remember too the storm in a teacup over Don Bennett's uncompromising attitude over sending people on courses. He claimed, with some justification, that anything other than bombing Germany was a waste of time and adequate training could be given on the job, or on an ad hoc spare time basis. That said, I managed a wartime CFS course before I took command of Warboys, otherwise I was on the sidelines in this

particularly heated exchange of opinion between Don Bennett and the
C-in-C.

I feel privileged now to learn of my AOC's uncompromising pursuit
of our interests which were of course to the benefit of Bomber Command as a whole, even if some people had difficulty in coming to terms
with this. It is fascinating to read some of the letters he wrote and to
have this further insight, both of a great commander and of the technique of war, with which he is so rightly identified. He was fearless in
his pursuit of what he believed to be right and his judgement in this
regard was usually impeccable. His sometimes outspoken comments
and relentless appreciations serve to underline the quality of the man
and I hope that John Maynard's book will preserve this aspect for pos-
terity. For me it serves to confirm, 50 years on, what we of PFF believed
all the time, that our greatest good fortune was to serve under Don Bennett. It was the time of my life, and this book captures it with the addition of some fascinating background detail.

Hamish Mahaddie
Bognor Regis
January 1996

PROLOGUE

T his is the story of a vital process of refinement which transformed a strategy of war from an almost symbolic irritation of a formidable enemy into a massive onslaught which destroyed his industry, sapped his vitality, and eroded his will to fight.

The strategy embraced the aerial bombardment of Nazi Germany by night and was sustained in an escalating campaign which lasted for most of the Second World War. For well over four years following Hitler's conquest of Western Europe in the early summer of 1940, the bombing offensive represented the only means by which the Allies could take the war to the enemy's heartland. Without this offensive Germany could have prospered, immensely strong and secure behind the defensive insulation of the occupied lands which surrounded her. Her citizens could have enjoyed the benefits of virtually undisturbed peace, their belief in the demoniac regime that governed them unshaken. Meanwhile that same regime would have felt unopposed in the pursuit of its ideological obscenities and in stripping the wealth, resources, and manpower from its defeated neighbours. Hitler's domination of Europe and his ambition to bring the world to his feet would have faced no obvious or immediate challenge to realisation.

The British resources committed to the bomber offensive were historically prodigious. In England's eastern counties, which became known with great justification as 'Bomber Country', there were some 50 fully operational bases. This number takes no account of the operational training units (OTU), the heavy conversion units (HCU), or of bases occupied by other vital components of Bomber Command. At one stage in 1942 at the very height of the construction programme, a new airfield was being opened almost weekly at the end of an average building time which amounted to only some 18 months. The massive paved runways, perimeter roads, and dispersals alone would occupy over one-third of this time, with the excavation of their foundations and the pouring of oceans of concrete. This immense effort was sustained in the main by manpower; great bands of men, perhaps reminiscent of the early days of railway building, were largely unassisted by the mechanical graders and earth movers of later years. In all, the civil engineering workforce contributed a total of 127,000 men to airfield construction. This was at a time when the total available building manpower nationwide of about a quarter-of-a-million was already stretched in erecting other military installations and the rudimentary repair of bomb damage. On top of this its fittest workers were frequently lured away to military service, perceived as a more heroic, if less well paid, way of life!

The manufacture of aircraft for the great offensive, the heavy night bombers, required the commitment of labour, finance, and purely material resources which amounted to nothing less than a miracle of sustained industrial endeavour. The aircraft industry became the darling of the war effort and, with the defensive line threatened in the Battle of Britain now much more securely in place, it was the output of bombers which inspired and gladdened the nation. Even the popular anecdotes of pampered, over-paid and strike-prone aircraft workers could not detract from the delight to be had in squadrons of excellent and, hopefully, invincible heavy bombers available to reduce Germany to ashes. Rates of production were generally admirable, and despite the occasional costly errors which allowed the manufacture of indifferent or unsuitable aircraft types, the industry did all that was required of it. Its successes were noteworthy, especially bearing in mind the vast gulf in terms of size, complexity and performance which separated the second generation of wartime bombers from those in production a mere six or seven years before.

The Avro Lancaster is perhaps the best example of this. It was a daunting weapon: its range, bomb load and general performance outstripped any other type, friendly or enemy, until the entry of the American Boeing B-29 Superfortress in to service in June 1944 (although the B-29 did not see wartime service in North West Europe). The overall Lancaster production programme including the Rolls-Royce Merlin engines, variable pitch fully-feathering propellers, electrical, hydraulic and pneumatic systems, gun turrets and armament, plus all the associated radio and radar equipment, would ultimately involve the full- or part-time efforts of well over one million men and women nationwide. In August 1944 a peak production rate was reached when 293 of the aircraft were delivered to Bomber Command in one month. A grand total of 7,374 of these superb machines was eventually built, but even this number was just the summit of a massive effort of aircraft construction.

Six other principal types of night bomber were flown against Germany together with a number of less significant, or less successful designs, some of American origin. In the big league, the so-called heavies, over 6,000 Handley Page Halifaxes and 2,000 Short Stirlings were built, the latter being an intermediate design bridging mid- and late-1930s technologies. Leading the medium bomber output, Vickers Armstrong and their sub-contractors made 11,400 Wellingtons. This aircraft, which made use of Barnes Wallis's inspired and strong geodetic structure, was by far the most used and most versatile of Bomber Command's early wartime equipment. In service alongside the Wellington were Handley Page's Hampden and the Armstrong Whitworth Whitley. Over 1,250 of the former were made but it was an unorthodox aircraft of limited bomb-carrying capacity, whilst the Whitley was conventional to the point of obsolescence, a lumbering cart-horse of an aeroplane which nevertheless pioneered the early night attacks on Germany; 800 of the latter had been made when production ceased in 1943. Finally, there was the de Havilland Mosquito, in many ways the shape of things to come and of future tactical thinking. Fast and small with a crew of two and an impressive range, its bomb load equated with that of the American Boeing B-17 Flying Fortress. It was perhaps the first multi-role combat aircraft and by the war's end it equipped no less than 15 of the squadrons of Bomber Command. Its operational loss rate of 0.63 per cent was by far the lowest experienced by any type in the Allied inventory.

Constructing a rough and ready balance sheet gives some measure of the national commitment in terms of bomber production against operational losses. Some 29,000 night bombers of all types were made and estimates of the number lost vary between 8,000 and 10,000 in the five-and-a-half years of the European war. Using an average crew size of six-and-a-half across all the main aircraft types (Lancaster, Halifax and Stirling seven each, Wellington six, Whitley five, Hampden four, and Mosquito two) against the total number of men killed or taken prisoner, which was almost 65,000, confirms the higher figure. Thus, over one-third of the bombers produced were lost in action and to these must be added machines damaged beyond economic repair, and those battle-weary aircraft which crashed in the course of their final service at OTUs and HCUs.

The cost of the strategy, in terms of the lives of the very best of young men from the British family of nations and their Allies, was in all con-

14

science well beyond what could possibly be deemed as acceptable. Almost by definition the aircrews of RAF Bomber Command were the cream of youth. All were volunteers, necessarily and demonstrably fit, intelligent and highly courageous. They were, in the main, a rich and poignant harvest gleaned from the survivors of the First World War. They had reached maturity in the years that were brightened by the romance of the air and enlivened by the achievements of airmen. They were certainly enthused by the prospect of a pure, almost clinical, war in the air, remote from direct contact with the enemy where skill and technological excellence would limit casualties and ensure success. Their courage was conspicuously complemented by a boundless enthusiasm. In the event 55,000 of them would die, far and away the worst casualty rate ever experienced within a sustained campaign by a British force before or since. Their loss is felt to this day, not only in the context of national and family bereavement, but even more vitally in the impact of their untimely deaths upon the stock and enduring fibre of their countries.

In cold statistics about 125,000 men flew at one time or another in bombers against Germany and Occupied Europe during the course of the war. Their chances of being killed were just a little better than even. Many died after a few, or very few, operations; the acquisition of experience conferred a degree of insurance, but such protection was fickle since many veterans were killed deep into their operational careers. Only some 10,000 became prisoners of war, thus confirming the dreadful difficulties involved in abandoning a spiralling, crashing heavy bomber whilst pinned down by violent G-forces and encumbered in a cramped fuselage by heavy clothing and a parachute pack. It is a matter of record that Bomber Command's British crews comprised some 2 per cent of the nation's armed forces, but the number killed amounted to 14 per cent of the total of those armed forces' war dead. If anything, this relativity was rather worse for Commonwealth aircrew.

Throughout the war there was general and informed awareness of the enormity of Bomber Command's losses. Much nonsense has been written claiming a conspiracy of silence to hide from bomber crews their marginal chances of survival. In fact routine wartime BBC news bulletins included remarkably accurate loss figures. Even after the disastrous Nuremberg raid of March 1944 this communiqué was broadcast: 'Last night aircraft of Bomber Command were over Germany in very great strength. The main objective was Nuremberg. Other aircraft attacked targets in western Germany and mines were laid in enemy waters. Ninety-six of our aircraft are missing.' There was no fudging, no concealment. Throughout the land there was ample evidence of heavy losses for all to hear, thus adding personal experience to official statistics.

Aircrew losses were not confined to those killed, injured, or taken prisoner in the course of the bombing offensive. There was another less visible and therefore more dangerous disability suffered by many in the course of the long campaign. The psychological disorders afflicting aircrew had first come to the notice of forces' medical officers in the generally unsympathetic climate of the First World War. In contemporary studies and in subsequent research between the wars the accumulative impact of oxygen starvation, extreme cold, and long exposure to noise and vibration on aircrew was identified as having both physical and serious psychological repercussions. However there was some optimism that the disciplined use of oxygen masks, coupled with the improved soundproofing of enclosed cockpits and electrically-heated clothing, would minimise both effects and for a while this appeared to be the case. However the early wartime evidence gleaned in disastrous daylight raids and long night leaflet dropping operations proved the extent of the pressures felt by even the most hardened and experienced regular aircrew. The influx of thousands of young volunteers from all walks and conditions of life heightened the problem to undeniable proportions. Eight hours of deafening noise endured in conditions of cramped icy darkness, stalked by the constant probability of a dreadful death took a great deal of surviving. It could perhaps be endured only as part of an operation which had an indisputable war-winning quality, and even then it would prove too much for some otherwise heroic men.

The national attitude to the bombing of Germany was direct and simple to the point of ruthlessness, at least when viewed at a distance of 50 years. There was little room for clemency, hard decisions had to be taken and followed through. There was only one objective, one compelling motivation, to win a war which had been forced upon the nation by a hideous and cruel regime from whom no vestige of mercy could ever be expected, least of all for Britain. Within this universal resolve there was also the deep conviction that the German people must pay for the obscenity of Nazism which they had embraced, and to this end any sacrifice was not only necessary – it was worthwhile. A sense of deep rage prevailed that Germany had again brought war to

Europe and one phrase of Biblical origin was particularly savoured. It was attributed in its modern context to Sir Arthur Harris when he became Commander-in-Chief of Bomber Command: 'Hitler has sown the breeze and now the German people will reap the whirlwind'. There were few, especially from Britain's many blitzed cities, who did not welcome the prospect of the utter devastation of Germany.

If the need for strategic bombing was universally accepted by the British, and if its heavy human and material costs were recognised, then the only remaining issue was to ensure that it was effective in bringing the enemy to his knees. Germany was a very large country, contained within boundaries having no natural definition deep within the European landmass. It presented none of the navigational simplicities available to an aggressor approaching the British Isles. The temptation to brush aside the difficulties by judging any bomb dropped anywhere on Germany as worthwhile was clearly ill-founded, as the witnesses of the Luftwaffe's blitz on Britain would readily confirm. Only such concentrated attacks as those on London's East End, Coventry, Southampton and Plymouth seriously undermined the public morale and impaired the will to fight. For the rest the BBC phrase 'bombs were dropped at random' entered the national vocabulary of humour. 'I hear "Random" got it again last night!', joked the radio comedians and the people laughed delightedly at the enemy's blundering inadequacy.

There was no question that the British wanted a programme of utter destruction to fall upon the cities of Germany and upon the people who lived and worked therein. The only detractors from such a policy were the politically devious, the religiously confused, and the internationally anarchical who eagerly went against the popular mood to foster their own bizarre independence of thought.

The public saw the airmen as their very special champions and ever since the combats of the Battle of Britain had been fought out in the summer skies of southern England, the RAF could do no wrong. Now the bomber crews were absorbed into the British countryside in a strangely personal war where only hours might separate relaxation in a country pub from a terrible death in a blazing aircraft over Germany. Their high spirits touched the villages and the country folk with a compelling, brief glamour, a kind of magic, and then they were gone. The sites from which they flew mostly live on in local legend, in stretches of crumbling concrete, and in scattered, stark, squat buildings. It is to be hoped that their memory will never fade.

CHAPTER ONE
THE ERRATIC OFFENSIVE

In the summer of 1939 RAF Bomber Command mounted a number of training exercises designed to develop the skills of crews, particularly in the operation of such recently introduced aircraft as the Wellingtons and Hampdens. A young flying officer with 83 Squadron recorded his experience on one such manoeuvre.

Piloting his Hampden, Guy Gibson joined a small force of bombers briefed to 'attack' London. Before coming in from across the North Sea they first had to fly out from their base at Scampton to a turning point close to the Dutch coast, whereupon they turned back towards the Thames estuary. Gibson experienced his baptism of fire on this occasion when Dutch anti-aircraft gunners fired warning shots to discourage the formation from wandering into their air space! The gunfire was highly inaccurate and the bomber crews were fascinated by their first sight of exploding shells, insubstantial puffs of smoke which seemed to imply no menace. More sobering was the fact that in broad daylight, and flying towards a well defined coastline, the bombers were off course and hopelessly late in executing their turn. But worse was to follow on subsequent occasions.

The increasing number of training sorties flown as war approached included several near disasters, occasioned by the navigational ineptitude of the crews and the mild hazards of European weather in mid-summer. Gibson flew with 83 Squadron to Paris in the company of a formation of Wellingtons and Whitleys from other units, later 'showing the flag' down in the south of France. In all these flights the prime purpose was to provide a demonstration of skill and professionalism which, it was hoped, would bolster the confidence of the ill-prepared and anxious French. In reality, these various sorties served only to confirm the extent to which aircraft performance had outstripped the techniques of aerial navigation and the rudimentary equipment which supported them.

The trip down to the Mediterranean presented many crews with their first experience of flying over a vast, largely featureless and strange land mass, which was often obscured by mist and haze and buffeted by variable winds. Many flights were delayed, diverted, or abandoned altogether because of the problems presented by indifferent weather conditions. Obviously such caution was entirely proper in time of peace. Guy Gibson recorded one flight he made from Scampton down to Tangmere where they were to refuel before setting out across the Channel to the Cherbourg peninsula. Soon after take-off from their home base they became lost over extensive early morning summer mist, but flew on hoping that some landmark would emerge to guide them. Eventually a tall spire appeared, somewhat dramatically, immediately alongside the aircraft which they assumed to be that of Salisbury Cathedral! Reluctantly they decided to return to Lincolnshire and on the way home grimly contemplated the imperatives of war, when the option of turning back would no longer be so acceptable.

From its earliest days the RAF had projected itself as an essentially offensive organisation. Trenchard believed in strategic bombing by day and by night as a means to victory in its own right. Between the wars a generous share of the limited defence budget was allocated to the maintenance of bomber strength. The biplane night bombers of the 'twenties and 'thirties impressed the crowds with their lumbering and awesome immensity, whilst their smaller daytime compatriots maintained law and order across the Empire, from the Middle East to the North West Frontier of India, at a modest cost and with high efficiency.

Trenchard was almost unique amongst the air strategists in his conviction that night bombing was a feasible proposition. The Americans virtually ignored the possibility, devoting their energies to perfecting the means of precision daylight attack, whilst the emergent Luftwaffe saw bombing largely as an extension to the Army's artillery and as a fundamental component of *Blitzkrieg*. Amongst the rest, Italy and Japan used aerial bombardment as an unassailable instrument of terror against primitive peoples as they set about acquiring their empires and subjugating their neighbours. In neither case did their bombers require the defensive cloak of darkness.

Operating the low flying, slow Virginias, Hinaidis and the later Heyfords, with the aid of flares the RAF's bomber crews were able at least to claim reasonable results on their exercises which were optimistically regarded as representative of war conditions. In fact they were no such thing. Anti-aircraft defences were not even in their infancy, searchlights hunted the skies using sound location as their totally unreliable guide, and any aircraft illuminated would have proved almost impossible to hit such was the inefficiency of range-finding and gun-laying equipment. The bombers had ample time to fix their positions, the distinctive coastline of the United Kingdom was never far distant from their area of operation, and the whole country was obligingly well lit. Even the most pessimistic strategist would have had to stretch his imagination to foretell a situation where British bombers would have to overfly hundreds of miles of enemy occupied territory before even reaching the borders of Germany.

The new generation of medium bombers – the 'heavies' of their day, Wellingtons and Whitleys, together with the smaller, cramped Hampdens, provided Bomber Command with aircraft of vastly improved performance. But their full potential was largely unrealised. Air Chief Marshal Sir Edgar Ludlow-Hewitt, Commander-in-Chief of Bomber Command from September 1937 to April 1940, was conspicuous by his good sense and realism when, in a secret and controversial report to the Air Ministry, he described his Command as a 'fair weather force'. Even assuming that his aircraft would be operating from advanced bases in France, he still had no faith in his crews' ability to mount night attacks deep into Germany against 'inconspicuous targets at the heart of a strange and hostile country'. The actuality of a six-hour journey to and from the target, being more or less wholly through enemy airspace once the British coast had been crossed, was obviously not foreseen by the C-in-C. He concluded his report by suggesting that, if nothing else, his crews should be provided with some better scientific means of finding their way home after a raid. Sadly as it turned out, this would be the least of their difficulties.

With some prescience, Ludlow-Hewitt's report covered in some detail the remarkable progress made in British civil aviation 'for the navigation of aircraft through every kind of weather'. He wrote: 'Today the airline pilots of all the leading European and American airlines are capable and accustomed to flying their aircraft for long periods and for long distances through thick cloud, fog, snow or other adverse conditions.' He might as well have been talking about a young Australian, Imperial Airways Captain, Don Bennett.

A US Navy navigational luminary, Commander Weems, once observed that there were four possible means of fixing an aircraft's position and that there were many times when all four were woefully insufficient! The systems to which the commander referred were those on which the RAF would depend until deep into the war when reliable radar aids finally became available. The first technique was basic map reading, making use of 1/1,000,000 or 1/500,000 scale maps which produced working scales of about 16 and eight miles to the inch respectively. Such maps were obviously useful in laying out routes, establishing turning points and so on, but large scale charts, or photographs, were necessary for the fine-tuning of target identification. The difficulties of map reading in a draughty, dimly-lit aircraft over, at best, a terrain made featureless by grey uncontrasted moonlight, require no exaggeration.

The second technique was that known with some optimism as dead reckoning, a description which implied a wholly spurious degree of precision. The navigator required access to accurate information on the aircraft's course and airspeed throughout the flight in order to achieve success using the technique. In fact, aircraft compasses were subject to many error-producing influences as indeed were airspeed indicators, and the lateral deviations caused by crosswinds introduced further mystery into the impossible equation. Obviously in the course of a long flight, dead reckoning would require frequent re-assessment by means of periodic checks on landmarks and topographical features which were likely to be almost indiscernible by night.

The third technique fundamentally involved the use of established nautical processes of navigation, using celestial bodies as points of reference. In theory this had a great deal more science about it than other methods. However, it was one thing to use a sextant to plot the position of a comparatively slow moving ship, but quite another to do so in an aeroplane proceeding at ten times the speed through turbulent air. In brief, the sextant was used to take sights measuring the angle of elevation of sun, moon, a planet, or a star relative to the aircraft. The exact time of the 'sight' was then noted from a chronometer and the two figures were plotted on a position line on a special chart. The whole process was then repeated using another celestial body and the intersection of the two plots would yield the aircraft's position, or perhaps more accurately where it had been some moments before. Sightings were taken through a perspex dome in the aircraft's roof adding problems of optical distortion, and obviously the whole practice was rendered useless by upper level cloud and by any hint of urgency!

Lastly, there was radio direction finding. This involved transmissions from the aircraft being intercepted by separate ground stations which would take bearings and thus establish its position at their point of intersection. This information would then be communicated back to the wireless operator on board the aircraft. A self-contained alternative involved the aircraft using a direction-finding loop to establish its own location relative to two known transmitters. This clearly avoided the back-and-forth communications essential to the use of ground stations. Although reliable and relatively uncomplicated, the system was vulnerable to jamming and other interference, as well as revealing the aircraft's position to anyone with an interest in finding it.

These totally depressing options led Bomber Command into the necessity of a daylight bombing offensive against its initial war targets, although the Whitley squadrons would go deep into Germany by night to drop leaflets, the release of which required scant precision.

The daylight attacks were an unmitigated disaster. Before the war, bombing tacticians evolved a variety of defensive formations whereby gunners in the individual aircraft operated as one in pre-determined cones of fire. Such a philosophy ignored the realities of combat and assumed that the intercepting enemy fighters would mount predictable copybook attacks against which a similarly inflexible defence could be mounted. Thus when 24 Wellingtons from 38, 115 and 149 Squadrons, engaged in armed reconnaissance off Heligoland early in December 1939, managed to drive off four intercepting Messerschmitt Bf109s, it was hailed as a vindication of the defensive strength of close formations. Some ten days later on 14 December, 99 Squadron responded to reports of several German warships at sea again in the vicinity of Heligoland and despatched 12 of its Wellingtons from Newmarket to deal with them.

Leaving their home base at 11.45hrs they sighted the enemy coast at 14.25hrs, although German *Freya* radars had already picked them up long before, while they were still far out over the North Sea. This time the enemy fighters were ready and fell on the bomber formation, shooting down five and seriously damaging a sixth which crashed on return to Newmarket. No bombs were dropped because no ships were seen!

The Air Ministry spent four days digesting this disaster and actually concluded that two aircraft had been lost by collision and one due to some catastrophic mechanical failure. This quite fallacious, but comforting, analysis led Bomber Command to repeat the attack four days later when 24 Wellingtons of 9, 37, and 149 Squadrons appeared on the German radar screens at Wangerooge at 13.23hrs. Again the aircraft dropped no bombs since no military targets were identified, and they were beginning their homeward journey when intercepted by a mass of German fighters over the chain of islands between Wilhelmshaven and the Dutch border. Twelve Wellingtons were destroyed in moments, consumed by searing fire since they had not yet been fitted with self-sealing fuel tanks. Three more crashed on reaching England and three were damaged beyond repair.

Daylight bombing was over for the RAF, other than as a purely tactical measure against accessible targets, until the future advent of high performance aircraft and the availability of escort fighters. Guy Gibson later wrote: 'I am not blaming the planners at the time. Then it may have seemed sound that a close formation of [bombers] could have protected themselves against repeated attacks by Me109s, but the proof of the pudding lies in the fact that a raid of that nature was never repeated.'

Considering the débâcle of the Heligoland raids, it was reasonable to expect that future loss rates would be in the region of 50 per cent or higher, if the original strategy was pursued, particularly insofar as attacks on the German fleet, or on Luftwaffe bases were concerned. By the same token any notion of devastating daylight attacks on the Ruhr valley were out of the question, and by night seemed unlikely to achieve anything of value. This austere judgement was confirmed in March 1940 when 50 Whitleys and Hampdens left their bases to attack the German seaplane base at Hornum by night. Encouragingly, 43 aircraft actually located the target since coastal objectives were always easier to find. But despite the claims of the crews which spoke of direct hits on hangars, blazing fires, and hefty explosions, the evidence brought back by a Blenheim photographic reconnaissance aircraft a week later confirmed German claims that only a sick bay had been hit and a few aeroplanes damaged.

In the raw cold spring of 1940 it was abundantly clear that Bomber Command could not operate effectively by day, and had even greater difficulty finding its targets by night. Only the tough, ageing Whitleys continued to shower leaflets on Germany, by night, largely unmolested and giving their crews, which included Leonard Cheshire, experience of operations in enemy skies. On one night the Ruhr was scattered with 3.25 million leaflets!

Ludlow-Hewitt's period of command ended as planned on 3 April 1940 and Air Marshal Sir Charles Portal succeeded him. Six days later Germany occupied Denmark and began her invasion of Norway. On 10 May the German Army launched its great offensive against France, Belgium and Holland and two days later most of the British light bombing component based in France, the Blenheims and Battles of the Advanced Air Striking Force, had been shot from the skies.

In the days that followed, the newly appointed Prime Minister, Winston Churchill, debated with his service chiefs the best means of retaliation against Germany. The options were depressingly few and most involved Bomber Command in night attacks either against the Ruhr, or against oil targets, the latter in the hope of impeding the German mechanised advance westwards. There was great concern about the impact of such attacks on the sensitivities of neutral countries and, it must be admitted, about the ferocity of the likely German response against the British Isles. However, the historic decision was made: Germany would be bombed on the night of 15 May by about 100 aircraft.

The bomber crews were briefed to go for military objectives including railway marshalling yards, steel works, and oil refineries. In the event 96 aircraft were assigned targets, 16 failed to find anything and dutifully returned with their bombs, and only two dozen of the remaining force claimed to have identified their objectives! During the remainder of May, 11 further attacks of similar magnitude were made without any perceptible effect upon the German advance through Europe, and without any adverse reaction from squeamish neutrals. For the moment Germany ignored the attacks. Hitler had other plans to fulfil and no retaliation was ordered against Britain.

It is tempting to dismiss this trifling foray as almost unworthy of note. It was as insignificant as a stirring of summer air at noon, but in dreadful reality it marked the moment of birth of a whirlwind.

Portal was not long at Bomber Command for on 25 October 1940 he took over as Chief of the Air Staff (CAS) from the affable and engagingly optimistic Sir Cyril Newall. Newall had been in the job for three years and had absorbed much of the criticism for the early shortcomings of the bomber offensive. The scheming Lord Beaverbrook who had become Minister of Aircraft Production in Churchill's coalition Government – and who disliked all senior officers, but Air Marshals most of all – formed an instant dislike of Newall and persuaded the Prime Minister to be rid of him. Beaverbrook was also entranced by fighter aircraft, the relative ease with which they could be amassed, and by the kudos that this had brought him in the summer of 1940. On the other hand, Newall's deep commitment to Trenchard's vision of bombing an enemy into submission did nothing for his own standing with the minister. The CAS's departure undoubtedly represented a setback for the fortunes of Bomber Command which was taken over by Air Marshal Sir Richard Peirse.

The next 14 months were spent by the new C-in-C in sustaining an offensive against Germany with all the means at his disposal. The importance of this period was two-fold. Firstly, although the raids were small-scale and largely ineffective, they contributed greatly to the maintenance of British morale and to some extent offset the fact that the war was going appallingly badly for Britain. Throughout 1941, incompetence, unpreparedness, and simple weakness produced an almost unbroken string of military defeats which was relieved only by news of the bomber war and the illusion that Germany, too, was suffering a blitz. Sadly, however, the losses of aircrew and aircraft were escalating rapidly as German defences improved in terms of deployment and of sophistication. (As a matter of record, 181 aircraft were lost in the first quarter of 1941; this figure had increased to 561 by the end of the second quarter and to 1,170 at the end of September!) This high level of attrition was unacceptable and unsustainable in its own right, bearing in mind the relatively modest scale of the campaign. But suspicions were growing that these heavy casualties were being taken without any really noticeable impact upon the enemy.

In August, Lord Cherwell, Churchill's Scientific Adviser, proposed an objective review of the results of bombing. When this was agreed a member of the War Cabinet Secretariat, Mr D. M. B. Butt, was allotted the task of analysing over 600 aerial photographs. These had been taken in the course of nearly two months of bombing operations in June and July involving attacks on no less than 48 nights. The results were awaited with considerable apprehension and the need for total objectivity placed an enormous burden on the analyst. It could only be hoped that any dismay which might arise from an unfavourable report would be offset by a speedy consensus on a means of improving bombing efficiency, but it was not to be.

Mr Butt worked quickly and well, and if his definition of success was undemanding this probably arose from the general need for measured optimism in an awful year for the nation. His findings were as follows:

1. Of those aircraft recorded as attacking their target only one in three got within five miles.
2. Over the French ports the proportion was two in three; over Germany as a whole the proportion was one in four; over the Ruhr in particular it was only one in ten.
3. In the full moon, the proportion was two in five; in the new moon it was only one in fifteen.
4. In the absence of haze the proportion was over one-half, whereas over thick haze it was only one in fifteen.
5. An increase in the intensity of AA fire reduced the number of aircraft getting within five miles of their target in the ratio of 3:2.
6. All these figures relate only to aircraft recorded as attacking the target; the proportion of the *total* sorties which reached within five miles is less than one-third.

These depressing figures might of themselves have halted the build-up of Bomber Command, but fortunately far too much was at stake. There was no other means of taking the war to Germany and the precipitate advancement of invasion plans whilst the enemy increased his strength unmolested seemed the clearest possible recipe for losing the war.

It must be said that Mr Butt's arbitrary use of a five-mile radius as defining the target success area was a classic example of putting the best gloss on things. In effect it meant that any bomb falling within a staggering 75 square miles was deemed to have struck home. Clearly, however, such an area was larger than many of the towns and cities attacked, let alone the defined targets within them. Setting this aside the best and most immediate impact of the Butt report was, to quote Lord Cherwell, 'Sufficiently striking to emphasise the supreme importance of improving our navigational methods.'

Almost as soon as Butt's conclusions became known two opposing factions emerged, each with their well defined agendas and supporting expert arguments to achieve bombing accuracy. The first, which comprised the majority of the senior group and operational squadron commanders, believed that the eagerly anticipated radar navigational and bombing aids, coupled with improved training and

the appointment of bombing leaders in the squadrons, would provide a speedy and durable solution. The second faction, centred on
the Air Ministry and the Directorate of Bombing Operations,
remained steadfastly unconvinced. Conscious of the massive build-
up in numbers necessary to turn the Command into a war-winning
force, they argued that the majority of wartime volunteer crews
lacked the navigational skills and the ability to make best use of the
new aids. The answer as they saw it was to create a specialist force of
'pathfinders' and target markers, both to guide the Main Force of
bombers to their targets and to ensure that these were so precisely
defined by flares and pyrotechnics that the average bomb-aimer's
task would be a relatively simple one. The gulf between the two arguments was further widened by the fears which were articulated by the
groups and squadrons, that the creation of the *corps élite* favoured by
the Air Ministry would destroy the morale of Main Force crews by
denying their professionalism and, perhaps, even their courage. They
would be turned into no more than delivery boys and both efficiency
and motivation would be lost.

The argument seemed set to run and run in the unhealthy conflict
between the Air Ministry office strategists versus the group and
squadron field tacticians. Portal faced an eventual moment of decision
one way or the other, but he was a wise enough commander to know
that a resolution reached by consensus was worth a thousand imposed
from above. Air Marshal Peirse at Bomber Command Headquarters,
High Wycombe, was exhausted and full of misgivings about the effectiveness of his Command.

Matters really came to a head on 7 November 1941 when 170 aircraft
were ordered by him to attack Berlin on an appalling night of strong
winds and freezing temperatures, whilst small diversionary attacks were
mounted against Mannheim and a number of other targets. The results
of these various activities were unremittingly awful. There was no evidence of any accurate bombing, aiming points were obscured by cloud
and aircraft were blown widely off course all over Europe. Worst of all,
when the returns came in from the squadrons and the stations to High
Wycombe it became obvious that a totally unsustainable rate of casualties had been suffered. Thirty-seven aircraft had failed to return, 21
from the attack on Berlin and the remainder from other sorties. Peirse
was stunned by the night's happenings and the apparent futility of it
all. He blamed the dreadful weather with some justification, but in the

end it had been his decision to proceed, despite the bad Met forecasts, and he had brushed aside the open opposition of 5 Group. The bombers' lack-lustre performance under his leadership and the increasing size of losses, coupled with the uncompromising nature of the Butt report, sealed Peirse's fate. He left High Wycombe on 8 January 1942 and his successor took up his post at the headquarters on 22 February. At the time someone remarked that Peirse had been the last of the admirable 'gentlemen', but with the appointment of Air Chief Marshal Sir Arthur Harris there could be no doubt that the bombing war had passed into the hands of the 'players' and the game would be pursued henceforward with unremitting ferocity.

Sir Arthur Harris had commanded 5 Group Bomber Command in the opening stages of the war and then went to the Air Ministry as Deputy Chief of the Air Staff. A thickset, forthright, imposing and outwardly austere man, he had an unshakeable conviction that his Command could destroy Germany and thus win the war without the imperative of a prolonged, and perhaps inconclusive, land battle across Europe. The stakes were high and so too, he knew, would be the human cost and the material commitment, but the prize would be well worth the likely sacrifice. Harris had experienced at first-hand the conflict of 1914–18 and he retained indelible memories of tens of thousands killed daily on the battlefield with no discernible gain for either side. He had resolved that air power could achieve a conclusive victory at a fraction of the carnage. Now he would focus the full fury of the onslaught upon Germany, demolishing her city by city if necessary, and purging the regime that had brought war, slavery and death to innocent millions.

He contemplated his task with a clinical detachment which accurately reflected the sentiments of his fellow countrymen and of their allies. His only regrets were centred upon the tremendous sacrifices that would be demanded of the bomber crews. He understood them well, sharing their laconic humour and their chilling realism. Like them he was a cynic, unimpressed by mock heroics and patriotic fervour, distrustful of quick fixes. He called the crews his 'old lags', a term which accurately reflected their unreformed long-suffering perseverance. They called him 'Butch' and delighted in the bloody-mindedness with which he always defended their cause. 'Harris stories' abounded, recalling his encounters with pale politicians and with other service chiefs who nurtured their own pet theories for winning the war. His scathing dismissals of 'panacea merchants' were legendary, as was his scorn for boffins who showered him with complex – sometimes useless – devices to refine the crude weapons of war. In all this he did no more than reflect the impatience and frustrations of his long-suffering subordinates. His exasperated demand to be allowed 'to get on with the war' was often heard at his headquarters as he faced yet another mire of mindless bureaucracy. The crews of Bomber Command had no doubt that Butch Harris's heart was in the right place. It was steadfastly with them.

CHAPTER TWO
'THE MOST EFFICIENT AIRMAN'

D on Bennett was four when he saw his first aeroplane, flown by an American and giving a display at Toowoomba, Queensland, Australia, where Bennett's father owned a cattle station in the remote Darling Downs. Don was the youngest of four brothers, and his mother, the daughter of an English doctor who had emigrated in the 1890s, brought him up to an independent self-sufficiency and quick wittedness which proved a practical alternative to his brothers' more academic leanings and achievements. By the time Don was ten, his eldest brother had already qualified as a barrister, and another brother would follow in this career, whilst a third became a doctor. There was some little concern about Don's lack of obvious scholarship and in later years he would describe himself as 'a bit of a loafer'. His parents were sensibly not over concerned about a future for their bright and confident son, there was after all an adequate living to be had in cattle rearing, or within the agricultural agency in which his father had an increasing interest. Finally, an impressively bad school report convinced his father that it was pointless to waste further time or money on Don's education, and that any thoughts of university were totally unrealistic.

The early 1920s saw the great pioneering flights which heralded the start of worldwide civil aviation. Australia was seen as an ultimate destination, an achievement that would really prove the value of air travel as a speedy alternative to the interminable sea journey that spelt lifelong exile, rather than emigration for so many English settlers. The brave quayside farewells at Tilbury or Southampton were more often translated into final partings by the tyranny of distance. As early as 1919 there had been the first dramatic and encouraging sign of what could be achieved when in June Alcock and Brown first flew the Atlantic eastbound in a Vickers Vimy. The successful flight was concluded with their aircraft upending into an Irish bog 16½hrs out of Newfoundland.

Some 18 months later Qantas (Queensland and Northern Territory Aerial Service) was registered in Australia and at the end of 1922 opened its first scheduled service between Charleville and Cloncurry in Queensland. In 1924 two officers of the Royal Australian Air Force (RAAF) circumnavigated the Dominion in a Fairey IIID in 90 hours' flying time. But it was not until 1926 that the first return flight to Australia was made by Alan Cobham in a de Havilland D.H.50, landing on the river Thames at Westminster on 1 October having left England on the last day of June. On 7 February 1928, Bert Hinkler departed from Croydon in an Avro Avian to make a pioneer solo flight to Australia, arriving in Darwin on 22 February after covering 11,000 miles in 15 intermediate stops! The age of long distance aerial navigation had arrived with a vengeance and it wove a rich pattern of ambition and endeavour in the mind of the 18-year-old Bennett, who always remembered Hinkler's arrival as the final trigger for his determination to fly. Hinkler's Avian aeroplane was placed in Brisbane Museum where it remains as a continuing inspiration to this day.

Despite his parents' gloomy prognosis of their son's likely fate as an airman and an effort by his second eldest brother, by then a doctor, to dissuade him, he applied for flying service in the RAAF. With the growing importance of aviation in the sub-continent, and the realisation by many that Australia would need to look increasingly to her own defence, it was to be expected that recruits would have been welcome at Point Cook, the RAAF's training airfield just outside Melbourne. However, Bennett's experience was a test of his enthusiasm, since he was at first adjudged medically unfit and advised to return a year later in the expectation that the shortcomings within his tonsils might have spontaneously cleared!

He was less than impressed by this suggestion and promptly arranged to have the offending organs removed the same day. This of course gave the Selection Board a measure of the man, but immediately ran him into a further rule which decreed a six-month wait after any surgical operation before a candidate could be re-assessed for service! Temporarily defeated he returned to Brisbane and a job in his father's office, until shortly before the end of the six-month wait he heard again from the RAAF who regretted that they were no longer immediately interested in him, but suggested he might like to apply again after a further year.

This was too much for him and, accompanying his mother on a visit to Sydney, he caught a train on to Melbourne and presented himself to the impressed if somewhat surprised Selection Board. He later assumed he was victim of a deliberate policy to discourage a surfeit of enthusiastic young men without revealing the true situation to them. In fact there was a desperate shortage of funds which precluded recruitment on other than the most modest scale. In some sort of demonstration of bureaucratic superiority the Board still sent Bennett away for another six months whilst assuring him that he was now irrevocably accepted, providing nothing else happened!

He spent an uncomfortable six months regarding official certainty as the most uncertain thing of all, until he reported to Victoria Barracks, Melbourne, in July 1930 where, apparently he was expected, much to his considerable relief.

Later, he found that his confidence about a career in the RAAF was entirely misplaced, since in the middle of the course he and the other 14 cadets were advised that Australia simply could not afford to employ them at the end of their training. Accordingly, the majority would be required to volunteer for service in the RAF in England once their flying training was completed. There was no alternative, other than a return to civilian life for a further indefinite wait, so Bennett made up his mind immediately and committed himself to future service in the RAF. It was for him a classic Hobson's Choice, but that made it no less momentous.

Bennett set out immediately with all but two of his original fellow recruits for Point Cook. The base combined a vast flying field unhampered by surrounding high ground or other obstacles, with a slipway and jetty on the western shore of Port Philip from which seaplanes and flying-boats were operated. Bennett was fortunate to complete the whole of his flying training on newly arrived de Havilland Moths, the purchase of which had survived the swingeing economy campaign only because of the dreadful safety record of their elderly predecessors. He quickly showed himself to be a meticulous pilot motivated by his own high standards of professionalism, rather than by the adventurous high spirits of contemporary aviation. He was mature and serious beyond his years and already commanded the respect of contemporaries. His aloof and apparently rather serious nature demonstrated its great strength, both in the meticulous way he acquired flying skills and in the absolute self-discipline with which he exercised them. He saw no value in taking risks; in his book dangers were best avoided and objectives achieved by planning and application. Blind confrontation was for fools. There was nothing remarkable to recount in his flying training, no near misses, no exuberant escapades, he took some eight hours to solo and he took equal care with theoretical studies. The outcome alone was worthy of note: he passed out a comfortable first in flying and second in the written examinations. It was thus with a sense of having fulfilled his early ambitions and having brought somewhat unexpected further credit to his talented family, that he set sail for England in late December 1930 on the steamship *Narkunda*.

His arrival in England in 1931 coincided with one of the RAF's most acute periods of financial constraint. The depression was affecting all aspects of national life and the defence of the realm attracted little government attention, or financial resources. After a period of acclimatisation at Uxbridge and a check on his flying ability at Sealand, Bennett was posted to 29 Squadron at North Weald flying the Armstrong Whitworth Siskin, a strange-looking biplane with sesquiplane-type wings, whose original design dated back to the latter years of the First World War. Like the other, pitifully few, fighter squadrons, No 29 was fuel-limited to the extent of restricting training exercises and the general accumulation of flying hours.

Despite such limitations, high standards were maintained and there were no limits to official expectations of the versatility and skills of the pilots. There was the annual opportunity to participate in the Hendon Air Display, although rehearsal time for this was jealously rationed, and late in 1931 it was decreed that 29 Squadron should add night fighting to its repertoire. Bennett was responsible for the demise of one Siskin when, with another pilot, he set out for the south coast on a navigational exercise which for once was not subject to official restriction. It was not a happy experience and Bennett never forgot the fact that stupid exuberance caused him to ignore the dangers and forego the careful study of route and wind and weather, to which he was normally so committed.

Flying home they ran into low, freezing cloud and, although the other pilot made it back to Essex, Bennett ended up inverted but otherwise uninjured within his wrecked aeroplane when the iced-up engine failed. He blamed himself and the economies that deprived him of the unlimited opportunity to practice the complex skills of airmanship. But perhaps fighters would never give him the fulfilment he most craved. He wanted to fly and navigate as a true professional, and to satisfy the ambition that had been triggered by the arrival of the early pioneers. Now as new routes were being opened up and new records broken with exciting regularity, it could only be a matter of time before long distance air transport became a reality. He was certain that he wanted to be a part of this promising future and so he decided to seek a transfer to a wider-ranging part of RAF activity as soon as his fighter time was up.

The Air Force took note of his wishes and obligingly posted him for training to one of the most famed flying-boat bases, Calshot, bordering the Solent. Here were based the great wooden-hulled, silver-painted Supermarine Southampton biplane flying-boats. There could hardly have been a more demanding transition for Bennett: he had been flying single-seat fighters and had never handled anything heavier than the Westland Wapiti at the end of his Australian training. Now he had to manage a multi-engined machine, demanding new techniques of airmanship and the subtleties of water handling, including seamanship.

Bennett rapidly concluded that navigation could become the central interest and driving force in his life. Under its spell his own intellectual capacity blossomed and his months at Calshot became some of the happiest of his life. He enjoyed flying with a crew, the greater challenge of the flying-boats and the elemental difficulties posed by wind and weather. He embraced the techniques of navigation with an enthusiasm which matched the fulfilment he now felt, and pointed the way to career possibilities which he found profoundly exciting.

After six months of learning at Calshot he moved to Pembroke Dock where he joined 210 Squadron. After a few weeks a new station commander was posted in, the then Group Captain Arthur Harris, who soon recognised in Bennett a man of single-minded dedication, a professional like himself, satisfied with nothing that fell short of excellence. He noted with approval the seriousness that dominated Bennett's personality, his clarity of thought and expression, and his impatience with the trivialities and the trappings of service life. He later wrote of the handsome young teetotal Australian, 'He was the most efficient airman I have ever met'.

Bennett quickly learned to master the Short Singapore four-engined biplane flying-boats with which 210 Squadron was equipped. He undertook fishery protection work which was, as ever, directed against Continental fishermen poaching British waters. He spent countless weeks droning up and down the south coast by night whilst engaged on an undefined exercise, the point of which was never explained to him, but it was all good practice. Finally the time came to leave and, with his skills now recognised, he was sent as an instructor to Calshot's School of

Navigation. Again, he looked back on a happy posting, this time made the more so by the encouragement and patronage of Harris. At Calshot he undertook various long trips around the British Isles and sometimes across to Continental Europe. He and his pupils would set off for days at a time, accompanied by a small ground crew and carrying a few spares to cover the possible need to replace vulnerable parts. It was a very self-sufficient existence where initiative, local knowledge, and good old-fashioned sea sense were married happily to aviation skills.

In 1934 he decided to sit for a First Class Navigator's Licence, largely because he was keen to participate in the England-Australia Air Race and wanted more to offer to a prospective sponsor than his RAF experience alone. He embarked on a period of study that bordered on the obsessive after persuading his commanding officer to excuse him from everything except his vital official duties. He passed the examination, becoming only the seventh man in the world to do so, and was accepted by an Australian competitor in the race as navigator of the Lockheed Vega monoplane he had entered.

On 20 October they left Mildenhall en route for Melbourne. Unfortunately the pilot experienced trouble with the aircraft's undercarriage and in attempting to land at Aleppo he overturned the Vega and Bennett severely injured his back, crushing three vertebrae. During a period of enforced – although far from idle – inactivity at Calshot recovering from the accident, he managed to acquire a Civil Class B Licence, an Instructor's Certificate, a Wireless Operator's Licence, and a Ground Engineer's Licence in three categories. He also met and married a girl from Switzerland and, he claimed, he taught her English into the bargain!

His decision to leave the RAF was made with some sorrow, but civil aviation seemed to hold considerable promise for the realisation of his ambition, not to mention greater recognition for his by now great skill and knowledge. He had not liked what he had seen of the Air Force's most senior officers, although he had full confidence in the next generation of commanders personified by Harris. It was indeed to Harris that he turned for support upon entering civil aviation, when he returned from Australia after a trip to allow his parents to meet his wife for the first time. The length of time that the journey took out of his busy life confirmed in full his belief in the future of air travel.

In January 1936 he joined Imperial Airways, having written his first book *The Complete Air Navigator* on the slow boat home! It remained in print for over 30 years. Soon he was flying as co-pilot on the majestic Handley Page 42s as they plied the route between Croydon and Paris. He went on to captain the last of Imperial's biplane flying boats back and forth over the Eastern Mediterranean using the long periods of inactivity, for which he was paid a retainer only, to write a second book, *The Air Mariner*.

In 1937 the Short 'C' Class Empire flying boats entered service, four-engined streamlined and beautiful monoplanes they transformed the airline's overseas long distance operations and gave Bennett his first modern commands. He next volunteered to pilot *Mercury*, the small four-engined float plane carried aloft as a piggyback mail plane by the *Maia* flying-boat, which was released from its parent at cruising altitude with a sufficiency of fuel to cross the Atlantic. After delays which he found insufferable, Bennett helped bully the Air Ministry into authorising a proving flight to Canada which finally took place in July 1938, and which was an outstanding and widely publicised success.

In early October, the Munich crisis having caused a postponement of the flight, Bennett took off from Dundee in *Mercury*, perched atop the parent *Maia*, and after separation set course for Capetown and a world long-distance record. Unfortunately the loss of an engine cowling caused increased drag and higher fuel consumption, with the result that although the seaplane record was broken the absolute record was not. Despite this disappointment, they had flown 6,000 miles in 42½hrs and Bennett had navigated his way down the length of Africa by sextant! Later that year he planned a *Maia/Mercury* flight from Durban to Sydney, but this was finally frustrated by the worsening international situation.

In the spring of 1939 he was involved in a new experiment conducted by Imperial Airways, comprising the in-flight refuelling of a 'C' Class flying-boat from a Handley Page Harrow, thereby securing the necessary range for trans-Atlantic crossings. Fifteen trial re-fuellings were carried out, but the dangers and uncertainties of the technique were such as to restrict its use to experimental flights across the North Atlantic. One such flight was scheduled to leave Hythe before lunch on Sunday 3 September 1939 with Bennett in command of the 'C' Class flying-boat. He took off shortly after hearing Prime Minister Chamberlain's announcement of the declaration of war on Germany. Later that day as they flew out over the ocean, they picked up an SOS from the passenger liner *Athenia* which had just been torpedoed by a German U-boat without warning. Bennett's war had begun with a stark reminder that there would be little regard for humanity.

Perhaps the obvious course for Bennett would have been to rejoin the RAF on the outbreak of war. However, his formidable reputation and accomplishments within Imperial Airways, and subsequently BOAC, made him an extremely talented loose cannon to be held available for a wide variety of assignments. For his part, he had no great desire to return to the RAF for routine squadron duties. He was conscious of having been a long time away and both his self-confidence and professional self-esteem caused him to bide his time for the right job to come along. In the meantime his contribution in the form of a number of special assignments was formidable.

In the early months of the war he retreated into the foggy world of special duties, centred upon monitoring the development of the enemy's submarine fleet. He was always remarkably reticent about this part of his career, but he wrote later of cloak-and-dagger meetings in London and elsewhere, all of which he described as 'real story book stuff'. Whatever he was up to, he gained great satisfaction from carrying it out to perfection using the precise techniques of airmanship in which he was by now an acknowledged master.

As the dreadful winter of 1939/40 drew to a close, Bennett returned to flying the routes just as Hitler launched his attacks on Denmark and Norway. Two months later, in June, he was flying back from Singapore in one of his beloved Empire boats when he landed in Italy on the very day that Mussolini decided to enter the war on the side of Germany. Ever resourceful, Bennett took aboard the local BOAC staff and left in good order for St Nazaire, itself resigned to the imminent arrival of the Panzers. The next few days were historic, with comings and goings surrounding the last-minute efforts to stave off the collapse and conquest of France. General Sikorski, leader of free Poland, sought Churchill's help in evacuating members of his country's cabinet and general staff from France where they were in danger of being caught by the German advance. Bennett flew back to a point just south of Bordeaux, taking Sikorski and landing him at midday with his aides, in the hope of contacting his now desperate fellow countrymen.

Deeply concerned about the deteriorating situation, Bennett gave the general until dawn the next day to return to the harbour. At 5.00 am three cars roared up to the quayside and the Polish party were quickly ferried out to climb aboard as the flying-boat's engines were started and she taxied out to begin her take-off run. As Bennett began his climb he saw the first German tanks approaching and on the way back there was ample evidence of the debris of war scattered beneath them. Their safe return to Poole was achieved despite the attempt of a Royal Navy cruiser to shoot them down, prompting an unsurprisingly sour comment from Bennett: 'fortunately the shooting was more or less of their usual standard and we were not hit'.

It was still a very peculiar war. Early in July, Bennett performed one of his last duties for BOAC by flying the Duke of Kent to Lisbon to attend an international exhibition. With the Battle of Britain being waged and the fate of civilised humanity hanging in the balance, propriety and national prestige still demanded that the King's representative should journey to the only European neutral well disposed towards Britain and the British Empire.

Bennett landed the flying boat on the Tagus river and went with his crew to the hotel where rooms had been reserved for them and, as it turned out, for the Lufthansa men who had brought in the German contingent. With the war situation at crisis point for Britain, and with final victory apparently in Hitler's grasp, it must have been the most fragile of international occasions. When they left Lisbon a few days later, lifting off the great river at nightfall, Bennett would have been saddened to know that he would never again command a BOAC aircraft.

Lord Beaverbrook, Canadian proprietor of the *Daily Express*, but then serving Churchill as Minister of Aircraft Production, was the next major architect of Bennett's developing career. Well before the outbreak of hostilities, the British government had embarked upon a controversial enterprise involving the acquisition of aircraft from the friendly but determinedly neutral United States. The controversy arose from the fact that many of the purchases were of inadequate aeroplanes which contributed little or nothing to the RAF's Order of Battle. There were, of course, notable exceptions which were urgently needed to fill vital gaps in Britain's defences. By 1940, however, the overriding problem had become one of delivery. North Atlantic convoys were increasingly hard-pressed by U-boat attacks, journey times were extended, and aircraft delivered by sea demanded extensive protection against the elements, with the larger types being, of necessity, carried as deck cargo. The majority were crated and therefore required reassembly and flight-testing on arrival, thus absorbing valuable man-hours and further delaying the aeroplanes' entry into service. In view of this it made a great deal of sense to contemplate flying the larger aircraft across the ocean to Britain. This would also provide the secondary advantage of releasing valuable shipping space in the hard-pressed convoys for the transport of other vital war materials.

The first aircraft to be delivered in this way were Lockheed Hudsons, developed from the highly successful Lockheed Super Electra airliner and ordered by the British Purchasing Commission in June 1938. By the early summer of 1940 many Hudsons had already been delivered by sea, but Lord Beaverbrook accepted that there had to be a better way and decided, with characteristic impulsiveness, to initiate an Atlantic ferry organisation to be set up in Canada by Canadian Pacific Railways. Three pilots were appointed at the outset, one of whom was Bennett, with the title of Flying Superintendent. His first step was to visit Lockheed and subject the Hudson to a demanding flight-test programme. The tests confirmed that, contrary to the manufacturer's belief, the aircraft would require the installation of an additional temporary fuel tank for the delivery flight. Lockheed, whose future had been assured by the British order, accepted Bennett's calculations and demands without argument and the new tank was installed overnight.

The niceties of United States neutrality, which were scrupulously observed, demanded that the Hudsons be flown across America by citizens of that country who were forbidden from delivering the aircraft directly to Canada. Accordingly, landings were made at a site in North Dakota adjacent to the 49th parallel. The Hudsons were then roped to a pair of horses, presumably regarded as devoid of nationality, and solemnly pulled across the frontier to start their journey to war! The remainder of the delivery would be the responsibility of British and Commonwealth ferry pilots and a collection of mercenaries – many of whom were American, and displaying less than attractive career backgrounds. To make matters worse, the loyalty of these foreign crews had hopefully been secured by the British government's decision to pay them significantly higher salaries than those paid to their own citizens doing precisely the same hazardous job. Bennett showed no hesitation in making his views known on this blatant unfairness, thus exacerbating the situation between him and his Canadian boss, of whom he later wrote, 'he was devoid of qualities either good or bad'.

For their part, the foreign civilian pilots found it hard to come to terms with a distinctly terse teetotal Australian, whose vocabulary verged on the puritanical and who demanded of them absolute perfection. In their more charitable moments they regarded him as a cold fish, but they quickly came to admire his airmanship. Thus, a hesitant working relationship eventually grew into a rather chilly mutual respect.

Bennett busied himself with the organisation of the North Atlantic Ferry, delegating the training of the pilots and radio operators for the long and dangerous flight, until by October 1940 a few Hudsons were ready at the newly established Gander airfield in Newfoundland. The possibility of a mid-winter trans-Atlantic crossing had not been seriously contemplated before now. In all conscience the dark ocean was a sufficiently terrifying prospect without the further hazards of cloud, icing, and the buffeting strong winds at altitude. Bennett had decided to use his own navigational skills to lead a first formation of aircraft across. He believed that this would inspire some much-needed confidence and was happier to trust his own ability, rather than relying on others to secure a successful outcome.

Accordingly, he flew into Gander on 9 November, immaculate and fresh as ever having signalled that he was hoping for an almost immediate departure. The weather decreed otherwise and some 24 hours elapsed before all the aircraft were cleared of a steel-hard layer of ice on their flying surfaces. Late on 10 November Bennett was first to take off, estimating a 9½-hour crossing to Aldergrove in Northern Ireland, allowing for a helpful 23-knot tailwind component. Each aircraft carried a crew of two pilots and a radio operator, the latter employed primarily to listen out and keep quiet. In the lead aircraft Bennett climbed to 16,000ft before handing over to his co-pilot and getting to work with his sextant. The six following Hudsons could hardly have been in better hands but, that said, it was a brave and infinitely hazardous enterprise.

Deep into the flight the formation was forced to break up as it entered an area of severe weather, but by that time the track was well established and all aircraft arrived safely. The final two landed well after the rest and, despite his exhaustion, Bennett remained staring out of the control tower until the seventh Hudson taxied in and stopped its engines. It is a measure of his professionalism, and no reflection on his humanity, to suggest that he was just as interested in confirming that his preparation and conduct of the crossing had been impeccable as he was in the safe arrival of the crews.

Almost immediately those who had made the crossing were bundled into a liner to make the even more hazardous return journey across the U-boats' hunting ground. They left Bennett to journey on to London where he launched a cogent and precise argument for the release of trained navigators to the ferry organisation. He had no intention of spending the duration leading gaggles of aircraft across the oceans, and anyway they had been fortunate to keep the first formation together as long as they had. The time would come when bad weather would make this system impossible from the outset. He also argued that it was absurd to fly aircraft across the Atlantic to avoid the menace of the submarines, and then to ship the even more valuable crews back through the self-same hazards. He had already looked at Consolidated Aircraft's B-24 Liberator long-range bomber and had judged it ideal for conversion to the transport rôle. Now he urged that a number should be purchased and this was agreed.

The matter of navigators for the ferry service was solved pragmatically. Newly trained men emerging from the British Commonwealth Air Training Plan navigation schools in Canada were to put their recently acquired skills to the test by joining a ferry crew for their return flight to Britain. Some of the lucky ones received brief additional training in their art from Bennett himself, and probably doubled their knowledge overnight at the feet of the master, but others were less able. The author recalls hearing of one freshly trained young man who joined a Catalina ferry crew much later in the war and became so overawed by the immensity of his task that he went and crouched in the tail, refusing to communicate with anyone. The gnarled pilot, who anyway regarded navigation as a pretty unworthy practice for a grown man, happily kept heading east and eventually arrived in Scotland!

As the months went by increasing numbers of Hudsons made their way to England. In December Bennett made his second crossing flying the much photographed aeroplane donated to the British by Lockheed and Vega employees, carrying an appropriate inscription on its side. During one visit to London he was invited to the Air Ministry, whose Directorate of Bombing Operations sought his expert advice on the problems of trying to ensure that bombers actually reached their targets. He was saddened but scarcely surprised at the paucity of the results being achieved. Bearing in mind his recent trans-Atlantic experiences, he suggested that as an alternative to improving general standards of navigation it should be possible to form a dedicated group of expert target finders, using 'fireworks' as he put it, to mark the way. He had no idea, as he returned to ferrying, whether his words had been received as prophetic, or merely bizarre.

During the course of 1941 the flight delivery of aircraft from Canada became increasingly accepted as commonplace, even if it never became routine and, inevitably, Bennett began to consider where next his talents might best be used. In the event his mind was made up for him as the whole basis of the organisation changed with the departure of Beaverbrook from the Ministry of Aircraft Production. At this point the Royal Canadian Air Force (RCAF) assumed responsibility for the ferry flights, and the United States became more actively involved as its neutrality became more openly benevolent towards the British cause. Bennett was replaced when Air Chief Marshal Sir Frederick Bowhill formed RAF Ferry Command on 18 July 1941 and he characteristically flew a new Hudson back over the Atlantic as his means of getting home.

After a number of dispiriting false starts, which must have brought back unhappy memories of his early days with the RAAF in Melbourne, Bennett found himself proudly back in the RAF and posted to Leeming in Yorkshire. After many frustrations with RAF administrative incompetence he assumed command of 77 Squadron equipped with Whitleys and operating within 4 Group RAF Bomber Command. He was totally confident of his ability to lead his squadron against the enemy and to imbue it with his own high standards of efficiency.

By the same token his flight commanders came rapidly to respect the somewhat complex Australian who now commanded them, and acknowledged that his background was the more valuable for its conspicuous non-conformity. He flew operationally with them from the outset and set about trying to improve the frankly minimal results that were being achieved. He approached all difficulties with a process of careful analysis, interrogating his crews, poring over target photographs, encouraging and criticising, always positive but always demanding. Unhappily, he did not have sufficient time with 77 Squadron to bring about the transformation that by now he knew he could achieve.

The new Halifaxes were beginning to be delivered in quantity when he was transferred to the command of 10 Squadron, also based at Leeming. It was April 1942 and the squadron had possessed its Halifaxes for four or five months when it moved on detachment to Lossiemouth, near Aberdeen, for an attack on the German battleship *Tirpitz* lurking in Foetten fjord, Norway. From its northern lair it posed a lasting threat to Britain's supply lines without ever needing to weigh anchor, until it was destroyed by the RAF in November 1944.

It was an operation almost tailor-made for Bennett, set at the very limits of range across the featureless sea to a pinpoint target on a rugged confusing coastline. The attack was to be made with mines and the landfall was excellent, enabling Bennett to lead his squadron towards the target precisely on track as the Germans put down a heavy smoke-screen. Unfortunately enemy anti-aircraft fire proved highly accurate and descending through 2,000ft to attack, Bennett's aircraft was hit on the starboard wing which began to burn fiercely. Nevertheless, he was dissatisfied with his run-in and nursed the Halifax round to line up with the target for a second approach. This time he managed to drop his five 1,000lb mines through the billows of protective smoke, but was always honest enough to admit that, despite having caught a glimpse of the battleship's superstructure, he had no idea how accurate his attack had proved to be. In fairness he had other things on his mind as he turned east towards neutral Sweden.

Just then the starboard wing flaps extended and the undercarriage flopped down out of its nacelles, making any thought of crossing the mountains between them and the frontier out of the question. By this time their airspeed was rapidly decaying towards a stall and asymmetric forces were increasing to the extent that Bennett was experiencing great difficulty in maintaining control. He gave the order to abandon aircraft.

CHAPTER THREE
GERMAN BEAMS AND BLITZES

The part played by Germany in the development of strategic bombing during the Second World War was a surprisingly modest one. However her near total disinterest in the proposition was not determined by any humanitarian scruples, but rather by a realistic appraisal of her requirements to ensure the success of the Nazis' basic war aims. The military planners in Berlin contrasted their conclusive victories of the Franco-Prussian war in 1870 with the strength sapping impasse of the trench-to-trench warfare of 1914–18 and determined upon the creation of a highly mobile army of overwhelming strength. This army would be supported by a tactical air force operating as an extension of the artillery and as a weapon of terror to strike ahead of the advancing ground forces.

The possible commitment of long-range bombers against industrial and civilian targets was largely ignored, despite a natural desire on the part of certain Luftwaffe generals to possess the prestigious capability of striking at the heart of any potential enemy. The concept of *Blitzkrieg* – or lightning war – now embraced by Hitler's generals would indeed involve indiscriminate attacks on civilians, but these were almost incidental, designed to generate hordes of refugees to clog roads, impede defences, and paralyse government.

Hitler needed to plan quick conquests if he was to keep the support of the German people, and he understood that the country's still fragile economic and political situation in the late 1930s would only tolerate spectacular success. This consideration above all determined his objectives, the strategy by which he would achieve them, and the choice of weapons that would be developed in their support. Strategic bombing did not fit easily into the German plans for it was by definition an instrument of prolonged warfare, needing to be sustained to produce even worthwhile results, let alone final victory. Furthermore it required an enormous industrial commitment to produce large and complex aircraft in even modest numbers, when the Wehrmacht was demanding that the Luftwaffe's contribution to *Blitzkrieg* should comprise squadrons of agile tactical machines.

There was another aspect of strategic bombing which was deeply unsettling to the Nazi leaders. Once practised it carried the threat of a response, large or small, sooner or later from the enemy. This response was bound to increase in intensity the more prolonged that hostilities became, and almost by definition strategic bombardment was an instrument of the long term. Such potential threats to the German homeland did not form part of the then German philosophy; to be acceptable, wars were to be fought outside her territory and her citizens were to be fed the fruits of proud conquest without any costly reckoning. Konrad Goseler had gloomily observed that there was no longer a clear separation between homeland and combat area, so once again, attacks on civilian populations had become the likely consequences of waging war. He drew some early comfort from this, suggesting that the widespread fear of attacks from the air might force politicians to abandon war as a means of settling international disputes. Although his basic proposition was rejected, it seemed in Berlin to confirm the wisdom of the concept of *Blitzkrieg*, for there would be nothing to fear from an enemy annihilated in just a few short days of fighting.

It was the open application of terror upon undefended centres of civilian population which really characterised the Nazi bombers and those of the broadly sympathetic Italian and Japanese warlords as the 1930s ended. Thus it was Guernica, bombed by the German Condor Legion in the Spanish Civil War, the earlier indiscriminate attacks by the Imperial Japanese Air Force on China, and the Italians' infamous mustard gassing of Abyssinia, that provided a grim prelude to the Second World War. It was hardly surprising that the gloom-laden predictions of Britain's Prime Minister, Stanley Baldwin, on the inevitability of air attack should generate the production of tens of thousands of cheap coffins as an essential element of preparation for war.

One or two voices continued to be raised to warn the military against over-enthusiasm for the quick-fix of bombing to achieve easy victory. A captain in the German Navy, Heye, spoke out against the Luftwaffe's involvement in Spain: 'Our attacks on objects of little military importance are not a suitable means of breaking an opponent's resistance' he said. 'The memory of the air attack on Guernica by the Condor [German] Legion still today affects the population and permits no friendly feelings for Germany in the population of the Basques, who earlier were thoroughly friendly.' His was another straw in the wind, blowing across German thinking, and seeming to confirm that such strategic bombing as might prove necessary should be seen as incidental, rather than fundamental, to the sort of war that Germany wished to wage.

Thus it was the dive-bomber – macho favourite of Ernst Udet, Director General of Luftwaffe equipment, and of Hermann Goering – which became the arrowhead of *Blitzkrieg* on 1 September 1939 when Poland was invaded, although medium bombers, the Heinkels and Dorniers, were committed to bomb the capital Warsaw. In making these last attacks the Luftwaffe, by prior arrangement with Stalin, homed on to the target city using Soviet radio transmissions to guide their way. This development was of the utmost significance. It not only concentrated German minds on the potential value of beam guidance, but also triggered a pre-planned British response in which all UK transmissions were confined to two synchronised groups on the erstwhile Northern and London Regional frequencies. The long-wave National programme from Droitwich ceased and when enemy air attacks began in 1940 transmitters near their approach routes were progressively shut down. By that time, however, the Luftwaffe's bomber squadrons based in Northern France had behind them a sophisticated system to guide their path to British targets.

The first of these systems was known by the codename *Knickebein* (translated as bent or crooked leg), although 'dog-leg' might be a more appropriate English colloquialism. British Intelligence first became aware of the likelihood of the existence of such a beam in the spring and early summer of 1940. This came about as a result of reported beam transmissions associated with German air activity, and of notes and jottings found on board crashed enemy aircraft. These seemed to confirm the existence of transmitting stations near Bredstedt, as well as near Kleve, and gradually a picture emerged of a navigation and bombing aid based upon the well established and widely used Lorenz blind landing system. If the enemy had indeed been able to develop the technology for even reasonably accurate bombing by night, or in bad weather, he would possess an enormous advantage and have the ability to re-direct a highly vulnerable summer daytime offensive into the comparative safety of Britain's winter night skies.

On the evening of 21 June, an RAF Anson flown by Flight Lieutenant H. Bufton with radio operator Corporal Mackie on board, left Wyton to fly up the east coast to attempt to locate the origin of the beams on which the Luftwaffe were suspected of operating. Just before 10.00 pm Mackie intercepted the transmission of a series of audible 'dots' which, as they flew North, merged to become a continuous note before slowly breaking again this time into dashes. On landing Bufton reported:

'(i) There is a narrow beam approximately 400–500yds wide passing through a position one mile south of Spalding, having dots to the south and dashes to the north, on a bearing of 104° to 284° true.

'(ii) That the carrier frequency on the night of 21–22 June was 31.5 Mc/s modulated at 1150 c/s and similar to Lorenz characteristics.'

It was immediately noted that the beam which actually had emanated from Kleve was aligned with some precision on Derby, the centre of Rolls-Royce aero engine production.

The ingenuity of *Knickebein* overcame the difficulty of transmitting a sufficiently long-range narrow beam by employing two beams, one comprising dots the other dashes, which when superimposed produced a continuous note. Thus, when the beams themselves were slightly overlapped, an extremely precise and narrow zone was produced down which a skilfully flown bomber could fly with enviable accuracy. This was in fact the well-known technique used in the Lorenz approach system developed and widely used before the war. The on-board equipment comprised nothing more superficially interesting than a standard Lorenz receiver, although closer examination revealed this to be much more sensitive than would ever be needed for the short-range requirements of blind landing. The final part of the system comprised a second beam on one side of the director beam, cutting across it to give the pilot appropriate warning that he was approaching the target, and giving him a usefully accurate indication of his distance from it.

Hardly had the secrets of *Knickebein* been unravelled when in August 1940 the Luftwaffe began to use two new and even more sophisticated bombing aids. By the late summer the British were jamming *Knickebein* with increasing success as well as evolving means of bending it, an obviously controversial process, or using it as a means of homing night fighters on to the bomber stream. The first of the new systems, known as *X-Geraet* or X-apparatus, was a complex arrangement involving a total of four beams, one aligned directly on to the target and the others coming in from one side, intersecting the director beam at various carefully pre-programmed points. The first of these would indicate that the bomber had reached a point 50km from the target, whilst the second signalled that there was 20km to go. At this point the aircraft's navigator started a clock rather like a kitchen timer. This was an essential element in the bomb release routine since when the final cross-beam was signalled 5km from the target, a second button on the clock was pressed stopping the hand which had been moving and activating another hand. When the two hands overlapped this indicated that the previously computed bomb release point had been reached and the bombs were dropped automatically.

On the night of Tuesday 13 August 1940, the *X-Geraet* beams were operated for an attack on Castle Bromwich where the main Spitfire shadow factory was located. Oddly enough this raid, which took place at the end of Goering's much vaunted *Adlertag* or Eagle Day, was a failure despite being entrusted to the redoubtable *Kampfgruppe 100*. The highly experienced German crews had great difficulty in the operation of the new equipment and only four positively claimed that their 1,400-acre target had been hit. The damage caused by the 11 x 250kg bombs was virtually indiscernible within the vast complex. Clearly the most ingenious apparatus and the best bomber crews were no guarantee of success. Undaunted, *KG100* made eight further raids on other targets before the end of August with varying degrees of success, and thereafter they continued to perform a very limited and specialised role – as close to pathfinding as the Luftwaffe ever came – during the night blitz of 1940–41.

Y-Geraet took beam technology one step further in terms of subordinating the contribution made by the bomber crews to target finding and bombing accuracy. The Y system used a beam of particularly sophisticated characteristics involving the transmission of 180 directional signals per minute and an on-board analyser to determine the aircraft's actual position. There was no navigational involvement on the part of the crew, simply because the signal's complexity took it well beyond human interpretation. The bomber's distance along the beam was established by sending a second signal which was radiated back from a further piece of on-board apparatus. The lapsed time between the sending and return of this signal gave a very accurate measure of its range, and in this way the ground station had all the information necessary to tell the crew precisely when to release their bombs. Of course, this was providing they had managed to fly a course which kept them within the comparatively narrow limits of the beam's radiation, and that they had responded accurately to the stream of information available.

Inevitably, the limitation of the system was the human element. The Luftwaffe quickly found that the two X and Y systems imposed a level of complexity well beyond the simple dot and dash constraints of *Knickebein*, making them best left in the hands of their most experienced crews. They were also uncomfortably aware of the susceptibility of such ingenious devices to jamming, bending and other highly effective disruption at which the British were proving most adept.

The cat-and-mouse game would probably have continued indefinitely, well beyond the night Blitz which followed the Battle of Britain. However, German war strategy had moved on and the first priority was the success of the invasion of Soviet Russia, a classic *Blitzkrieg* which suited Goering by taking the pressure off the Luftwaffe and its less than successful efforts to bomb Britain into submission. In the last days of the Blitz of 1940/41 the Luftwaffe's best squadrons, inevitably including *KG100*, had used the beams to guide them in early pathfinding and the release of flares, or fire-bombing to mark targets for the main bomber force. Oddly this gave some solace to Sir Henry Tizard, Scientific Adviser to the Air Staff and a devout sceptic of German beam technology, who claimed that the enemy's frequent use of flares and fire-raising was proof that they lacked sophisticated navigational aids. He dismissed any suggestion that they might in fact be using such aids to place the flares and the incendiaries with consummate accuracy.

The severity of air attacks on Britain diminished as the demands of the war on the Eastern Front made increasing inroads into German war resources. There was also some shift of emphasis by Germany on to the Atlantic war, where it was hoped their U-Boats would ultimately sever supply lines to the extent of causing the British to sue for peace. The Luftwaffe excelled in its operations against Russia, supporting and supplying the army as it struck eastwards. There were no plans for the evolution of new types of strategic bomber and certainly no plans to build up a force of such aircraft. However, by 1942 major industrial centres in the Ruhr, and indeed throughout Germany, were beginning to experience increasingly determined attacks by night from RAF Bomber Command. The attacks on the ancient Baltic cities of Rostock and Lübeck particularly angered Hitler and he demanded revenge.

His choice of targets in Britain singled out for revenge attacks were a handful of ancient cultural cities with Exeter, Bath, Norwich, York and Canterbury taking the brunt of the onslaught between April and June 1942 in what became known as the Baedeker Blitz.

Once the pattern of the attack became apparent at the end of April, Intelligence sources began to monitor the air waves for indications of beam directions so that targeted cities could be identified and the defence forces deployed accordingly. It was known that the enemy had modified *X-Geraet* by the use of an inaudible ultrasonic beam superimposed on the original frequencies, but no trace of any transmission was found. For a while it was assumed that the lead German squadrons had access to some new device to achieve the accuracy required to mark their targets with the concentrated release of incendiaries. Yet another theory was that the enemy was relying on eyeball navigation since all the targeted cities lay close to distinctively shaped coastlines. However, this held true for most centres of population and industry within the British Isles since none lay more than 50 miles from the sea – a permanent advantage to the Luftwaffe.

The actual solution to the puzzling silence was more prosaic. It emerged that the apparatus used to detect the beams had been incorrectly modified to meet the ultrasonic characteristics of the new enemy equipment, and so was missing them altogether. Whilst this was not a disastrous error it temporarily boosted the sagging morale of the Luftwaffe by perhaps allowing its bomber crews to believe they had for once maintained a brief lead in the battle of the beams.

Following the Baedeker raids Goering balefully took stock of the RAF's night offensive against his country, and the escalating mighty impact of the American daylight raids. Until the end of 1943 and with all attention in Germany turned to fighter production and the defence of the Reich, attacks on Britain became desultory, generally small-scale and almost totally random. There were a few larger raids, for instance on Cheltenham on 14 April, but the Luftwaffe's loss rate was climbing and *X-Geraet's* use had been abandoned in favour of the Y system, despite the fact that the RAF's 80 Wing was achieving great success in jamming it. *Knickebein* was still in use, but with increasingly disappointing results.

To maintain pressure on Britain's defences, numbers of Focke-Wulf FW190s were deployed at night for scattered attacks designed to disrupt and disconcert, whilst more conventional bombing raids became ever less frequent. However, in August 1943 the Luftwaffe attacked Portsmouth and made use of techniques closely similar to those of the RAF's Pathfinders. Flares were dropped, followed by target markers and a final cluster of illuminators, before a Main Force of about 90 aircraft moved in to attack. A few nights later a similar number set out to raid Lincoln, but the attack went disastrously wrong and no bombs actually fell within the city, perceived by the Germans to be at the very heart of Britain's bomber country!

As the year drew towards its close the enemy's bombing campaign almost faded away, but Goering remained under strong pressure to avenge the devastation being wrought nightly on his country by the RAF. Accordingly, the Luftwaffe were instructed to mount a further major assault on London using a newly developed blind bombing system, *Egon*, similar to the British Oboe and making use of *Freya* ground radars sited in France. In addition certain bomber crews had a further device, *Truhe*, which poached transmissions from the British Gee navigational system and used them to provide highly accurate positional data. This aid was restricted to the Luftwaffe's own pathfinders, both to reduce the chances of its discovery by the British and to retain its operation in the most expert hands. However *Truhe* was soon blown and counter-measures in the form of artificial delays in the radiation of Gee slave station pulses were introduced. These distortions were corrected by RAF crews using data provided to them at each day's briefing.

The new German attack on the capital was codenamed *Steinbock* and was mounted six weeks later than originally intended, on 21 January 1944. A total of 227 bombers were involved in a two-phase attack amounting to some 450 sorties. Great lines of white flares were dropped by the Junkers Ju188s of *KG66*, pointing the route from the south across Kent and East Sussex, and further distinctive clusters coloured white and green fell in London around Waterloo station to mark the aiming point. Despite the large scale of the attack by German standards, the bombing accuracy was poor. This was also the case during a second attack in January and in five further raids on London during the first half of February. Indeed it was not until the 18th of that month that the Luftwaffe managed to effect a damaging and well disciplined raid. Four more followed on consecutive nights, culminating in a final one on the 24th when the bombers followed red and white markers circling round High Wycombe, before turning to approach London from the north. As they neared the city they saw Westminster bathed in an unearthly red glow from cascades of markers, pin-point dropped from 29,000ft by Junkers Ju 188s of *KG66* Pathfinders. When *Steinbock* ended the Germans had lost more than 300 aircraft and had forfeited the advantage of all its new bombing and navigational devices to British jamming. Some 1,600 civilians had been killed and 3,000 more badly injured. Only 40 per cent of the bombs intended for London actually fell within the boundaries of its civil defences.

Within three months a new assault would begin which made no claim of precision, had no purpose but terror, and required no skilled crews nor electronic aids. The flying bombs and the rockets were Hitler's last, wild throw.

CHAPTER FOUR
PLAYERS VERSUS GENTLEMEN

Group Captain Hamish Mahaddie recalls that his first experience of any disciplined process of target finding was in June 1940 when serving as a pilot in 77 Squadron on Whitleys. Flying Officer Jimmy Marks, later to lose his life when a Wing Commander and CO of 35 Squadron, suggested that the great fires still burning from the Luftwaffe's attack on Rotterdam might be used as elementary signposts for night bomber aircraft attacking targets deeper into continental Europe. He proposed a carefully timed flight commencing over the Rotterdam blaze and ending with the release of flares to pinpoint the target and allow for a reasonable concentration of bombing. All the crews agreed that this was a splendid idea and in the ideal conditions of an early summer night, facing little or no opposition, they set out to put it into effect.

Each aircraft in the elongated stream of 12 or so thought they did precisely what had been agreed, but not one single crew member saw any of the flares dropped by their squadron colleagues and accordingly dropped their bombs on an unscientific best-estimate of the target's location. Marks was frustrated but undismayed and secured his squadron commander's agreement for a repeat performance the following night. This time only four aircraft participated with the four most experienced navigators and great care was taken to re-calibrate the Whitleys' airspeed indicators and re-swing their compasses. Stopwatches were used to time the flight in from the still-burning Rotterdam fires, and at the end of the timed run the agreed signals of Very lights and flares were visible to all from aircraft which were within a three-mile radius of one another. One flare clearly illuminated the target, a concentration of armoured vehicles and troops in a distinctive area of woodland, and more flares were dropped before bombing began. Mahaddie believes that an effective attack resulted, proving the value of disciplined navigational skills exercised by a small number of experienced practitioners.

By 1942, however, there was an increasing number of rebels within the middle ranks of Bomber Command who shared the concerns expressed by the Butt Report, although they might have lacked the mass of detail evidence to which he had access. These men with operational experience knew the daunting difficulties faced by crews, and suspected that many of the claims made of targets located and destroyed were no more than the products of wishful thinking.

The great prejudice that existed amongst senior officers of the RAF against the creation of a bomber *corps élite*, was naturally at its strongest amongst the group and squadron commanders of Bomber Command. They held – with some justification – that the singling out of experts or supermen, far from encouraging the less proficient airmen to try harder, was more than likely to have the opposite effect. Furthermore it was absolutely certain that the squadrons would be weakened by the loss of their best crews, taken to create the new force. Therefore it was argued that the whole exercise could well be self-defeating. It must have required considerable courage on the part of the Deputy Director of Bomber Operations at the Air Ministry to cast his lot with the rebels, but that is precisely what Group Captain Syd Bufton did on 17 March 1942.

The Buftons were within the new genre of RAF families of which the Atcherleys, the Dundas and the MacRoberts were amongst others. Sydney Bufton had an overwhelming desire to see his service make the vital contribution to victory, and was dismayed at the way in which its courage and material resources were being squandered. He had the added advantage of knowing precisely what he was talking about, having commanded 10 Squadron from July 1940 until April 1941 and thereafter, briefly, 76 Squadron. His brother John died flying Hampdens with 83 Squadron, and just before his death wrote to the girl he hoped to marry. In one sentence he poignantly and precisely defined Bomber Command's awesome responsibility and the indisputable justification for its every action. He wrote: 'We're the only active force operating against Germany and as it's the only way of striking directly we'll be exploited more and more, especially as the force grows. The RAF fighters and bombers combined will undoubtedly win this war in time, but the end isn't nearly in sight yet and before its all over the losses will be enormous...'

In his paper written in March 1942, Bufton recorded his dismay at the inadequacy of bombing aids, particularly of the flares that were available, and he contrasted this with the quality of the German defences. Since arriving at the Air Ministry in November 1941 he had participated in many discussions about the extremely poor results being achieved. He was convinced that the solution lay in selected crews being used to co-ordinate the offensive by finding and marking targets with flares, and by preliminary incendiary attack to guide in the Main Force. He rejected the notion that jealousy and poor morale would be experienced by run-of-the-mill crews and suggested that any dilution of squadron expertise by creaming off their best men would be transitory and survivable. He further argued: 'Our present inability to effect a decisive concentration [of bombs] must completely outweigh personal and administrative considerations, particularly in view of the critical period which is now upon us and the urgent necessity of providing conclusive evidence of the value of our strategic bombing force to counteract political and other forces aiming at its disruption.'

Bufton was well aware that the Admiralty harboured great ambitions to assume control of a dramatically enlarged Coastal Command to pitch against the U-boats in the North Atlantic. At the same time the Army clamoured for tactical bombing support in North Africa. Both of these objectives, if agreed by the War Cabinet, would have been at the expense of Harris's new generation of bombers and his aim of having a force of 4,000 strategic bombers to take the great offensive to Germany. Sceptics abounded and Churchill's support for the bombing offensive was only durable for so long as he could be assured of its ultimate effect upon the enemy.

At the end of his paper, Bufton summarised his views. He proposed that six squadrons should be designated to a target-finding role and they should be located on airfields reasonably close to each other to encourage the growth of a cohesive unified force. Geographic proximity would make easier the force commander's co-ordinating task as well as helping him to develop and refine its tactical efficiency. There should be no difficulty in assembling an armoury of markers and illuminating flares on the back of the well-established pyrotechnic industry. In particular Bufton favoured the development of colour-coded marking backed up with a deluge of incendiaries, a technique which had already produced encouraging results in limited squadron use. Handled in the correct manner he believed that the creation of the proposed force could be a positive inspiration to Main Force crews. However much they might grumble that their skills were being impugned, Bufton guessed from his own experience that many would be relieved that some of the burden of responsibility was being lifted from their shoulders and that someone else was going to seek and find their targets.

There had never been a war campaign before, reasoned Bufton, where a strategy whose purpose and method were determined at the highest levels, was eventually left for its execution in the hands of small groups of men, each one operating in near total isolation hundreds of miles away from any structure of command. There were no great battlefield generals wheeling formations, or plugging gaps in the line, no gallant admirals conning majestic lines of ships and executing precise manoeuvres. The bomber war was remote and infinitely lonely, depending for its success on the very individual effort, perseverance and bravery of men whose youth made the doom which confronted them the more poignant. Anything that could be done to relieve their task, or to make it more effective, was really a vital imperative alongside which considerations of vested interest, tradition, or inhibiting convention were as irrelevant to this war as a cavalry charge.

No doubt with some apprehension, but with the utter conviction that he was right, Bufton circulated his paper to a limited number of his most senior superiors. Harris replied on 17 April, the day on which 12 Lancasters from 44 and 97 Squadrons had set out for a 1,000-mile round trip at low level to Augsburg to hit the MAN U-boat engine factory, a target of great interest to the Royal Navy. It was hoped that the fast modern aircraft with their heavy bomb load could not only evade the defences, but could also hit the factory hard in the high visibility of an early spring afternoon before returning home as darkness came to defend them. Five Lancasters eventually came back, three from 44 Squadron to Waddington and two from 97 Squadron to Woodhall Spa. The operation's leader, Squadron Leader J. D. Nettleton, who survived the raid was awarded the Victoria Cross. The production of MAN U-boat engines proceeded without noticeable interruption. Clearly the option of attacking German targets at low-level in daytime was no more practicable in 1942 than it had been at the very start of the war, despite the superior aircraft available at the time of the Augsburg attack.

Harris must have pondered this latest disaster to befall his squadrons as he prepared himself for the next onslaught from the Air Ministry on the target finding issue. He was under continuing pressure from his group commanders to resist the proposals which, as each day passed, became even more justified. The C-in-C had gone so far as to write to Bufton on 17 April that he had an open mind on the issue, but was not as yet convinced. He claimed he had discussed target marking very thoroughly with his various senior field commanders down to station level and that they were almost universally hostile. He believed their reasoning was sound and supported their deep dislike of the *corps élite* concept. He reported that henceforward photographs taken by aircraft at the moment of bomb release (an automatic process) would be carefully analysed squadron by squadron and at set intervals, a winning squadron would be announced and designated 'raid leader' for the following period. He saw in this scheme a means of securing expert target finding on a competitive, and therefore morale boosting, basis.

Any commander would have the utmost sympathy for Harris's predicament. He depended absolutely upon the commitment and support of his field commanders, and morale amongst them was already sufficiently low without the turmoil that would be caused by a cautionary sacking or two. They were, after all, living closer to the operational squadrons than he was and they should therefore be accurate barometers of attitude and opinion. And yet there was a diametrically opposing view in the Air Ministry and a sensitivity to the broader politics of waging the war which Harris would be crazy to ignore. His dilemma was how to respond positively to the Air Staff whilst retaining the trust and support of his command. He was in the limelight in the middle of the stage and the audience was waiting with mounting expectation for something rather better than the 'raid leader' speech.

Harris was well aware of Churchill's interest and had reacted angrily to the intervention after the Cologne raid of Air Vice-Marshal C. E. H. Medhurst, acting Vice Chief of the Air Staff, who suggested a list of 'standard towns' for elimination following the success of the first 1,000-bomber raid, the results of which amazed him. Such a concentration of explosives could, he suggested, wreak havoc on towns of between 2–300,000 population within 400 miles of Mildenhall. The list included Kiel, Kassel, Magdeburg, Frankfurt, Mainz, Saarbrücken, Karlsruhe, Osnabrück, Dessau and Schweinfurt. He advocated five such attacks on Hamburg alone to lay waste to it. Harris took the opportunity to complain that everyone seemed to want to get in on the act, to the extent that he had to wait up to a fortnight to see post-raid target damage photographs. He required them to establish whether second attacks were needed, yet all the emphasis seemed to be on presenting the Prime Minister and others with beautifully mounted photographs in great leather-bound volumes! Harris said he was sick of his headquarters being full of 'goofers' who seemed to have absolute priority for information. Medhurst pointed out in a diplomatically written response that the 'goofers' seemed to comprise His Majesty the King, the Prime Minister, the Secretary of State for Air, and the Chief of the Air Staff, all of whom failed to merit the C-in-C's description.

On 8 May 1942, Bufton wrote a further paper saying that he was convinced his ideas, if put into effect with the total commitment of all concerned, could treble or quadruple the impact of Bomber Command's attacks. He argued that this scale of improvement could be achieved almost immediately without waiting for more aircraft, bigger bombs, or better navigational and bomb-aiming devices. It was simply a case of doing everything to ensure that current efforts with all their shortcomings were not wasted. Accuracy would have the same result as multiplying the strength of the bomber force three or four times over.

Reviews of recent raids amply illustrated the deficiencies. Between 8 March–12 April 1942 Essen, which was heavily defended, had been attacked eight times at a cost of 77 aircraft. From these losses only 110 crew members survived and 354 died. The 122 photographs analysed showed that only two aircraft had actually bombed the target, two had got within one mile of it, eight between one and five miles, 104 between 5–25 miles, and six between 25–100 miles. In short 90 per cent of the aircraft had bombed between 5–100 miles from the target.

Perhaps it could be argued that Essen was, for the time, extremely well defended and therefore presented particular problems. In view of this it is worth considering a contemporary attack on Rostock which was far distant, but lightly defended by any standard. Here 72 target photographs were taken of which only 16 were recognised as actually depicting Rostock. Wasted effort accounted for 80 per cent of the operation, much of this being due to the bombing of decoy fires and conflagrations caused by previously mistaken bombing. One obvious conclusion would be that defences and distance were the inhibitors of accuracy, but an attack on Genevilliers, a comparatively close and well-defined target, produced equally lamentable results. Eighty-five aircraft took a total of 91 target photographs of which only 11 were recognisably accurate.

With all the zeal of a prophet Bufton waded into the attack once more, going as close as he dared to rubbishing the 'raid leader' idea which Harris had grasped as one way through the impasse. He argued that all squadrons comprised good and bad crews and could be called upon to attack targets ranging from the easy to the impossibly difficult.

These variables plus those imposed by wind, weather and defences made the selection of leaders on the basis of aiming-point photographs a highly unscientific process.

He suggested that the very mention of a *corps élite* appeared to give rise to a vague antagonism in some quarters. Yet, to take the issue to its logical conclusion, Bufton claimed that current policy was synonymous to seeking to defeat 'the rival school by turning out the best house team' rather than fielding the School First XI. Sir Henry Tizard, the Air Ministry's Chief Scientific Adviser, later developed Bufton's analogy saying: 'I don't think that the formation of a First XV at a school makes the small boys play rugby any less enthusiastically.'

Bufton must have regarded the increasingly frequent arrivals of Harris at the Air Ministry with some disquiet at this time. The C-in-C possessed a formidable reputation for putting subordinates in their place but he was generally a fair boss, appreciating those who stood up to him and he was never afraid to admit that he was wrong. One morning at this time he encountered Bufton in the entrance lobby of the Air Ministry and fixed him with a baleful stare. 'Good morning Bufton,' he growled, 'and what are you going to do to me today?' It was a *bon mot* which rightly passed into the folklore of the RAF.

On 22 May Harris wrote to his AOCs in the aftermath of an attack on Mannheim on 19 May which had cost a further nine aircraft. He told them that the attack had caused virtually no damage to the city or its suburbs, although there was evidence of large fires in a nearby forest which could, he assumed, have been the result of effective decoys. Reports from the squadrons had indicated the expectation that this was a good raid but, Harris wrote, it was no more than a fearful waste of effort, lacking in skill and full of carelessness. Crews should not bomb blazing fires. What was the point of adding to an existing inferno with further incendiaries, or of pouring high explosive on to fires? There had also been earlier wild bombing at Rostock, but subsequent attacks on that city had shown great improvement. The C-in-C was tempted to think that only when crews realised they would have to return again and again to cities until they had inflicted the required measure of destruction, were attacks diligently pressed home. Harris concluded this bitingly critical letter to his commanders by reminding them that even at the height of war there remained influential people who wanted to destroy Bomber Command, if not the RAF, and evidence of inaccurate bombing was all the justification they required. In a last paragraph he recounted the story of one squadron commander's impassioned recommendation for an award to a pilot for pressing home a successful attack. Subsequent photographic evidence showed him to have missed the target altogether!

On 11 June, Harris met Air Chief-Marshal Sir Charles Portal, Chief of the Air Staff, who questioned him closely about the great debate. The next day he sent Portal two examples of the analyses conducted by Bomber Command into each and every raid. 'We try to extract all possible lessons from any operation,' he said, 'and to profit by them.' He went on to report that he had met his group commanders that morning, together with their best 'target finding' squadron commanders, and 'all were utterly opposed to the formation of a Target Finding Force on the lines which hold favour in the Air Ministry. Briefly their arguments (were) that we already have a Target Finding Force by a process of electing the best squadrons and best crews to lead attacks. All were insistent that there was nothing particular to be gained from these selected crews belonging to one unit and living on one aerodrome. There were, on the contrary, overwhelming considerations against the proposal from the point of view of morale, practicability, etc. etc.'

Harris went on to say that he had persuaded the raid leader squadrons to get together, perhaps twice a month, for the purpose of comparing notes and improving techniques. Warming to the support of his highly experienced subordinates, he recorded the general view that so-called 'starred raid leaders' and their crews should have a special badge, perhaps a gilt eagle to be worn below brevets and medals. Despite himself, Harris found that he was using the phrase 'esprit de corps' whilst still eschewing the 'corps élite' designation! The universal opinion at the C-in-C's meeting was, he said, 'that the trouble is not "*finding*" the target, within very narrow limits using TR 1335 (Gee) or other means, but in "*seeing*" the target when you get to it on the average dark night through the haze and in the face of the vast searchlight glare common to all highly defended areas. The general argument was that the target-finding expert has no greater chance or ability to *see* under such conditions than anybody else.'

Harris added that most people at his meeting thought that due to permanent haze over the target the only effective technique for striking at the Ruhr was area bombing. 'We have always said this,' he insisted, 'it will remain so until the Force is so large that major conflagrations result from... the first [phase] of any attack.'

If proof were needed that area bombing was a necessity forced by the lack of adequate technology, it was here for all to see. The critics of such bombing miss the point as surely as so-called precision bombing missed its target for most of the Second World War. Harris concluded his letter with the following sentences:

'My existing Raid Leader Scheme provides all the requirements of the Target Finding Force fanatic, but living together in special units. All my AOCs and all the best squadron commanders who attended my last conference see no gain to be obtained from this getting together requirement. They were all decisively and adamantly opposed to the proposition... The only dissenter was an ex-squadron commander from Feltwell (where the Target Finding Force idea originated), now on 3 Group staff. But he could offer no reasoned argument for the constitution of such a special force beyond asserting that he wanted to find the target as often as possible, which naive statement received of course the chorused reply of "and so say all of us".'

Two days later Portal replied. He was an excellent CAS, combining an agile mind and great firmness of purpose with a strong streak of humanity and understanding of the problems of his subordinates. Above all he was very perceptive and a seasoned diplomat, both qualities being vital in the dangerous high ground surrounding his job. His letter ran to five pages of reasoned counter-argument to Harris's spirited defence. He suggested that there was nothing between their respective analyses of the problem, the waste of effort involved in imprecise attacks, adding: 'I take it that you agree that something must be done to prevent less expert crews lighting fires in the wrong places...' Portal next commented on the fact that although Harris claimed all his command representatives were utterly opposed to the formation of a separate target marking force, they 'seemed to admit the need for such a force and present no reasonable argument [against it]'. In fact, wrote Portal, they seemed enthusiastic about apportioning the task to the best crews and now even proposed a special badge! Surely this went against the supposed opposition to a *corps elite*. He noted that the C-in-C's attitude had subtly changed since March, from total rejection of the target finding suggestion to the current raid leader concept. 'Surely,' wrote Portal, 'it was not logical that [Harris] should now reject the final and essential step of welding the selected crews into one closely-knit organisation which, as I see it, is the only way to make their leadership and direction effective.'

He continued:

'I cannot believe that your compromise will give equal results. You say that there is nothing particular to be gained from bringing the selected crews into one unit and locating them together on one air-field. As we see it this is the essence of the problem. Without this close association there could be no continuity of technique; there could be no day-to-day improvement of method; we could not ensure that the plans and briefing for each individual operation were similarly and clearly interpreted and acted upon by the force as a whole. In effect it would mean perpetuating the present rule-of-thumb tactical methods by segregated crews, rather than introduc-ing the finesse and polish which one would expect from a well trained and co-ordinated Target Finding Force. The problem con-fronting us is clearly so great that nothing less than the best will do.'

Portal had seized upon a way through the impasse by identifying the areas of agreement between the factions, and suggesting that the tangi-ble differences were now too small to be of concern to a warrior like Harris. He thus sidelined the great unspoken issue that the squadrons sensed their ability, professionalism, and even their courage was being somehow denigrated by the formation of a Target Finding Force. Portal continued:

'There is one further point which I particularly desire to emphasise. Your raid leader scheme would depend for such success as it might achieve largely upon the assistance of [Gee]. We have already had the equipment in use three months. We cannot expect immunity from interference much longer. When it is denied to us as a target locating device it is clear that your proposals could not ensure to the bomber force the leadership which they must have if the aver-age crews are to overcome their great and increasing difficulties.'

This was a master stroke. It was true that Harris was relying on the suc-cess of Gee, and if this was effectively jammed by the enemy (in fact the first sets had fallen into enemy hands almost a year earlier) then some other expertise would be needed and a new approach justified. Portal thus provided Harris with a means of losing the argument with honour.

In conclusion, Portal disposed of further points made, without too much conviction by Harris, which had concerned the use of Commonwealth and foreign crews outside of their 'own' squadrons, and the availability of suitable aircraft. The letter ended with just the right measure of the diplomacy which had put Portal in his job: 'Although I do not consider the proposals which you have so far made go nearly far enough, I am reluctant to impose the Air Staff proposal upon you while you object strongly to it. I would therefore like to discuss the subject with you tomorrow as a preliminary to holding the conference arranged for next Thursday and I hope we shall be able to formulate an agreed scheme.'

The arguments were nearly finished when a report commissioned by the Joint Chiefs of Staff and conducted by Mr Justice Singleton really left nothing further to be said. Referring to Gee, Singleton wrote that two experienced operational officers had told him 'it will take you within four miles of the target longitudinally with a possible error of two miles laterally. It is in the last few miles that the real difficulties arise and they can only be overcome by determination and willpower. The crews are not by any means of the same calibre and the officers to whom I refer are firmly convinced of the desirability of a specially trained Target Finding Force which, they believe, would lead to greatly increased efficiency in bombing.' In referring to Singleton's words, Portal told Harris 'any failure on our part to effect a radical improvement may well endanger the whole of our bomber policy'.

Bennett had stayed with his blazing Halifax until the crew had baled out and, as he jumped dangerously close to the ground, the starboard wing broke away. On landing he buried his parachute in the Norwegian snow and quickly headed east away from the crash site and towards Sweden. Shortly afterwards he joined up with his radio operator. Despite the intense cold and the ever-present risk of detection the two men eventually established contact with a Norwegian family and, through them, with Resistance workers who guided the airmen to the Swedish border. There they were first officially placed under arrest and then generously entertained before being placed in internment by the friendly and sympathetic authorities. Don Bennett was delighted to see his second pilot and his flight engineer who were already in the camp, and to learn somewhat later that the other three members of his crew had survived to become prisoners of war. It had been a typically efficient example of survival, with evasion and escape for some of them.

After some negotiation between the British Embassy and the Swedish authorities, it was agreed that Bennett be repatriated. He was flown back to Leuchars in Scotland in a Lockheed 14, the civil equivalent of the Hudson he knew so well, and was mildly discomforted by a 'hair-raising flight', as even he described it, through hundreds of miles of enemy air space. The forecast weather was said to comprise moderate cloud, but in the event they completed the most dangerous part of the journey in clear bright conditions before night provided them with some welcome protection.

By the time that Portal had written his letter to Harris, Bennett had just resumed his command of 10 Squadron.

CHAPTER FIVE
'GIVE US THE TOOLS'

A British early wartime publication describes a fictitious approach of a night bomber to its designated target: 'The observer strains his eyes in the darkness and momentarily catches a gleam of water. He alters course to bring it dead ahead, but now he can see nothing. Then again he spots the glint of the water reflecting the light from the beam of a searchlight. He sees that it is indeed the lake for which he has been looking. He alters course still further to starboard to bring the estimated position of the target dead ahead and strains his eyes once more to find the river and the acres of workshops which are his objective. In order to help in this each bomber carries a number of powerful parachute flares which can be released by the bomb-aimer. When one is dropped it falls for a pre-arranged time after which the parachute opens and checks its descent. At the same moment the flare begins to burn with a light equal to several hundred thousand candle power... in clear weather conditions the ground will be sufficiently well illuminated to enable the bomb-aimers to pick up the target.'

This poignantly naive projection of a night bomber's mission had been totally confounded by Bomber Command's experience in the 20 months of war up to the late spring of 1942. When Harris had assumed command in February, it was of an increasingly dispirited force bearing an enormous responsibility for taking the war to the heart of Germany, but lacking any real prospect of doing so in any decisive manner. The squadrons were a long way from fulfilling the war-winning role that Trenchard had foreseen for them, and the depressing war situation in the early months of the year only added to the pressures on the new C-in-C who seemed no more likely to succeed than his ill-starred predecessors Ludlow-Hewitt and Peirse, both of whom were broken by the bleak enormity of their task. Such a judgement did not take account of Harris's Olympian determination, or of the sheer strength of his personality. He committed himself to the single shining objective of defeating Germany outright by aerial bombardment.

He determined a two-fold policy, comprising both the wholesale destruction of the enemy and the resultant resurrection of British morale from a graveyard of two years of almost uninterrupted defeats. He started with two advantages: the unswerving commitment and bravery of the bomber crews, and the quality and growing numerical strength of the aircraft they flew. Typically, as a mighty overture to the campaign he would fight for the next three years he staked both in a single throw.

On 30 May 1942 Harris assembled 1,000 bombers for an attack on Cologne. He committed every suitable aircraft from his own and other commands, and from operational training units, to make up the magically significant number. In a sense Cologne was both a beginning and an end: it concluded the years of strategic equivocation over the bombing of cities, and introduced a more realistic assessment of what were and were not legitimate targets. Certainly, no right-minded analyst could conclude that 1,000 aircraft might be engaged on the precision bombing of military and industrial objectives in a single city on a single night. Equally, he might well have concluded that the destruction of life and habitation associated with war industries in so vital a centre as Cologne represented an entirely reasonable extension to the harsh realities of total war.

Whatever the conclusion, the truth was that 00.47hrs on the morning of 31 May 1942, when the first bombs fell on Cologne, marked the moment when Germany's cities began to die in a manner which her leaders had never even contemplated as possible. Bomber Command lost 40 aircraft in the attack, an 'acceptable' 3.8 per cent, made the more so when the diverse make-up of the force and the inexperience of many of the participants were taken into account. The target had been marked by the Wellingtons and Stirlings of 3 Group, making good use of Gee. Next day the cameras of photographic reconnaissance aircraft recorded heavy damage, but the devastating big bombs – the so-called 'block-busters' – were still months away from delivery to the squadrons, as were the aircraft to carry them.

Capitalising on this success, two nights later Harris sent 956 aircraft to Essen, but despite brave attempts at accurate marking the raid was a near disaster, with bombs scattered far and wide and the towns of Oberhausen, Duisburg and Mülheim all being severely hit. Thirty-four aircraft were lost and three weeks later, on 25 June, a record total of 1,123 aircraft were despatched against Bremen for the loss of a further 50. As with Essen, Bremen was a disappointing operation and the absence of any profoundly encouraging outcome from these three immense operations must have hit Harris more than anyone. He had been at Bomber Command for some four months and, like the professional he was, had weighed all the evidence, listened to all the arguments, explored all the possibilities. He now perceived, perhaps against his own deep beliefs, that the magnificent men, fine aircraft, and increasing technology under his command were inadequate to make a decisive – perhaps the decisive – contribution to final victory. The problems of night bombing were too profound and the objectives too elusive for a mass of courageous, enthusiastic and utterly committed warriors to be sure of achieving them, consistently.

The harsh fact was that the bombing offensive had depended for its success upon bravery, persistence, luck and, not least, good weather. Much more certain means were now being developed both to assist navigation to the target area and to ensure its precise identification on arrival. With a reluctance that never really left him, Harris accepted that he must henceforward rely on the emerging industry of electronics to substitute science in the hands of his best crews for blind courage and fickle chance. It was not a situation that he savoured: his career experiences had taught him to distrust all gadgets and purveyors of quick fixes. He only became enthusiastic when convinced that the inventors had come up with something practical which would improve efficiency and the safety of his crews. If it was reasonably easy to make, so much the better.

Before the war he had visited America on a mission designed to form a judgement of that country's military aeronautical expertise. Whilst immensely impressed by the huge potential that then lay dormant in the USA, he was suspicious of his host's worship of complex technology and dismissive of the quality of their contemporary aircraft and engine designs. He was told of the supposedly miraculous Norden bombsight, but was forbidden any information about its design or operational capabilities. Irritated, with some justification, he assumed it to be yet another flawed panacea. He was always an unsympathetic observer of the scientific and industrial community, to an extent which came within an ace of damaging his own best interests. One can understand his impatience, but he was fortunate to have amongst his subordinates younger men with more scientific understanding and a clearer vision of what might ultimately be achieved.

The first navigational aid to become available to Bomber Command was Gee which contributed to the success of the first '1,000-plan' raid on Cologne. Devised by the Telecommunications Research Establishment, it was described as a system by which an aircraft navigator could calculate the position of his aircraft by observing the time taken to receive pulse signals from three different ground stations, radiated in a complex and pre-determined order. In essence, the Gee transmitters set up a vast radio grid over those parts of Europe within its range which normally extended for some 400 miles from the closest transmitter. The aircraft's navigator had on board equipment to analyse the incoming signals and to produce a reading which he then referred to a Gee map upon which he could fix his position. The system was accurate to within about half-a-mile close to the transmitter, but precision fell away with increasing range, to an accuracy within some six miles at maximum range.

In terms of the findings of the Butt Report it was a most useful improvement, and was first used by the Wellingtons of 115 Squadron flying from Marham in July 1941. Gee had benefits similar to those of the German beams, but used less easily jammed radar pulses. Its three transmitters gave it a universality which the single-beamed *Knickebein*, focused on a single target, obviously lacked. The device secured its first success during the attack on Lübeck on 28 March 1942. A relatively small force of 200 bombers attacked on a clear night and achieved an attack, the concentration and ferocity of which saturated the defences and tore the heart out of the ancient Baltic city. To the Germans it was a first indication of what lay in store for them, and its lessons in terms of civil defence and the deployment of anti-aircraft and nightfighter resources were quickly absorbed. Bomber Command lost 14 aircraft on the long trail to Lübeck, an unacceptable 7 per cent of the force despatched, and from these only five crews survived, some later dying from their injuries. The losses comprised four Stirlings, eight Wellingtons, one Manchester and a Hampden, a near-precise microcosm of the make-up of the command's order of battle at the time.

The most widely used of all the bombing aids was the centimetric wavelength radar known as H2S which represented a revolutionary advance in Bomber Command's armoury and offensive all-weather capability. A rotating scanner mounted in a perspex blister under the bomber's rear fuselage transmitted radar signals to the ground over which the aircraft was flying, and the returning echoes were displayed on a cathode-ray tube on board. The echoes were strongest from buildings, less so from open land, and weakest from water, thus it was possible to create a good image of the terrain below over a 10-mile radius. Comparisons could then be made by the set operator with maps or target area photographs to establish position, regardless of either the weather or of conditions of minimal visibility. Furthermore, the equipment was self-contained within the bomber, being independent of any input for ground stations. Thus it was virtually impossible to jam or mislead.

However, there were drawbacks. H2S was both bulky and relatively heavy and the Germans soon found a means of homing their nightfighters on to its transmissions. Especially in its early forms, the picture presented on the cathode tube was coarse and required considerable interpretative skill in the absence of prominent or well defined target characteristics. However, as time went on wavelength refinement and other improvements greatly enhanced the display. The bombers' vulnerability to attack by nightfighters 'seeing' the H2S pulses was lessened by the practice of turning the equipment on and off to obtain periodic fixes en route to the target. It was an unfortunate limitation, but one which paled into insignificance compared to the advantages which possession of H2S conferred.

Much more debilitating was the device's initially bad serviceability record, which caused many frustrations in target-marking the deep penetration raids. H2S almost succumbed to another British-imposed limitation. Its effectiveness was largely due to the development of the Magnetron valve which made 10cm wavelengths a practical possibility. The cavity Magnetron as a means of generating considerable amounts of power on a wavelength of 10cm or less had been discovered by Randall and Boot, working at the University of Birmingham in February 1940. It revolutionised the quality and precision of radars being first used within British nightfighters' Airborne Interception (AI) sets against the Luftwaffe's bombers. In this form it achieved escalating success, superseding the earlier 1.5m AI from March 1942 onwards.

However, in October 1941 tests were initiated using a centimetric airborne system mounted in a Blenheim to establish the feasibility of detecting and identifying towns and landscape features in any weather, day or night. As will be seen, development proceeded apace despite the disastrous crash of a trials Halifax and by July 1942 the Magnetron was established as the core component of British airborne radars, with Bomber Command as its principal customer.

But this was not without opposition from a number of quarters, both on grounds of security and priority utilisation. Security rightly assessed the secrets of the Magnetron as being of the utmost interest to the enemy. Fighter Command's nightfighters using centrimetric AI were warned against the pursuit of enemy bombers out over the North Sea, or into continental airspace; and the prospect of the inevitable loss of bombers carrying Magnetron H2S was deeply disturbing to the War Cabinet. As one solution, explosive devices were fitted within the H2S installations and designed to detonate in the event of a crash or forced landing, but to the dismay of all concerned the Magnetron proved remarkably resilient and defied anything approaching total destruction. As an alternative the use of the far less efficient Klystron valves was contemplated, since their characteristics and availability were both widely known. However, by mid-1942 the Klystron's shortcomings were showing no signs of alleviation which led to a decision in July to proceed with the Magnetron, regardless of the concerns.

In January 1943, H2S was used for the first time for an attack on Hamburg and some aircraft carrying it were immediately lost over Germany. Amazingly, all the British concern proved ill-founded. The Germans had no knowledge of the techniques and qualities of centimetric radar and dismissed the Magnetron as a gimmick, perhaps deciding to investigate it later. At all events the valve was quickly submerged in the usual welter of jealousy and suspicion in which relationships between the Luftwaffe and its supporting industry and scientific services were immersed.

The priorities for the use of the new radars posed irritatingly intractable problems for the RAF, since Coastal Command with the strong support of the Royal Navy demanded that Air to Surface Vessel (ASV) sets be made available to them incorporating the high definition qualities imparted by the Magnetron. In the event Bomber Command's offensive was judged marginally the more vital, and it was not until March 1943 that the first centimetric ASV came into operational use over the waters of the Bay of Biscay.

Of all the bombing and navigational aids, Oboe was undoubtedly the most widely respected. This device operated in conjunction with two separate ground stations. The first known as 'cat' ensured that its controlled aircraft maintained a constant range flying along an arc which, if followed, would take it directly over the target. Signals were superimposed on 'cat's' radar pulses so that the pilot would hear dots or dashes if he strayed either side of the perfect track. When he was on track he would hear a continuous tone, the same method of course maintenance used earlier in the war in German radio beam technology. The second ground station was known as 'mouse' and followed the aircraft round its arc until it calculated, on the basis of airspeed and weapon ballistics, the precise moment when bombs or target markers should be dropped. At this point the bomb-aimer would receive a pre-arranged signal from the 'mouse' station which determined the point of release. This near perfection of bombing technology was range-limited to an arc of 280 miles from the most distant transmitter, and could only be used to control one aircraft at a time. However, the modest size and weight of Oboe's airborne component made it ideal for operation within the fast, high-flying Mosquitoes of the Pathfinder squadrons, two of which became indelibly associated with precision marking. Their equipment's accuracy was such that 50 per cent of their TIs could be almost guaranteed to fall within 400yds of the target, an achievement that was unsurpassed at the time and remained so for years to come.

The next challenge to be met was the marking of the target. By 1942, Bomber Command's arsenal included an increasing range of pyrotechnics which, by the war's end, had burgeoned into an incredible variety of devices some of truly daunting size. Bennett had spoken of 'fireworks' in his discussions with Bomber Command's Directorate of Operations just before he re-joined the RAF. Certainly, the description was prescient of what would be achievable using the accumulated knowledge and experience of centuries of firework manufacture, and the consummate skills of the British manufacturers, in particular those of the Brock Company. The potential for sophistication well beyond the entertainment of bangs and flashes was clearly there to be drawn on.

In fact there were three main challenges involved in the design of precision target markers. Firstly, there was a requirement for extended 'burn' endurance. Although ground and air markers could always be 'freshened' during an attack by further drops, it was obviously desirable that the illumination should be both long lasting and relatively impervious to blast from nearby bombs, although none could survive the snuffing impact of a direct hit! Secondly, the enemy had already shown himself a master of disguise and deception. From the very first days of the war elaborate schemes of camouflage had been adopted by the Germans to hide ground targets and to modify natural and man-made landmarks, or geographic features. In Hamburg, for instance, rafts carrying dummy streets and houses were moored on the Binnen Alster, a lake in the middle of the city across which ran a prominent and important railway link bridge, the Lombardsbrücke. A dummy replica bridge was then assembled a few hundred yards away across an adjacent lake, creating there an almost identical urban panorama to the original when viewed from a few thousand feet. There were also many examples of spoof towns and factories constructed of flammable materials outside German cities and industrial centres which were used time and time again to distract and deceive the bombers. Obviously there would be no insurmountable problems involved in home defence units igniting appropriate fake 'markers' in open country, once the direction of the incoming bomber stream had been established. For all these reasons the pyrotechnics used by Bomber Command had to have easily recognised and, if possible, unique burn characteristics.

The attacking stream of aircraft could well take up to an hour to pass over during a major attack on an important city. In the course of such an operation it could well prove necessary to mark more than one target, or turning point, simultaneously, or to 'move' the bullseye from one point of a city to another. In addition there had to be means of signalling corrections and of countering misleading indications developing in the heat of the attack. Whilst the principal colours of red, yellow and green provided reasonable scope for varying combinations, it quickly proved inadequate. But the manufacturers were soon able to offer a range of markers which changed from one colour to another in the course of ignition, and others which signalled by emitting dots and dashes whilst they burned.

The basic building block for marker bombs and sky markers was the candle, most rudimentary of which was the Type 'A' which ignited instantaneously for a 3-minute burn and was just 11.7in long and 1.8in in diameter. Type 'B' candles offered colour options and provided various lengths of delay capability, varying from 2.5mins to 5mins for the Bl's, and up to 33mins for the slightly larger B3. More ingenuity conceived the Type 'C', a delay flare which after an initial burn fell dormant for 10mins before blazing briefly into renewed light. The sinister Type 'D' was specific in deterring Civil Defence workers from any attempt to extinguish markers, since it burned normally before exploding, whereas Type 'E's included delayed action of up to 31mins, a burn-time of some 3mins and then they too exploded.

Type 'G's' were simple skymarkers whereas Type 'H's' changed colour from red to yellow, or red to green, or from yellow to green. Each colour burned for 15secs before changing and the whole candle had a life of some 5.5mins from first ignition. This candle was 23.3in long, twice that of the normal. It consisted of two single candle cases joined end to end, each case containing 11 flare pellets. The joint between the two cases was covered by a calico-laminated tinplate sleeve and the candle was protected against impact damage by a further sleeve and an end diaphragm, both of tinplate. The device was ignited by a quickmatch projecting slightly through the diaphragm. The flash from the impacting quickmatch would ignite a small quantity of gunpowder held in place by book muslin and a millboard washer. This ingenious but standard pyrotechnic device initiated a process which set off the first 'colour' pellet, which in turn ignited the second and so on, until all 11 of the initial group of pellets had burned. The last one fired a further quantity of powder which lit an instantaneous fuse running through a separator comprising a wooden disc and connected to the first of the eleven pellets producing the second colour. All in all, it was a virtually foolproof system of elementary fusing!

Other candles were variations on the foregoing themes, up to the Type 'R' which transmitted Morse dots or dashes to a pre-determined programme. The Type 'S' generated green, blue or yellow smoke and the Type 'T', the final designation, red smoke, all of these being obviously for daylight use.

The individual candles themselves, in their multitude of capabilities and purposes, provided the filling for most of the big TI bombs, the majority of which were 250lb in weight, although the B2 to B29 series were massive 1,000lb markers of various capabilities.

No 1 TI bombs weighed 250lb and were filled with 60 candles in any of the available colours, or combinations thereof. A burn time of up to 5mins was available for these, mainly ground markers, but its candles did ignite in free-fall. The bomb case comprised a steel tube on the end of which was welded a hemispherical sheet steel nose. The bomb's tail was secured by six brass rivets. A burster charge in the nose was designed to explode and activate an ejector plate, making it slide up a central steel tube (carrying the candles, packed in corrugated paper strips and wooden battens) at high velocity towards the tail which would shear off under their impact. The candles would thus be hurled into the air to descend, falling free in a dense cascade either instantly ignited, impact ignited, delayed action, or a mixture of all three.

No 2 bomb included four explosive candles in its load and 56 non-delay candles which burned for up to 5mins, starting in free-fall. Nos 3, 4, 5 and 6 provided varying combinations of delay and non-delay, whilst No 7 bombs provided flashing candles to foil enemy attempts at decoy deception. A different principle was involved in the No 8 bomb, which contained a great bale of cotton wool impregnated with a flammable substance designed to burn in selected colours for up to 60mins. Photoflash bombs, designated No 11 for a white flash and No 12 for red, green or yellow, produced an awe-inspiring flash illumination of 1/10th sec duration! No 13s simply exploded with a devastating report and were designed to disorientate and dismay ground defences. And so the long list of specialised ingenuity went on to a total of 28 types, including the No 23 providing delays of 2.5, 5, 7, 9 and 11mins; and No 19 delays of 13, 15, 17 and 19mins. A veritable fuse maker's benefit!

Perhaps the prize for cleverness should go to the No 19 bomb designated as a sea marker. A canister was ejected by this bomb in free-fall and its case included a number of holes covered by hessian. On hitting the sea salt water would penetrate the hessian and react with a chemical to produce phosphine gas in clouds of dense white smoke and a luminous flame. The big league comprised 1,000lb weapons which generally mirrored the attributes of selected 250lb bombs whilst releasing up to 200 candles in various combinations. One exception to this was the marker designated B.29, rather engagingly known as the 'Skymarker Puff', which was used for daylight raids and was designed to burst in mid-air creating an immense cloud of dense colour above a target and coloured red, green, yellow or blue. Finally, flare clusters were available in almost infinite combinations and the path of descending bombs could be followed by red, green, or white light tracers attached to their fins.

The Pathfinders would soon develop specific tactics and marking techniques to suit varying targets and, most importantly, the vagaries of North European weather conditions. Don Bennett used to tell of the occasion when it first became necessary to allocate codenames to the three main systems to be used, and he asked a member of his Head-quarters staff, a New Zealander Squadron Leader named 'Pedro' Ashworth, where he lived. The Squadron Leader replied 'Wanganui' and

Bennett – 'to keep the balance', as he put it – proposed 'Parramatta', a city near Sydney, as the second codename. He then asked his WAAF clerk, Corporal Ralph, for her home town and this turned out to be Newhaven in Sussex. They may not have been the most easily pronounced, or starkly unambiguous names in military history, but they had about them both a patriotic romance and a happy international diversity.

Thus it was that 'Newhaven' involved ground marking by visual methods and Main Force crews simply aimed at the TIs burning on the ground, which would be replenished until fires were sufficiently well established to make the aiming point obvious. 'Parramatta' comprised ground marking in indifferent visibility, or broken cloud, where the TIs were dropped using H2S radar operated by Pathfinder aircraft to the maximum degree of accuracy. Again the Main Force would aim straight at the burning markers. Finally, 'Wanganui' was sky marking in really poor visibility with the TIs, similar to parachute flares being released using Oboe blind bombing radar. Bombs would then be dropped through the descending flares which would be frequently replenished until the attack was well and truly established. The prefix 'musical' to the codename indicated that Oboe was to be used to ensure accurate placing of markers.

Many are the contemporary descriptions of the markers falling out of the sky, the brilliantly coloured heralds of death. There may have been air-raid sirens, the sound of distant gunfire, the vision of searchlights criss-crossing the black and threatening sky, even the ominous escalating roar of 2,000 and more aero engines coming in from the far horizon. Whilst there were only these things there was hope, selfish hope that someone else, some other town or factory would vanish that night into choking rubble or searing fire. But once the red cascades burst in the night sky overhead, or the spluttering green pools of unearthly light turned streets into ghostly canyons, then both doubt and hope were gone. Despair and hate alone, those most negative of emotions, would occupy the final seconds before the first shattering explosions drove away all reason and let in abject terror.

The enemy applied all of his ingenuity, his scientific expertise, and the undisputed courage of his nightfighter pilots to counter the onslaught of Harris's offensive, by destroying the vulnerable bombers. The energies of pioneering British radar research, and of the growing industry it supported, were committed to overwhelming the German defences and thus reducing the unsustainable loss rates the bombers were encountering, particularly on the deep penetration raids. As a frightening example of this, an attack on the Skoda armament works at Pilsen on the night of 16 April 1943 had resulted in the loss of 37 aircraft out of a force of 327, a rate of 11.3 per cent.

An early defensive measure had been the modification of the 1.5m AI radar used by British nightfighters in the winter of 1940, to enable it to be fitted on RAF bombers. This adaptation provided a cone of radar coverage at the tail of the bomber and the 'echo' from an approaching fighter was translated into a series of 'pips' on the aircraft's intercom, which increased in frequency as the range closed. Codenamed 'Monica', this system, though useful, had significant drawbacks. In the first place it was entirely non-selective and therefore any aircraft entering the radar cone emanating from the bomber would excite the warning pips. It requires but little thought to imagine the cacophany of noise that could readily result from bombers within a dense stream triggering one another's warning systems. However, that said, Monica was certainly better than nothing, importantly it kept crews alert and the more experienced were able to deduce that an unchanging pip rate was likely to indicate another bomber maintaining station, rather than a predatory defender. Those who switched off Monica did not live long, for the Luftwaffe crews naturally picked on the 'easy' bombers and did not waste time on the gut-churning corkscrew manoeuvre of the alert crews.

Monica was a rough and ready ally and clearly more sophistication was needed. Monica could not give any indication of the speed, height, or bearing of an approaching aircraft, neither could it interrogate the dangerous killing ground immediately under the bomber's belly which was so fruitfully exploited by the nightfighters. The answer to these shortcomings came in the form of modifications to the basic H2S system. It became possible to display on a separate indicator tube the airspace extending thousands of feet below and around the bomber, without encountering the first ground returns. On early trials, Mosquito nightfighters acting as the attackers appeared as vivid spots of light on the cathode ray tube, giving precise indications of their range and bearing.

Thus 'Fishpond' was born and fitted to Bomber Command's 'heavies' to be 'read' at the wireless operator's position. It gave an accurate indication of all aircraft within a five-mile radius of the bomber and, again, with experience its operators could assess the one piece of information not available, namely, the elevation of an approaching aircraft. They could also usually determine whether it was hostile or friendly by watching its response to a course change by the target bomber. 'Fishpond' went operational in October 1943.

'Boozer' was a 'bargain basement' warning system which picked up the signals from German radars which might be 'holding' the bomber in which the device was installed. The great ground-based *Würzburg's* beam would light up a red lamp on the bomber's instrument panel, the airborne *Lichtenstein* a yellow one. In either case violent evasive action was called for, but unfortunately this passive system was dogged by false alarms from the mass of enemy radar signals in the hostile crowded skies.

As time progressed a specialist group was formed, 100 Group, under the command of Air Vice-Marshal E. B. Addison, to be a single centre of all activities designed to jam, dislocate and confuse the enemy defences on the widest possible scale. The group's aircraft were normally painted black overall, and included Liberators, Fortresses and Stirlings as well as the more usual Lancasters, Halifaxes and Mosquitoes. They sowed the skies with 'Window' radar-jamming chaff, carried high-power 'Mandrel' transmitters to swamp the Luftwaffe's early warning system, 'Jostle' which radiated ear-blasting noise on enemy fighter control channels, 'Cigar' which disrupted VHF communications, and 'Piperack' which jammed the most sophisticated of German airborne radars, SN-2.

In this deadly tit-for-tat combat there was an inevitable downside: the Germans developed *Naxos* which enabled fighters to home on to H2S transmissions, and *Flensburg* which homed on Monica. The Luftwaffe also dispensed with widespread ground control and deployed 'Wild Boars' – or free-ranging Focke Wulf 190 nightfighters – to stalk within the crowded bomber streams, selecting and destroying targets of opportunity.

Finally, there were the raid tactics evolved in the hard clear light of experience and perfected under the precise professional control of the Pathfinder Force. Rarely was a target approached directly. There were feints which involved the bomber stream approaching a city, only to veer off and attack another; dog-legs and spoofs, where subsidiary attacks were mounted to draw defences away from the main attack. There were also the phantom deceptions where a handful of aircraft dropping 'Window' could develop the picture on enemy radars of a substantial attack and vanish into the night after dropping a full pattern of target markers, heralding an attack which would never come.

The enemy kept constant watch on his radars, mounted in endless profusion along the sandy, wind-swept, Dutch North Sea coastline. He would 'see' the bombers air-testing in the morning over the eastern flat-lands of England, and he would endeavour to seek out further information from any careless radio transmissions. Later he would follow the fast tracks of the Pathfinders across the cathode tubes, before the swamping echoes from the Main Force filled the radar screens. The controllers would then endeavour to predict the target city and arrange the best disposition of nightfighters to defend it. Many times their deductions were correct, many times they were not. Either way it must have occurred to them all that, right or wrong, they were in the safest place and those dear to them were in the most dangerous of all.

CHAPTER SIX
A FORCE IS BORN

There is no record of the conversation that took place between Portal and Harris when next they met. The CAS knew his man well and would have anticipated spirited argument and fervent support by Harris of the views which had been so emphatically expressed by his subordinates. In the end, however, Portal was confident that he could persuade the C-in-C at least to give the target-finding force a trial, and he anticipated that once this was done there would be no turning back. He was certain of Harris's loyalty not to some vague concept of service or country, but to the men of his command whose wellbeing was his greatest imperative. He would not resign over this issue, it was not his style, rather he would stay on to ensure that the ideas of Bufton and the rest were implemented in a way most beneficial to the bomber crews and to the progress of the campaign.

Harris was shrewd enough and certainly experienced enough in command to know that once he had conceded the point and embraced the ideas now clearly being forced upon him, he would be left to get on with it and higher command would move on to some other area of concern. After all, the point at issue was not the need for bombing accuracy, but the means of achieving it. A pragmatist would also recognise that Harris's acceptance of the Air Ministry view on this issue could win him the support he required, and for the resources and the freedom of action to pursue his concept of the great war-winning campaign against Germany.

Portal would probably have started by reminding Harris of the War Cabinet's deep concern about the bombing offensive and the poor 'value for money' that it currently represented. He had been having a difficult time, both with the Prime Minister and the other service chiefs, to the extent that it would not take much to dislodge the bomber offensive from any priority status in the overall war policy. He would have emphasised that some major tactical shift was needed to overcome the problems of target-finding, and that ingenious electronic bombing aids might prove unreliable short-term benefits unless handled by the most experienced aircrew. Harris would also have been challenged to explain what significant differences of task existed between his Raid Leaders and the proposed Target Marking Force. The only difference that Portal chose to identify was that of a scattered band of disparate experts against a highly trained cohesive group, serving a single commander. Surely, Harris would have to agree the advantages of the Air Ministry solution. He may also have emphasised that Gee had already been compromised, and that sooner or later all the other gadgets likely to be employed against so technically ingenious an enemy as Germany were likely to suffer the same fate. Finally, there was no chance of more than a small number of H2S sets being available for many months to come, and Oboe would be limited by its inability to control more than one aircraft every 10mins.

In his book *Bomber Offensive*, Harris wrote about the formation of the new force:

'I was over-ruled by the Air Ministry. In other circumstances I should not have accepted the position, but we were now faced with the fact that Gee had failed as a bombing aid and that the new radar aids, Oboe and H2S, which had been promised for the autumn of 1942, were not now to be forthcoming until the end of the year. For the time being it was essential to improve our methods of finding the target visually and marking it, and this seemed to require the whole time activities of a specialised force.'

He now had a compelling reason to give to his group commanders to deflect any suggestion that he may have let them down, or shown weakness in the face of Air Ministry pressure. Typically he now put all the weight of his personality, authority, and enthusiasm behind what was now required of him.

In retrospect Harris was somewhat harsh about the limited availability and utilisation of the various new radars; furthermore, Gee was never regarded as a 'bombing' aid, its purpose being entirely navigational. Certainly no promises were ever made by the industry for H2S and Oboe sets being widely available for the autumn of 1942. Air Vice-Marshal Michael Hedgeland recalls that new ground was being broken all the time and the best measure of progress was the setting of broad targets which often proved wildly optimistic. H2S was first demonstrated as feasible in November 1941, and flight-testing began the following April. In May 1942 a Halifax carrying one of the two competing systems was lost after a mid-air engine fire. The aircraft crashed in the Wye Valley and all on board were killed including five crew members, the Bomber Command liaison officer, and no less than five irreplaceable design team members and scientists from TRE and EMI. Despite this disaster, training on the first H2S sets began in 35 Squadron on 5 November 1942 and in 7 Squadron just a month later. All in all it was a quite remarkable achievement.

Harris wrote to his group commanders on 20 June 1942, telling them that he had strongly represented their common views in the course of the debate on the problems of target finding. He now had to tell them that he had agreed to test the value of an independent group, to be known as the Pathfinder Force. Interestingly Harris had insisted on this title, suggesting as it did a navigational aid, rather than the targeting function of his raid leader scheme. Thus his preferred solution was left to one side, and remained unchanged, while the Air Ministry's proposal was adopted lock, stock and barrel. If anything went wrong the concept of raid leaders, already tried, could be dusted down and re-introduced without loss of face by anyone, except of course the Air Ministry! Harris was careful to use the phrase 'will be tried out' when he announced the decision to raise a Pathfinder Force.

The C-in-C proposed four Pathfinder squadrons and at this stage qualified his support only to the extent of excluding from their number any of the new Lancaster units, reserving these superb aircraft for the Main Force. Thus the pathfinders would go to war with the workhorse Wellington III and the four-engined Stirling which had proved somewhat of a disappointment in squadron service. There were advantages however in both types, the Wellington was exceptionally rugged and well-liked by its crews, while the Stirling was a good performer at medium altitude and combined this quality with unusual manoeuvrability for its ungainly size. Both aircraft were technically obsolescent and soon would be totally eclipsed by the Halifax and the Lancaster. Certainly, there would be less reluctance on the part of the AOCs over giving up squadrons of these aircraft to the Pathfinder Force.

Harris selected 3 Group as father of the new organisation, conceding the value of its squadrons being stationed either all on one airfield, or on two in close proximity to one another. He was, however, careful to credit the Air Ministry with the authorship of this particular philosophy with which he still – somewhat surprisingly – disagreed. At this time 3 Group was under the command of a legendary RAF character, Air Vice-Marshal J. E. A. 'Johnny' Baldwin, with its headquarters at Exning in Suffolk. However, the Pathfinders initially would be under the direct control of the C-in-C Bomber Command, relying on 3 Group only for administration, 'pay and rations'. This arrangement ensured that plans for the establishment of the Pathfinders were rapidly put into effect, despite any residual lack of enthusiasm on the part of Groups unhappy at parting with their most experienced crews.

Initial instructions called for the AOC of 3 Group to accommodate two Stirling and two Wellington III squadrons, and to locate them on adjacent airfields. He was to see that squadron and flight commanders were of the highest calibre and should any not measure up he was to arrange for substitutions via his colleagues heading 1, 4 and 5 Groups. Having established the top echelons, he was to weed out any unsuitable crews and acquire new ones through the same process of substitution. The other AOCs were required by Harris's order to select their outstanding crews in advance and to prepare to post them to fill possible vacancies in the PFF squadrons.

'In future,' wrote Harris, 'aircrew of particular ability or experience may wish to volunteer for Pathfinder service.' In fact it was expected that those finishing operational tours would prefer to carry on with the new force, rather than spend time on the comparative tedium and hazard of the operational training units (OTU)! Although this would be encouraged in the case of the better crews, the C-in-C anticipated that some could find the stress of a further full operational tour too much, and he decreed that they should be allowed to stand down at any time during the second half of this double-dose. He insisted that no shame should be felt or implied in such circumstances.

In the squadrons there remained some considerable misgivings about the creaming off of the best operational crews for pathfinding, and in response to this Harris proposed that some novices should be posted to PFF squadrons direct from the OTUs. This set an impossible task of selection since it was acknowledged that only newcomers of 'great promise' should be chosen, which caused one hard-pressed instructor to observe that it was a process somewhat less reliable than that of sexing day-old chicks!

Finally, by Royal Warrant, Harris secured authority for PFF crews to wear a small 'golden' eagle on their lefthand breast pocket flaps. He also thought he had Air Ministry agreement to promote them all by one rank on joining, but he under-estimated the inertia of vested interest and dusty tradition. He was forced to add a postscript to his orders to the groups which admitted to 'some difficulties [having] arisen regarding promotions' and that they should not mention this aspect for the time being.

Harris had already addressed the question of a leader for the new force and found this to be the easiest decision in the whole series of problematic issues which had faced him. It was at least a comfort to be given a more or less free hand over the appointment, although there was some astonishment and resentment over his selection of a 32-year-old Wing Commander whose RAF career had been broken by a period in civil aviation.

Even in 1942 there were many in the RAF who regarded civil aviation in much the same disagreeable light as the Royal Navy viewed the Merchant Service. To such men it was deeply upsetting that the plum job of directing the improvement in efficiency of the RAF's bombing offensive should pass into the hands of someone other than a so-called career officer. The fact that Don Bennett was an Australian hardly helped matters. Harris did not even consider another candidate and in one way his apparently bizarre decision was notably shrewd. Had an able squadron commander been chosen, his qualities could almost certainly have been matched (in theory anyway) by a dozen others and rivalry, if not jealousy, would have tarnished the decision. Don Bennett was in many ways unique through his prowess and authority as a navigator, his experience of long-distance flight, his independence of thought and, above all, his formidable professionalism. He was 'an airman's airman' and whatever criticism might be levelled against his appointment there was no denial of this simple fact. It is wholly realistic to conclude that Harris's final decision to yield to Portal's pressure was to a very large extent determined by the availability of Bennett, 'the most efficient airman I have ever met'.

In fact, on 4 July, Bennett was at Hurn airport having said farewell to his wife before taking 10 Squadron and its 16 Halifaxes to the Middle East for operations in support of the North African campaign. He was not in the best of tempers, having little faith in the value of sending squadrons of bombers to support Army campaigns, rather than attacking Germany. At the very last moment a signal came through ordering him to report to Bomber Command Headquarters at High Wycombe, and to hand over command of his squadron to the senior flight commander, Flight Lieutenant Seymour-Price.

After a brief exchange of greetings, Harris left Bennett in no doubt about the deep trouble that now threatened Bomber Command's very existence, and the whole future of the bombing war. He outlined the many arguments that had been raging within and without the RAF, and identified their various exponents before outlining the broad consensus of agreement that had now been reached. A cohesive specialised force would be created to make best use of the various bombing and navigational aids now available, and to prepare for the arrival of even more sophisticated equipment. This could only be achieved by putting such technology generally in the hands of highly experienced crews under a single leadership. Harris emphasised that he was firmly committed to giving the new policy a trial, although he was temperamentally more closely aligned to certain AOCs who remained distrustful of *corps élites* and nervous of the damage they could do to general morale.

Bennett learned that several operational squadrons had already been earmarked to form the nucleus of the force, which henceforth would be known as the Pathfinder Force (PFF). The C-in-C was now seeking a commander for the PFF, a man he could trust implicitly and whose commitment to the highest standard of professional airmanship was absolute. The task was nothing less than to bring a precise and ferocious accuracy to the process of bombing Germany into submission. Bennett had been chosen to bear this responsibility and with effect from 5 July 1942 he was to command PFF. He would report direct to the C-in-C at High Wycombe and as a first step would be promoted to the rank of Group Captain. He was assured of the support of all senior commanders and had their total confidence, said Harris. The time for argument was over and the common strategy was now firmly in place.

Bennett left High Wycombe, moved by the C-in-C's confidence, but inevitably mindful of the enormity of the task he had been given. He knew how much depended upon him – the confidence of superior officers could be highly transitory and was durable only to the extent of the subordinate's success. For his part he would be relying on a relatively small force of young men, most of whom had already earned the name veteran and were unlikely survivors against all the odds. The small golden eagle now proposed as their badge of distinction was scant return for what was being asked of them. They would always be first over the target; a resourceful enemy, aware of the vital part they played, would react ferociously against them; they would often need to loiter throughout the raid in the hostile, lethal skies until their marking work was complete; and their operational tour would be twice the length of that of their Main Force comrades.

Bennett had to be the inspiration of these men, their driving force to give nothing but their distinguished best. He weighed up his own qualifications. He was without doubt a brilliant professional airman, his personal standards and integrity now matched by a unique breadth of experience, but at the same time he was about as far away from the popular image of the extrovert devil-may-care flyer as it was possible to be. A quiet, highly intelligent, and always positive man, his leadership qualities sprang from a calm, measured self-confidence which was immediately apparent to all from the first moment they encountered him. Many thought him cold, whilst austere was another widely held first impression. But he was neither of these things. He had both a deep regard and a ready concern for his fellow men. Anyone who patently did his best, no matter how indifferent the result might be, had nothing to fear from Bennett provided he was willing to learn and improve. He would take endless trouble to unravel complexities, explain strategy and justify policies to anyone who showed interest, however lowly their position or mundane their responsibilties. Only the idle and the arrogant, the poseurs, and wiseacres, who inevitably infested the complex machinery for making war, had cause to fear him. He would expose them without a moment's hesitation and then ignore them. His anger was spectacular but instant; he bore no lasting grudges and harboured no resentments.

He loved the good company of intelligent, thoughtful people and found it in abundance amongst the enduring friends that he and his wife made. He was a very private man, drawing much of his confidence and motivation from the stability and warmth of his own family life. He was an unrepentant, passionate patriot, but he understood that the fundamentals for which he and his crews were prepared to fight, and probably to die, were far more personal and immediate than brave considerations of King and country. In the end it was all about the private liberty, peace and happiness contained within a few million homes and families. Their right to live and prosper in a well-ordered, law-abiding world was close to Donald Bennett's heart.

He had a great sense of humour and he was an accomplished tease, but he found parties and socialising for its own sake something of a burden. He had no capacity for small talk, no empathy for the stupidities and superficiality of forced party conversation. His attention and his gaze would wander hopelessly around the room, whilst his expression of ill-concealed boredom would only soften when the time for departing drew near.

For all the hectic activity and forced companionship of war he remained at heart a lonely man, detached by his very seniority from the community of the squadrons. He maintained a punishing schedule of visits to the airfields, and his subordinates knew that they could retain an absolute confidence in his uncompromising loyalty. Typically, he never questioned the support he could expect from his own commanders, but in this respect he would be proved, sadly, naive and unmindful of politics.

His personal honour was a shining, admirable quality, but it ill-served his interests. As his responsibilites grew and the pressures upon him increased, he turned more and more to his wife to talk through the problems that beset him. She helped him order his thoughts, distil the host of alternatives that always demanded consideration, and, finally, to seek the best solutions. In their conversations he invariably observed the absolute demands of security. His own self-discipline and unswerving loyalty to his country and his command would have allowed nothing less. So they often talked in abstracts, respecting one another's opinions, whilst their differences and spirited arguments helped him relax and unwind in the loving, unthreatening atmosphere of his own home. He was horrified on one occasion when Ly named a puppy he had given her Tinsel, coincidentally the codename for a jamming device to combat enemy nightfighters. He forbade her to use the name, but would not tell her why until long after the war was over!

Within a few days of his conversation with Harris, Bennett set out to meet the group commanders, one by one, in their various headquarters. As ever, he had ordered the priorities in his mind well in advance. First he must handle positively, but with some circumspection, these very senior, experienced, and opinionated men who remained fundamentally opposed to the concept he had been appointed to put into effect. All in all, the outlook could hardly have been less promising for the 'young upstart'. The *Tirpitz* episode, he thought gloomily, almost made him into one of those 'one-op heroes' so comprehensively derided by the tour-expired veterans in the squadrons.

In the event Bennett had reckoned without two factors, the first being the regard felt by the group commanders for their C-in-C, and for the fearless way in which they knew he would have represented his views and their own to the mandarins of the Air Ministry. If 'Bert' Harris – as they knew him – had accepted defeat, that was good enough for them. Therefore, they were well aware of their duty to make the new policy work, and work supremely well. After all, that would show the armchair theoreticians the true mettle of Bomber Command. Secondly, the groups had their own misgivings about the heavy losses being sustained. They recognised that these were further multiplied because the squadrons had to return to the same well-defended targets in their efforts to inflict the destruction that should have been caused in the first place. If this man Bennett could point the way ahead with his centralised force he could count on their enthusiastic support from now on.

No 1 Group's headquarters was at Bawtry Hall near Doncaster in Yorkshire. The Group had originally spawned the Advanced Air Striking Force in France in 1939-40, and after Dunkirk had received back the sad remnants of its shattered Fairey Battle-equipped squadrons. By 1942 it was mainly operating Wellingtons from airfields at Binbrook, Elsham, Snaith, Holme, Hemswell, Lindholme and, most recently, Breighton which had opened in January. The first 1 Group Lancaster squadron was working up for its initial operations when Bennett arrived to meet the AOC designate, Air Vice-Marshal E. A. B. Rice, who was in the process of taking over from his predecessor Air Vice-Marshal R. D. Oxland. Rice had been the Wing Commander (training) on flying-boats at Calshot during Bennett's time there, and his maritime background was marked by his nickname 'Winkle'. As a consequence of this association, Bennett's reception, he later recorded, was 'fairly friendly' although Rice was careful not to be drawn on his views about the new force. But he assured his visitor that he would do nothing to inhibit the natural flow of volunteers for pathfinding and went on to nominate Wellington-equipped 156 Squadron to join Bennett's organisation. Interestingly, 156 was hardly 'in' 1 Group at all – it was operating out of Alconbury where it had re-formed in February 1942 and which was a 3 Group station, and would eventually move to Warboys. Thus Rice's donation to PFF was, at best, of a unit which had been merely destined to come under his command. Bennett recorded that Rice 'expressed very little in the way of views either way' and this seems amply confirmed by this rather equivocal gesture of support, which in fact involved no sacrifice.

On the other hand the AOC of 4 Group, Air Vice-Marshal Roderic Carr, had been a very enthusiastic supporter of group-based target finding, and had confided to Harris that he had earmarked one of his squadron commanders to do the job – one D. C. T. Bennett. He did not favour the independent force and made no secret of the fact. However, Carr was a big man and an admirer of his one-time subordinate and 10 Squadron commander. Consequently, he was now generous in his support and nominated one of his Halifax Squadrons, No 35 based at Linton-on-Ouse, but which then moved to Graveley to join the new force. Harris had not originally considered ceding a Halifax unit to PFF so this was an advance, although not perhaps so significant as Air Vice-Marshal Alec Coryton's 'donation' of 83 Squadron, to be based with its Lancasters at Wyton, again in Huntingdonshire, as 5 Group's contribution. In Bennett's view, Coryton was the most outspoken critic of all that was now proposed and this made his action the more admirable.

This left 3 Group under the command of Johnny Baldwin charged with nursing the Pathfinders into existence, but not spared from making its own contribution to the force which turned out to be the Oakington-based Stirlings of 7 Squadron. Finally, 2 Group came in with 109 Squadron, which had been carrying out trials duties at Boscombe Down since December 1940, with various marks of Wellington, the most recent of which were the strange looking pressurised Mk Vs and VIs. No 109 Squadron had been re-formed as a squadron out of the old Wireless Intelligence Development Unit and engaged on trials of radio countermeasures and radar aids including the superb Oboe. On joining PFF it moved from Boscombe Down to Wyton and continued with its Wellingtons in the operational development of Oboe, until re-equipped with Mosquitoes later in the year. Another of Syd Bufton's brothers, Hal, was a leading light in proving the new precision radar device when serving as second in command of 109 Squadron. Pathfinding was almost becoming the family business!

Thus were assembled the five squadrons, 7, 35, 83, 109 and 156. The Pathfinder Force officially came into existence on 15 August 1942 with its headquarters at Wyton, and its squadrons based there and at Oakington, Graveley and Warboys. All were within 3 Group as originally decreed, and all within easy reach of one another to the north-west of

Cambridge, close along the course of the River Ouse. This was the heart of Pathfinder country, and the squadrons which flew in that day were held available for immediate operations.

Wyton itself had opened in July 1936. The station had made history when one of its Blenheim IVs had flown on the very first sortie of the Second World War to reconnoitre the disposition of the German fleet. Oakington had opened in July 1940 housing 3 Group's Blenheims and Wellingtons before the Stirlings and Lancasters arrived. Warboys and Graveley were operational from September 1941 and March 1942 respectively, the former as a satellite to Tempsford and the latter to Wyton within this runway-crowded part of England.

On 1 August 1942 Bennett wrote to the C-in-C outlining what he referred to as the 'initial ability and methods of the Pathfinding Force'. He listed comprehensively the target finding methods:

(i)   Visual medium/high level by moonlight
(ii)   Visual medium/high level by flare
(iii)   Visual low level by moonlight
(iv)   Visual very low level by dusk
(v)   Visual very high level by dusk
(vi)   Using direction finding loop
(vii)   Using astro navigation
(viii) TR 1335 (Gee) fixed-precision procedure
(ix)   TR 1335 (Gee) homing, with precision ETA as check
(x)   Oboe within 300 statute miles
(xi)   H2S

He noted that (x) and (xi) were not yet available and that there had been no training as yet on (iii), (iv) or (v). Training was to become the dominant area of Bennett's concern, particularly the time needed to replace the continuing casualties.

Next, Bennett listed the means by which the accurate release of bombs was being achieved:

(i)   Visual – by moonlight
(ii)   Visual – by flares
(iii)   Visual – at dusk
(iv)   Blind TR 1335 (Gee) precision procedure
(v)   Blind TR 1335 (Gee) – homing

(vi)   Oboe

(vii)   Visual by flares or moonlight with H2S confirmation

(viii)   Blind with H2S

On the matter of target marking Bennett was particularly grim in his assessment of the means available to him, and stressed the vital need to improve output. It was a subject to which he would return with increasing vehemence, but for the moment he identified:

(a)   Illumination by reconnaissance flares in strings or bunches

(b)   Sky and ground-marking by 250lb marker bombs. Three colours and white

(c)   Ground marking with 4,000lb Gel bombs producing a mass of white flame

(d)   Ground marking with salvoes of 2,000lb Gel bombs

(e)   Ground marking with 4lb incendiaries

(f)   Intensive fire-raising for 45 minutes before an attack

(g)   Sky-marking using high altitude dropped flares over cloud

Towards the end of this letter Bennett floated an alternative policy of mounting a series of multiple attacks against smaller and less well defended towns, with the dual objectives of destroying enemy morale and of overwhelming his defences by an unremitting onslaught on the broadest possible front. He nominated towns of between 6,000 and 20,000 inhabitants, many of which could be identified as having military or industrial relevance. As an option it had huge attractions, but it was opposed by Harris who decreed a continuing and intensifying campaign against the great manufacturing and population centres.

Bennett concluded by proposing six weeks of comprehensive on-the-job training, which would obviously not exclude frequent operations which were essential to maintain the momentum of the PFF's build-up. He also had in mind a sophisticated operational planning system which would leave the techniques and processes of route planning, and all aspects of marking, exclusively in the hands of PFF who were the best able to concentrate on the problems involved. They would, however, maintain the closest contact with the Main Force squadrons and with changing operational conditions. It was essential, he wrote, that HQ Bomber Command identified to PFF each morning as soon as it became known, the target for the forthcoming night, and that the need for goodwill and backing for PFF's endeavours should be impressed upon all concerned, particularly the operating groups, as a vital ingredient for success. Bennett was clearly aware of the many mischievously jealous eyes that were upon him.

As good as his word, on 18 August 1942 Harris sent a signal to the Group Captain in command, PFF, Wyton:

'The force under your command makes its debut in the vitally important role for which is has been raised. I am optimistic that the selected crews under your command will achieve all that skill and determination makes possible of achievement. All the crews of Bomber Command now look to the Pathfinders for a lead to their future objectives and will ensure the maximum infliction of damage on the enemy with the greatest economy of force. They will, I know, not be disappointed. Good luck and good hunting. Harris.'

Between 21.30hrs and 23.30hrs on the night of 18 August 1942, Pathfinder aircraft of 7, 35, 83 and 156 Squadrons left Graveley, Oakington and Warboys to mark the target for the Main Force, which was Flensburg, to the north of Kiel. Flight Lieutenant G. P. Greenup, flying a Wellington III of 156 Squadron, believed that he and his crew were the very first Pathfinders to enter enemy air space preceding 30 other aircraft from the four squadrons. Flensburg was due to be marked with flares and incendiary bombs, but weather conditions were generally very unfavourable and the operation was far from being a good start. Only 16 of the PFF crews claimed they had successfully marked the target. Sadly, too, the PFF experienced its first loss when Halifax W1226 of 35 Squadron succumbed to nightfighter attacks and ditched. All the crew survived and were taken prisoner, but one died later in captivity when the working party of which he was a member was attacked by Russian aircraft. Such were the unending hazards of war. No other PFF aircraft were lost. (In July 1995 the rear gunner of W1226 was still alive aged 81 and living in Queensland, Australia.)

The second attack using the new technique took place on 24 August when cloud obscured Frankfurt and results were at best highly marginal. Of the 16 bombers which failed to return that night, five were PFF aircraft; four were the victims of nightfighters, as was another

Stirling of 7 Squadron which crashed near Abingdon shortly after midnight, fortunately without injury to the crew.

In a report to Harris, the two PFF operations were assessed chillingly as failures, and as having no effect whatsoever on the accuracy of the Main Force bombing. It was a dismal start and no doubt the absence of further written comment within surviving files merely confirms that people were prepared to reserve judgement until further experience had been obtained. However, Bennett later complained that the Flensburg marking was carried out by operationally experienced – but otherwise untrained – crews, without the benefit of any of the radar aids and suffering a hopelessly inaccurate weather forecast into the bargain. The result was, he said, 'exactly what one would expect', and he feared that the Command's cynics were by now rubbing their hands and saying 'there you are, I told you so; the Pathfinder Force won't work.' Fortunately it was a pessimistic assumption.

On 27 August the PFF went to Kassel, but was judged to have had no effect on the bombing results achieved by the Main Force. The frank opinion was that in moderate weather and bright moonlight the PFF techniques had again been only partially successful. However, some concentrated bombing was achieved by the Main Force, including damage to the Henschel Aircraft Works which disrupted production at three factories in the city which made the Hs129 ground-attack aircraft, then coming into service on the Russian front. Out of a high total of 31 aircraft lost, three were 156 Squadron Wellingtons from Warboys, all of whose crews were killed.

The effort put into training the Pathfinder crews was now redoubled, both on the ground in the navigational classrooms and in the air. Also introduced was a system of flying 'supporters' dropping conventional bomb-loads alongside the first waves of experienced markers. This gave the newcomers some feel of the problems of leading a raid, of receiving the undivided attention of the defences, and of the calm precision needed to carry out their task efficiently. However, Bennett recorded there was a snag to this means of induction: the supporters' high explosive bomb-load tended to raise clouds of smoke and rubble dust, as well as having the propensity of snuffing out the early and inadequate ground-marker flares. Also used to ease in newcomers to the force were 'Freshman' raids, defined as relatively 'easy' attacks on well defined and perhaps lightly defended targets. The supply of such objectives was limited almost by definition. Later, Harris was to dismiss the Freshman approach saying, with some justification, that additional training was worth a score of unrepresentative and undemanding attacks. He added that there were no easy targets left, 'except Italy'!

On 28 August the Main Force were led by PFF to Nuremberg and would use for the very first time 250lb target indicator bombs. This time the raid analysis spoke of success in the austere terms of Bomber Command, and of the 'improved' impact of PFF techniques on the bombing results on a night of good weather and bright moonlight. The downside of the operation was a very heavy loss rate. As a later raid would tragically demonstrate, Nuremberg was a distant, dangerous target offering little scope for spoof diversions to confuse defences. In the event a total of 20 bombers went missing including a 7 Squadron Stirling, two Halifaxes from 35 Squadron, and a Wellington from 156 Squadron.

On the raid against Frankfurt on 24 August an 83 Squadron Lancaster was lost, crashing in Belgium, killing four of its seven crew, including Flight Lieutenant Angus Buchan DFC, the PFF's Navigation Staff Officer. He died observing the principle laid down by Bennett that there were to be no armchair warriors in the headquarters, and that all aircrew on his staff should fly 'moderately frequently'. The dangers of this necessarily 'hands-on' approach were all too apparent by the end of August 1942, as was the chilling observation of the PFF commander that 'there will only be posthumous VCs in my squadrons'. Even his most devoted admirers were somewhat taken aback by this, but he always maintained that his intention was to discourage the 'glory boys'.

In all conscience there were going to be enormous demands made upon the heroism of his crews, without their actively going out looking for more. He was seeking the most demanding quality of all, the cool and ceaseless application of the highest standards of airmanship, regardless of the strength and accuracy of the defences. Thus night bombing required a very particular continuum of courage and Bennett would not tolerate any crew having their lives put at risk by the pursuit of momentary valour. That said, it was an almost unique example of something that Don Bennett might have put rather better!

CHAPTER SEVEN
HARD LESSONS

Saarlouis lies in the valley of the River Saar some 20km to the north-east of Saarbrücken, close to the French frontier. On 1 September the Pathfinders led in the Main Force and one aircraft released its markers over the centre of the town. The main weight of the subsequent attack fell with great accuracy on Saarlouis which was a comparatively small, though well industrialised, centre. Other Pathfinders flew on to mark the correct target, Saarbrücken, but few of the bombers responded to their TIs. The PFF lost only one aeroplane, a Wellington, which crashed soon after take-off from Warboys, killing three of the crew.

Bennett faced a new situation when the raid photographs were analysed, showing a well-marked and subsequently disciplined, heavy and accurate attack by the bomber stream. But the embarrassing fact was that the raid had been carried out against the wrong target, due entirely to the release of markers far too early. The word spread around Bomber Command like wildfire but, oddly enough, although there were many guffaws of laughter there was also a large measure of under-standing and goodwill. The 'experts', now firmly in the limelight, had 'put up a black'. But everyone knew that this was all too easy and, pro-viding PFF learned from their mistake, it was probably all to the good. Harris received a deeply worried Bennett and 'was very kind about the whole thing', taking the view that the enemy had been hit hard in a heavy and accurate raid on a town with an industrial centre. The only misfortune was that the scale was far beyond what was necessary, or jus-tified, for Saarlouis.

Hamish Mahaddie, when on the PFF staff as an unconventional recruitment officer – or 'horse thief' as he preferred to be known – found some advantage in describing the errors as well as the successes that had come their way. He used the Saarlouis attack to demonstrate how even the best of them could make mistakes, even with the assis-tance of Gee and good weather. All in all he received a more than sym-pathetic hearing from those whose very creed was 'There, but for the grace of God, go I'.

The Saarlouis incident had one further long-term effect in that it provided Bomber Command's more revisionist latter-day critics with vivid evidence of the damage which could arise from mistaken marking. However, such incidents were so rare as to be insignificant and the Pathfinders' target finding usually left nothing to be desired, to the extent that their contribution to accuracy was unquestionable. There was far more chance of death by misdirected bombing in Germany before August 1942 than ever there was thereafter.

Bennett set himself a most taxing schedule from the very start. He seemed to be omnipresent on the airfields and in the headquarters, added to which he maintained a flow of precise clear memoranda to Harris and to the groups, pressing the needs and promoting the achievements of his units. Occasionally the asperity of his comments exceeded what was acceptable for his comparatively lowly rank, but the seniority and considerable experience of his C-in-C and the other Group commanders held no fear for him. He was a past master at chivvying and pressing his requirements on an opportunistic basis. He also rapidly acquired the very necessary facility of judging Harris's moods and anticipating the moment when he should back off. It was always better to leave the door slightly ajar at High Wycombe, rather than have it slammed shut behind him!

Examples of this were the series of memoranda written by Bennett to further his wish to fly on the occasional operation. On 24 April 1943 he wrote to Harris with what he defined as 'a small request' which probably put the C-in-C immediately on his guard. 'I would like to go on a raid to Berlin' he wrote, 'and to direct it by R/T describing to the main force aircraft the TIs at which they should aim'. This early suggestion of what was to become the Master Bomber role found no favour with Harris, who wrote 'I am sorry I cannot agree to your proposal, although I fully appreciate your motive for making it'. Bennett was back with a further probe. This time he wanted to fulfil the role of 'commentator' as he put it, covering a raid 'on the Baltic coast' planned for a moonlight night, where he believed he could be invaluable as a sort of airborne master of ceremonies. This was in August 1943 and it is almost certain that he was referring to the attack on the V-weapon test site at Peenemünde which actually took place in bright moonlight on the 17th of the month.

Harris by now was less patient, pencilling a note to his Senior Air Staff Officer, Air Vice-Marshal Robert Saundby, on Bennett's letter of request: 'No, he can find another good commentator!' Later the C-in-C put his instructions in clear terms. Bennett must give up the idea of accompanying a raid. 'You are', he said, 'very important to the whole outcome of the war.' Backing up these words he added that his further concern was that Bennett knew too much and the enemy were fully aware of the job he did. Harris had no doubt that if captured he could anticipate an extremely unpleasant death under investigation by the Gestapo, since it was unlikely that he would be left in the hands of the more gentlemanly Luftwaffe. Interestingly, many Pathfinders are convinced that their chief went on a large number of operations flying high in his personal Beaufighter, or with the Mosquitoes. As proof of this it is said that on occasions he would appear at a de-briefing dressed as if he had just emerged from his office, but would let slip a comment proving he must have been over the target. The crews knew better than to draw attention to his trips, but in his autobiography he writes 'I also went out occasionally in person and saw how things were going actually on the targets themselves'. It is a strange way to put it, but the meaning seems abundantly clear. In his time he was probably the most senior officer to fly over Hitler's Germany.

His other means of keeping in close touch with his men were less dramatic, but equally effective. The early concentration of PFF airfields within the narrow confines of Cambridgeshire Pathfinder country was well conceived, and paid off in precisely the way intended. No one ever quite knew when Bennett was likely to turn up in the squadrons to see and be seen, his invariably immaculate uniform standing out amongst the more unconventional dress of the operational crews. He was at his very best on these visits; direct, approachable and always a good listener. He was, nevertheless, demanding to a fault. Nothing seemed to escape him, he had an uncanny facility for overhearing all the 'wrong' observations, and seeing everything which had been carefully hidden from him. Oddly enough those irritating characteristics made him the more welcome. Bland or gullible visitors wasted everyone's time, but changes for the better invariably followed close on the heels of Don Bennett.

Bennett tried each day to be present at a briefing at one airfield, a departure on operations at another, and the final de-briefing at a third. It was an unquestionably punishing schedule, especially since in between the whole complex operational machine had to be managed in all its diverse manifestations. The morning at Wyton would begin with Bennett in the operations room waiting for the first intimation from Bomber Command Headquarters identifying the target for that night. This would normally be conveyed by a telephone call from the command's Senior Air Staff Officer, Robert Saundby, who would also give an indication of the size of the planned attack. Bennett recorded that his own first concern was almost invariably the weather, since this would determine the marking technique to be employed and its intensity. His own meteorological team was probably the best in the service of the Crown and it carried a tremendous responsibility. With the marking decided the next job was to plan a route. By this time of the war an immense amount of intelligence existed about the disposition of enemy defences, the coverage of ground-to-air warning radars, the Luftwaffe's nightfighter bases and patrol areas. There was even detailed knowledge of dummy fire zones, spoof targets, and other attempts at deception revealed by the probing cameras of the high-flying Spitfires of the Photographic Reconnaissance Units. Thus the weather and the defences were the principal determinants of route, but there was a third important consideration.

As the offensive built up from 1942 onwards, the Germans became increasingly adept at second guessing Bomber Command's targets. This process was further refined by increasingly sophisticated radars set in a long chain down the sand-duned coast of Holland, and down through Belgium and deep into Northern France. The great *Freya* aerials were able even to detect bombers forming up before they left the skies of eastern England. With all this science and the growing skills of anticipation marshalled against them, the attackers entered the deadly game of cat-and-mouse with feints, setting courses which seemed to betoken a raid on one centre suddenly diverting towards another, and with diversionary attacks by small forces of aircraft flooding German nightfighter operations rooms with misleading indications. Many of these elaborate tactics were to be masterminded by the Pathfinder Force, although the bomber group headquarters were reluctant to lose their grip on these more cerebral aspects of the job of delivering high explosives and incendiaries to a target. Bennett had a hard struggle in persuading the operationally experienced commanders that they should defer to the central detail planning of his force. For many months he had to cope with outright opposition, foot dragging, and a certain amount of deception as the struggle against him and PFF burned out. And even as it seemed he had won the struggle, 5 Group, still unconvinced, managed to shoot a great hole in his organisation. But in the autumn of 1942 that was still months away.

A detailed attempt was made after 21 November to analyse the Pathfinders' achievement up to that date. (A summary of this exercise is given in Appendices F and G.) The objective was to establish the extent of the PFF's success and to attempt a forecast of the likely impact of H2S if it were to be carried by the whole bomber force or, alternatively, by the Pathfinders alone. Interestingly, the failure rate of H2S on operations before the target was reached was assessed at a high 30 per cent. However, it should be no surprise that the autumn weather in northern Europe was the biggest single factor affecting the success or failure of an operation. Of 18 attacks on Germany in the review period seven were deemed to be entirely successful, that is 30 per cent of the aiming point photographs taken were within three miles of the target, and all seven took place in good to moderate weather conditions. Similarly, the partially successful raids, six in number, all took place in weather judged moderate or better, and the five failures were all in moderate to bad conditions and included the cities of Flensburg, Frankfurt, Saarbrücken (a second, correctly identified attack), Cologne and Hamburg. Hamburg in particular on 9 November was the target on a night of bad weather and with no moon. No identifiable aiming point photographs whatsoever were obtained and the contribution of PFF was deemed non-existent. This harsh, but sadly accurate, appraisal pays no regard to the cost of the night's activities in which 7 Squadron lost three of its Stirlings and all of their crews perished. The Main Force losses amounted to a further 13 aircraft, mainly Lancasters and Wellingtons. Of the crews of these 13 aircraft, only three men parachuted to safety and survived to become prisoners of war.

Bomber Command's analyst turned next to the degree to which the Main Force crews believed they had been helped by PFF. The responses of those questioned were probably objective, despite the fact that most crews actually wanted the Pathfinders to succeed and looked forward to a time when their own task would be made a little easier. In just over half of the 18 attacks covered in the review, the work of Bennett's new group was judged of positive value to them all. Encouragingly, all the raids judged as successful were those in which the Pathfinders' contribution was acclaimed as decisive. The analyst summarised his findings with: 'Success by the PFF in executing their planned technique has almost always resulted in an improvement in the results achieved by the main force. Where PFF have failed the main force has never been able, by its own efforts, to improve upon expectation.' Taking the new definition of success (ie, within three miles of the target) – an arguably realistic one, at least on large conurbation's such as the Ruhr – on the night of 4 September, 58 per cent of the aiming point photographs of Bremen were within this radius. Over the whole period, 24 per cent of all photographs achieved the same standard of accuracy, showing something like a 40 per cent improvement. The Osnabrück raid on 6 October demonstrated expectations improved upon by a factor of three, but it was relatively small-scale and although six Main Force bombers were lost, all the Pathfinders returned home more or less unscathed.

Completing his review of operations to date, the author of the report turned his mind to future possibilities. These were early days not only for the crews developing their expertise, but also for the radar aids and the pyrotechnics. The custom-tailored target and sky markers were under trial and development, so adaptation was the order of the day. The attack on Düsseldorf on 10 September had initiated the use of the so-called 'Pink Pansy', a massive weapon comprising a 4,000lb bomb case stuffed with an appalling mix of benzol, rubber and phosphorus, which exploded in a great pink flash, standing out amongst surrounding conflagrations, and spreading burning phosphorous to ignite new fires. Longer-lasting was the 'Red Blob', based on the 250lb incendiary but which lacked the unique attention-attracting qualities of the bigger weapon which was clearly visible to approaching bombers for miles around.

As 1942 drew to a close with the heartening prospect of victory in North Africa, Bomber Command looked forward to a substantial improvement in its fortunes and in the results being achieved. However, as both H2S and Oboe began to enter operational use, a new argument raged over the deployment of H2S in particular. The benefits of equipping all of Bomber Command's heavies with the capacity for blind bombing were, in theory at least, obvious, but Bennett saw greater value in leaving the temperamental new equipment in the hands of his crews. The last three months of 1942 had produced some improvement in accuracy, to the extent that some 24 per cent of bombs dropped fell within three miles of the target and five per cent within one mile. The Pathfinders believed that if they marked using H2S they could secure a 50 per cent improvement in these figures, with a reasonable number of bombs likely to fall within the hitherto largely unobtainable one-mile radius. Trials had shown that it was possible to get all bombing within two miles of the aiming point. Realistically however, when due account was taken of operational conditions, equipment unserviceability, and the generally low standards of bomb-aiming, even 70 per cent accuracy seemed almost beyond reach. However, if it could be achieved it would represent an amazing three-fold improvement. Only in the clear moonlight of northern Italy against insignificant opposition had the bombers achieved accuracy at these levels. In October and November 1942 the Pathfinders had led raids on Genoa and Turin which achieved 80 per cent accuracy and, on 15 November, an extraordinary 91 per cent. These raids, ordered to Harris's fury – he regarded them as yet another distraction – were intended to demonstrate support for Allied landings in Morocco and Algeria. They had the benefit of surprise, but against this exposed the participating crews to the intense fatigue inherent to sorties of some 10 hours duration. After November the mid-European winter brought the raids on Italy to a close.

At this time 109 Squadron was busily working up its Oboe Mosquitoes for their operational début. The long trials carried out in Wellingtons had been beset with the inevitable problems of unserviceablility, and even less tractable ones of signal interference, the solution of which absorbed much time and effort. Oboe was a most promising device. The compact size of its airborne elements meant that it could be accommodated easily within a Mosquito, and therefore benefit from that aircraft's enormous advantages of speed and comparative invulnerability. These factors, combined with an excellent high altitude performance and a very respectable bomb capacity, inspired Bennett to consider a whole range of possibilities for the aircraft on PFF service as will be seen later.

By Christmas 1942, Bennett's determination to weld the disparate veterans of four squadrons into a cohesive war-winning force was beginning to bear its first fruits. By the most superficial judgement bombing was 'going better'; under more detailed examination the trend was even more encouraging. The gritty professionalism of the Pathfinders was starting to rub off on the Main Force crews whose growing respect for PFF inspired an improvement in their own skill and the accuracy of their deliveries on to the target indicators, put down with such precision for their guidance.

But there was another sign which was less felicitous, but increasingly apparent to the men who flew most nights to Germany. The defences were strengthening and the Luftwaffe was making great – and ultimately dangerous – strides to increase the size and effectiveness of its nightfighter force, and of the long, deep radar chain which extended from Norway to the Bay of Biscay. In addition there were the guns. Much of the terrifying flak was generated by the Germans' most spectacular artillery success, the 88mm heavy gun with a maximum altitude range of 20,000ft. The '88' was a versatile weapon later much in demand by the Wehrmacht as an anti-tank gun. It was however denied to them in the battle-winning numbers they sought by the priorities of home defence. In the end the four-unit batteries of the Luftwaffe's standard flak defences absorbed some 20,000 88mm guns and, each night 18lb steel high-fragmentation shells without number. In Germany there was a growing clear understanding that unless they took desperate measures, Bomber Command would surely finish them.

With this in the background, Bennett measured his resources against the growing demands made on him and the sadly lengthening casualty lists in his handful of squadrons. He was becoming a victim of his own success. He wrote a paper outlining his philosophy to Harris and his senior colleagues. He wrote:

'The success of the Pathfinder Force obviously depends very largely on the navigational skill of the captains, navigators and air bombers. Particular attention is therefore given to the navigational training of these three aircrew members. There is, however, nothing particularly abnormal about the training used.

'A proper appreciation of what navigation is has been the first point made clear to new crews. It is stressed to them that all observations, or all calculations, are done for a purpose and not merely to please the Station Navigation Officer. Wind velocities are to be found when required and not otherwise. The importance of the ground plot, ie tracks and ETAs and the time-distance scale, is stressed before all else.

'Teamwork, by enlisting the aid of all crew members for observations, is encouraged to a maximum provided it is on an organised basis and the observations are not too frequent.

'In order to assist the captain and bomb-aimer, the navigator when giving an ETA always gives the track and the ground speed required at the same time. It is a rule that there shall be no bombing before ETA is reached, unless it is proved to be wrong without

the slightest doubt. Evasive action (it is calculated) will reduce groundspeed in the following proportions:
Slight Evasive Action reduces groundspeed to 97 per cent. Add 1 minute in 30-minute run.

'Moderate Evasive Action reduces groundspeed to 87 per cent. Add 12.3 minutes in 30-minute run.

'Heavy Evasive Action reduces groundspeed to 71 per cent. Add 12.3 minutes in 30-minute run.

'Every effort is made to make navigation as simple as possible. Small modifications to the navigational layout of the aircraft have been incorporated. Nautical miles and knots are used exclusively, scaled miles and ground speed dividers are issued, clocks with centre second hands (running in phase with the minute hand) are installed for the use of navigators who work to the closest one-tenth of a minute for all purposes. Pilots, navigators, air bombers and flight engineers are encouraged to take their sextant sights through open windows, rather than through the astro-dome. Stress is laid on the importance of compass accuracy, and compass checks in the air are taken when possible.'

Bennett went on to describe an ideal PFF squadron briefing:

'The Squadron Commander opens the briefing with a statement of the intention, the number of aircraft, the method of the Pathfinder Force, and the part to be played by the particular squadron. The Met Officer then describes the weather completely, the Intelligence Officer describes the target and a series of target maps are displayed on each of which one phase of the Pathfinder technique is illustrated. This is done by the use of strings or coloured pins to indicate how and where flares and/or markers are to be laid. To each of these maps is attached a large notice on which is printed a brief description. The Navigation Officer gives a full statement on the availability of observations, the best times to find winds, state of the moon, and various data such as astrograph, Gee, Splashers, etc. The Signals Officer makes a statement as to whether there are any abnormalities. The Bombing Leader makes a statement on the load with particular reference to the height fuses set for flares. Finally, the Squadron Commander sums up, repeating the essential items...'

Next came Bennett's definition of various roles and specialities evolved from experience in the first operational months:

'*Qualified Pathfinders* are those aircrews who are permitted to undertake finding, illuminating, or marking duties. It does not necessarily mean that they have been awarded the Pathfinder Force badge, though this qualification is held by most of them.

'*Finders* are aircraft who [sic] are detailed to drop a long stick of flares at a big interval of time (usually between 6 and 10 seconds) along a given geographical line at a particular time (at zero minus one or two minutes) without positive identification of the target itself. The important point for a finder is that he must put down his stock on time and may, if necessary, do so on dead reckoning.

'*Illuminators* are those aircraft which drop bundles of flares (at three- to six-second intervals) in or around the aiming point only when it has been positively identified. The essential point of an illuminator is that he identifies the target before dropping his flares.

'*Blob Fire Markers* are those who drop a large load of aimable incendiary bombs exactly on the aiming point in one salvo (using the Mk XIV bombsight). This causes an immediate, large and distinctive fire. Blob Fire Markers must only drop their loads when they have positively identified the aiming point.

'*Ground Markers*. The same rule applies as with Blob Fire Markers, but the load dropped consists of a coloured or variable pyrotechnic of a distinctive nature which lies (burning) on the ground.

'*The Sky Marker* is an aircraft detailed to drop a flare or flares of a distinctive nature and at a particular level above the ground to indicate (a) that the aiming point has been found; (b) that the aiming point lies between two such flares; (c) that the illumination amongst which the marker flare lies is not over the target, but at some other point (see next paragraph); and (d) to indicate a release point at high level.

'*Local Landmarkers* are aircraft who are detailed to drop illumination and sky markers over a prominent local landmark such as a lake or inlet, or the like, only when it has been positively identified. This is to permit all aircraft to make an accurately timed DR run from this landmark to the target, thereby ensuring navigationally that dummies are avoided.

'A *Datum Light* is a bundle of three or four 4lb incendiaries dropped through the flare chute so as to mark the ground. This is used to assist the aircraft (when for instance it is too early and needs to circle a point, or return to cross it later) without losing their navigational accuracy.'

Bennett concluded his paper by stressing the need to anticipate likelihoods and plan their impact out of the equation. Thus he would eliminate unreliable types of aircraft from operations only requiring a small number; weather-sensitive airfields from the unique provision of a vital component of an operation; bad timekeeping, since, he argued, to arrive early necessitated time killing and hazardous dawdling near the target, whereas to arrive late was useless; finally, and unsurprisingly, he reiterated the vital necessity of basic accurate navigation, regardless of the ingenuity or availability of wireless or electronic aids.

In that autumn of 1942 there remained a shortage of crews in the four PFF squadrons; 109 Squadron was still working up. It had been established that there would always be a split of intake, as between experienced crews and those coming in straight from the OTUs. However, 35 Squadron was short of eight pilots and 17 navigators and was hoping for 16 of this joint total to be operationally experienced. The other units had similarly ambitious demands covering 64 pilots and navigators, whilst the PFF as a whole remained 130 engineers, wireless operators, and gunners below their required establishments.

Bennett continued to argue that many members of the Command's aircrew remained totally ignorant of how they could volunteer for pathfinding, and what their conditions of service in the force were likely to be. The C-in-C, however, was unconvinced that there was a real problem and was increasingly impatient at Bennett's dogged pursuit of PFF's best interests. In fairness, Harris had a vast hard-pressed war machine to run and he managed to do this with as much even handedness as the many priorities and demands on him would allow. He could not respond to all of Bennett's jostling and he refused to do more than urge his group commanders to transfer some of their best men to pathfinding duties. At the same time he was never slow to point out that the donation of good Main Force crews to PFF was in a very real sense an act of enlightened self-interest.

Harris was already sensitive of the extent to which he had allowed his early stance against *corps élites* to be compromised, now even to the extent of proposing a unit badge, unique in the RAF's history. He had no problem in justifying this and, in later writing, acknowledged that the Pathfinders 'were running even greater risks than the squadrons of the main force, to work longer tours and probably to miss promotion in their parent squadrons... It was also desirable for recruitment to arrange for the Pathfinder squadrons to be given adequate publicity in the press and by the BBC, but this was prevented by the security aspect of the matter... the enemy made a card index of all the names and details about aircrew they could get from our newspapers and found this very useful in the interrogation of prisoners.'

Later, matters were eased when in the early part of 1943 Hamish Mahaddie came off PFF operations and became Bennett's headquarters personnel specialist. He entered the job with a bubbling enthusiasm that has never left him. He had enormous advantages, extrovert, sociable, good humoured, but obstinately tough he was the archetypal irrepressible Scot. He seemed to know everyone in Bomber Command and those he didn't know knew him! He lectured, travelled, listened, and talked, he encouraged volunteers with all the guile he could muster under the baleful gaze of their squadron commanders. By the skin of his teeth he avoided most accusations of poaching, but he left no one in any doubt that to be accepted as a pathfinder was the greatest accolade available to an airman. He admitted to only one defeat in his attempted acquisition of talent, but philosophically came to view it as having been for the best. The episode concerned a young Australian pilot who had served with 106 Squadron at Coningsby, and who had acquired a formidable reputation for meticulous flying and courage well beyond his 20 years. At the end of his tour with 106 he volunteered for pathfinding and actually got as far as a posting to Warboys before his one-time CO, Guy Gibson, intervened with Harris's full authority and snatched him back to Scampton, 617 Squadron and the Dams raid. David Shannon would have enhanced any unit and Mahaddie particularly regrets this one that got away.

All of this was still months away when, towards the end of 1942, Harris visited Wyton and PFF for the first time. By all accounts he was impressed with almost all that he saw and heard. Like most senior commanders he welcomed these all too infrequent days at the sharp end of the war effort and obviously showed his appreciation. After he left, Bennett wrote him a fulsome letter of thanks: 'The personnel at PFF are all most impressed by the interest you are showing in their work and results. This is a tremendous incentive. I trust we may be fortunate enough to have you visit us again some day.'

As the year ended Harris wrote to Bennett and the other group commanders on the subject of awards and decorations. He observed that throughout his months at High Wycombe he had argued for an even higher allocation for the heroic crews of Bomber Command. Now he had discovered that only some 88 per cent of the command's entitlement was being taken up. 'It's up to you', he told Bennett and the AOCs, 'to ensure we're over-subscribed in future...' The year 1943 would see the start of the great offensive.

CHAPTER EIGHT
STRUGGLING FOR PERFECTION

Bennett chaired a meeting at Wyton on 28 November 1942, consisting of 20 of Bomber Command's most experienced men. Their objective was to consider the progress of pathfinding since August, to establish the way ahead, and secure the best possible results for the Main Force. Two future commanders of 617 Squadron were there, Leonard Cheshire, then with 76 Squadron, and 'Willie' Tait, then at the Air Ministry. When, in July 1944, Harris finally decided to take Cheshire off operations, with his score at an unbelievable one hundred in July 1944, Tait took over the Dambusters.

Bennett's meeting started with a lot of criticism about the concentration of flares and the fact that many of them were bursting far too high. (Harris was already complaining to the Air Ministry about the unreliability of barometric fuses), and Cheshire ruefully commented that the high-bursting flares did a great job for the enemy in illuminating the bomber stream. He went on to praise the ground marking, particularly of landmarks, which was greatly appreciated by all his crews. In making this point he crossed swords with 5 Group's SASO, (Senior Air Staff Officer) Harry Satterly, who argued strongly for sky markers, but quickly found himself in the minority.

All praised the Lancaster now being delivered in increasing numbers. Its power and performance meant that real precision was possible in timing and the attainment of altitude, whilst its crisp response and manoeuvrability, even when fully laden, made the accurate holding of a course a practical proposition even in the most adverse circumstances. The snag was that the non-Lancaster squadrons were beginning to detect their own comparative vulnerability, particularly those with Stirlings. Bennett took up the question of flares again before inviting further comments and promised better fusing and the availability of hooded flares reducing all-round illumination. He added that his squadrons were experimenting with new drop patterns around, rather than on, aiming points, as well as downwind of them to avoid the problem of their heavy smoke omission obscuring the clear view of the target.

As the meeting ended Cheshire responded to Bennett's worries about the continued shortage of Pathfinder crews. No one was more conscious of the vital contribution of squadron loyalties and personal friendships to the maintenance of morale, and in Cheshire's view these bonds should not be lightly broken. However, he acknowledged that there was a great conservatism and resistance to change amongst aircrew. Perhaps, he suggested, an element of detailing men to PFF should be introduced, but only if numbers were seriously short. He was convinced that most would volunteer to serve Bennett once they had completed their tours, but to ensure this the maximum internal publicity should be given to the work of the force.

Bennett considered all the possibilities. The overall loss rate across his squadrons which was approaching 4.2 per cent, against the Main Force's 5 per cent average over an equivalent period. He suggested to Harris that there should be no further direct intake from the OTUs and that a new system whereby crews undertaking their first tour were detailed to the force should be considered. They would complete their tour without the PFF badge to a total of 45 operations and then be awarded the eagle permanently. Another suggestion he made was for each squadron in the command to contribute one crew per month as a matter of routine. The debate rumbled on, the very last thing that Bennett wanted was to have below standard personnel diverted to his élite force, and his selection processes were carefully designed to screen such people out. At the same time he could only attract the best if the force became recognised as a team of high achievers using the most modern equipment available. This, in turn, required an input of skill which was far from assured in early 1943, despite the still fragile truce that had broken out amongst the high commanders over pathfinding. It was a classic, if no longer vicious, circle. Eventually the lure of the force – even the glamour – pulled in the people that Bennett so keenly wanted, particularly after PFF acquired Group status and a burgeoning reputation. Time was needed to see the realisation of all this and time was the item in such critically short supply.

The previous autumn a story reached Harris via sources in Turkey. The Portuguese ambassador in that country had told of a recent conversation he had had with von Papen, a German aristocrat and diplomat who endeavoured always to put a seedy respectability on the Nazi party. The German had spoken of the bombardment of the Rhineland by the RAF and the thousands rendered homeless by it. He said that there was a belief within the Nazi party that unless Russia could be defeated before the spring of 1943 there would be real fears for the future. Von Papen had his own reasons, no doubt, for stressing to a committed neutral the impact of the bomber offensive upon German civilian populations and even exaggerating this. However, no exaggeration would be necessary of the devastation that was soon to be inflicted upon industrial Germany.

January 1943 was a month of appalling weather, but using the sky-marking Wanganui technique in conjunction with 109 Squadron's Oboe Mosquitoes, which had attacked Düsseldorf for the first time on 31 December, several raids were mounted against Essen. Despite inevitable failures and unserviceability of the new radar aid, good results were achieved, but Hitler still refused to accept that Bomber Command had the means to attack with accuracy in such dreadful conditions. Magnetron H2S was now coming on stream in increasing numbers, the aircraft so equipped being distinguished by the large opaque perspex blister under the rear fuselage. On Lancasters, H2S-equipped from the spring of 1943, it occupied the position once intended for ventral defensive guns and, although these were probably of dubious value, the bomber's underbelly remained a lethal blind spot. The great number of aircraft which fell to the German night-fighters' upward-firing *Schräge Musik* guns, without their crews ever knowing what had hit them, bears terrible witness to this.

In the midst of frequent attacks upon Essen the decision was taken to acquaint the British public with the weight and new effectiveness of bomber operations. To this end it was decided to allow a BBC war correspondent to participate in an attack on a city, and Berlin was chosen for the obvious symbolic and newsworthy reasons. It was the first attack on Berlin for almost a year and, with only some 200 aircraft participating, it was not a particularly heavy raid. Richard Dimbleby flew in a 106 Squadron Lancaster from Syerston, taking off late on a winter's afternoon. It was a very long haul and by the time they arrived cloud was partially covering the target area and the red markers around the aiming point, Alexanderplatz railway station. Dimbleby's Lancaster made two bombing runs before releasing its single 8,000lb bomb. He was immensely impressed with all that he saw and experienced; the precision which was practised regardless of the hazard, the weight of the flak (it was actually judged light that night!), the cheerfulness of the crew, despite the terrible conditions in which they worked, and the devastation of parts of a city which he was witnessing. He later summarised his feelings and his fear, adding his thanks to his pilot, the squadron commander, for this 'unique chance to see for myself what is being done week after week in the name of Freedom'. It captured perfectly the public mood and the general grim pleasure at what was being done to Germany. The RAF was determinedly lifting the profile of Bomber Command and in so doing focused upon it publicity and thus the acclaim of the British population. Harris accepted this distraction as yet another of his burdens and, as ever, got on with the war. Dimbleby's pilot that night had been Wing Commander Guy Gibson.

On 5 March 1943 the first Oboe-controlled raid was launched against Essen. Eight Mosquitoes of 109 Squadron based at Wyton marked the target with red TIs dropped with great accuracy. They were backed up by 22 Lancasters and Halifaxes dropping greens. The main force of 400 heavy bombers followed and tore the heart out of the heavily defended, haze-covered target. At its centre lay the Krupps factory which, together with hundreds of acres of the rest of the town, burned on for more than two days. Subsequent reconnaissance photographs established that Krupps, more or less untouched in two-and-a-half years of war, was severely damaged, but importantly the area around the Oboe aiming point was 'virtually devastated'. As if this was not achievement enough, the loss rate on the attack was 14 aircraft, just over 3 per cent. It was said that Alfred Krupp, Germany's grim armourer through two world wars, never recovered his reason after seeing the destruction that had been wrought.

Essen was more than another attack, it was the start of a campaign that would become known as the 'Battle of the Ruhr'. Actually about half of the 43 major attacks in the period concerned were on areas outside Germany's industrial heartland, and the loss rate of bomber aircraft sadly crept upwards. By the end of the battle, 872 aircraft had failed to return from 18,506 sorties, a loss rate of 4.71 per cent. Over 2,000 more came back variously damaged, some beyond economic repair.

Oboe Mosquitoes were distinguishable by having their normally transparent nose, the visual bomb-aiming position, painted over and the airborne element of Oboe mounted on a small platform behind it, evidence again of the valuable 'portability' of the device. The Essen results seemed to portend that Oboe would be a war winner and its limited range still placed the vital Ruhr targets within PFF's grasp.

So valuable was the new radar's potential that considerable concern was expressed about security. Obviously the concept of a secret weapon is to some extent a contradiction in terms, since it is unlikely that the enemy will remain long in ignorance of any device being used against him. However, the longer he was relatively unaware of the source of his misfortune the better. The Mosquitoes which dropped their Tls on to the precisely Oboe-indicated objective, usually from altitudes of 28,000ft or more. The German nightfighter force had great difficulty in detecting these aircraft let alone catching them, and shooting them down, with the result that their loss rate remained just above the half of one per cent. Since comparatively few were employed, and they were operated by a two-man crew, they ranked high in the list of truly economical weapons of war. Saundby, Harris's SASO, wrote to Bennett with an expression of pleasure at Oboe's success, but sounding a note of caution and a call for every effort to be made to keep the device out of enemy hands. In all conscience its aircraft-installed paraphernalia was relatively inconspicuous and likely to be rendered the more so by crash impact. Saundby added that the longer the enemy thought they were relying entirely on H2S the better.

In fact the Germans were already aware that high-flying Mosquitoes were marking targets with some accuracy, even if they did not know how. Accordingly, the Luftwaffe's effective Junkers Ju88 workhorse was being tuned up for another task, that of the high altitude interception of fast moving targets. By the autumn of 1943 the Junkers Ju88-S1 was being produced, powered by two BMW 801 G-2 engines with the GM1 boosting system. This system involved the injection of nitrous oxide into the superchargers, providing additional oxygen for combustion. This addition of 'laughing gas' made Mosquito interception possible and earned the Luftwaffe soubriquet 'Ha-Ha' for the high-flying Junkers. Less amusing was the enormous explosion that would blow the aircraft to smithereens if the nitrous oxide tanks were breached by battle damage, or in a crash landing.

The fires of Essen remained clearly visible from the Dutch coast as the Main Force returned home in a state of high euphoria. Before the end of March Munich, Nuremberg and Duisburg had all been successfully marked and bombed. On 25 January, PFF had been translated into No 8 Group Bomber Command and Group Captain D. C. T. Bennett was promoted to Air Commodore. The change gave him equality of function, if not of rank, with the other group commanders; this apart it was an accolade, a symbol of success, a promise of permanency. By now the group headquarters staff was becoming well established and Bennett had taken great care to ensure that all the major staff appointments were filled by men with recent operational experience. It was not a situation mirrored in the other groups, where key jobs at headquarters and in command of stations were more often than not occupied by men who had never flown against the enemy.

It is unlikely that these had a particularly adverse, or indeed any, effect upon Bomber Command's pursuit of its war objectives, despite the enthusiasm of some authors to label them as out of touch, mannered, and conservative. There were not too many 'old fogeys' in the RAF, certainly not in comparison with its sister services. Senior officers were used to quick radical change, they had grown up with it, and they had a deep regard for the young men they commanded. The important thing was not that Bennett thought very differently from most of them, but that the whole mighty organisation was sufficiently flexible to contain and to use profitably all colours of experience and thought. The 'Service Establishment' made little secret of their views about the rapidly promoted, self-confident Australian, but they were well aware of the immensity of his contribution – whether they liked him or not was hardly relevant.

In March, Stalin recognised that something important was at last happening in the West. Despite his continual pressure for an Allied invasion of France to create 'The Second Front', demanded by Britain's noisy Communist nuisances who spanned a wide swathe from the intelligentsia to the reserved occupation industrial workers, he wrote a message for Bomber Command: 'I welcome the bombing of Essen, Berlin, and other industrial cities of Germany. Every blow delivered by your Air Force to the vital German centres evokes a most lively echo in the hearts of many millions throughout the length and breadth of our country.'

The new 8 Group was busy establishing its maintenance facilities for Lancasters at Wyton and Mosquitoes at Upwood, whilst two more stations at Bourn and Gransden Lodge to the east of Cambridge moved in under Bennett's control, extending the close-knit community that was Pathfinder Country. Co-incident with these moves, 97 (Straits Settlements) Squadron moved from 5 Group to 8 Group, taking up residence as a Lancaster-equipped marker squadron. Another new unit was 405 (Vancouver) Squadron RCAF with Halifaxes, but shortly to re-equip with Lancasters at Gransden Lodge. Last, but by no means least, of the newcomers were the Mosquitoes of 1409 Met Flight. The study of the weather was a great and understandable obsession with Bennett. In the midst of his developing menu of tactics, blind-bombing on dark and moonless overcast nights was becoming increasingly possible and attractive.

The ubiquitous Mosquitoes of 1409 roamed over the Western Approaches and the near and far continent right up to the moment raids were launched. Thereafter, as the bombers neared their targets, the Met Flight aircraft would bring forecasts up to date with commentary on changing winds, cloud cover and temperatures. In the colourful language of the Pathfinders' art and services, these were known as Zephyrs. The Met Flight also often photographed targets the day after attacks to secure an early assessment of results.

Early in the month of April, on the night of the 3rd, Essen was once again the target for a force of some 350 Lancasters and Halifaxes, but typically the weather left something to be desired. The Pathfinders dropped skymarkers as well as the usual TIs but the target eventually turned out to be clear, giving the strange aspect of the markers in the sky drifting down to those on the ground. The Wanganui system was not easy for bomb-aimers. Flares were floating down under the force of gravity whilst being blown potentially in any direction by the wind. With the aircraft moving forward and almost certainly drifting into the bargain, aiming became an infinitely variable process. But whatever the difficulties, the results were a quantum improvement over what was being achieved even a year previously.

On 14 April, Stuttgart was attacked by over 450 aircraft. On this occasion a new technique was used, marking blindly using H2S. The first Pathfinders would drop TIs and flares, enabling the second wave to pick up the aiming point visually and mark it with greens. Unfortunately the Main Force got it wrong and started to bomb the reds. Almost immediately they were instructed to aim on the greens, but at this point a stray green fell on a suburb which, fortunately, was highly industrialised. Heavy bombing took place in spite of the obvious presence of a far greater concentration of greens further into the city at the correct aiming point. This incident highlighted, if it were needed, the tendency for the average bomb-aimer to release at the closest apparent target, whether this was a marker or an incendiary conflagration. This phenomenon, known as 'creep-back', would become well known and target photographs frequently displayed a long line of intensive damage stretching back from the target in the opposite direction to the bomber stream's approach.

One cure for this was greater discipline; that bomb-aimers must await positive identification of the target either visually or blind by H2S, before releasing their bombs. It was simple, also, to suggest that a target left 'unfinished' would need to be re-visited, and that the next time the weight of defensive fire would be even greater.

The veterans could well understand the pressures on a 19-year-old bomb-aimer in a Lancaster making its slow dead-straight approach to the target as the flak burst all around. He would be lying on the cardboard-thin metal floor gazing at the twinkling fires thousands of feet below through the great perspex nose dome. He would know that the intricate structure in which he flew was immensely strong, so long as it held together. He would understand that a near miss from an 88, or a burst from an unseen fighter's battery of 20mm cannon, would turn the contraption into a spiralling confusion of wreckage blazing from a thousand gallons of aviation fuel, or blown apart by its own load of high explosive. He would hope that the new agility and the keener performance about to be given to his aeroplane, by the simple action of his pressing a button to release five tons of bombs, would prove sufficient to evade the defences and enable him and his crew to head for home. Such a man would not be doing what he was doing in the first place unless he had courage, endurance, and a sense of duty well above normal. There would be little point in discussing the need for discipline with such a man. The best that could be done to help him perform his unimaginable job was to perfect the technique of Pathfinding through equally brave, but more experienced, men and training them to mark the target accurately, promptly and unambiguously.

On 20 April over 400 aircraft went to Stettin and Rostock, a long haul with the targets being approached over Denmark and the Baltic. The emphasis on this raid of feints and diversions was early evidence of the way Bennett's mind was working. Mosquitoes of 2 Group attacked Berlin as the main force was approaching the Danish coast at low level and, as it turned out, this was an unfortunate ploy. Far from protecting the mass of aircraft from the probing German radars, they ran into well-placed flak ships around a convoy which put up a lethal barrage and forewarned the coastal anti-aircraft belt. That night some 14 aircraft were shot down by flak, almost half of the total number which failed to return. The Pathfinders' marking, on the ground this time, was excellent at Stettin, but at Rostock a well placed and dense smoke screen caused major problems for the marker Stirlings. One of the principal targets, the Heinkel Works, escaped unscathed.

The two new PFF squadrons, 97 and 405, had their baptism of fire as part of 8 Group on the 26th of the month when they performed their role well in the marking of Duisburg. The technique employed was Oboe directed blind ground marking, now dubbed Musical Parramatta, and throughout the attack aiming points were replenished with fresh TIs. Apparently, there was a well-founded degree of elation when the main force crews returned claiming a savage, concentrated attack. But it was the unhappy task of photographic reconnaissance aircraft next day to prove otherwise. The great weight of the attack had fallen outside the city, back along the approach path of the bomber stream.

Creep-back remained the implacable foe of accuracy. This was proved again when 120 Lancasters from 5 Group made a return visit to Pilsen on 13 May, the prime objective being the Skoda works on the very edge of the town. Harris was always against making aiming points of targets so placed, but unfortunately he allowed himself to be persuaded. A previous attack in April had been disastrous with nearby Dobrany receiving the bulk of the bombs and 11 per cent of the bombing force being lost. This time at least the attack was concentrated and well disciplined, but all Harris's fears were realised when the photographs showed devastation of open countryside and the Skoda works untouched. It seemed that a new fundamental had been established in that well-marked targets were still being missed by Main Force crews; perhaps saturation bombing was the only way ahead.

Two months earlier Bennett had chaired a meeting which agreed that the entire Lancaster force, with the exception of the single 8,000lb-bomb capacity aircraft, should be modified to carry H2S radar as should all Halifaxes. The advantages of this massive programme (up to then only 1,500 H2S sets had been ordered) were seen mainly as providing the Main Force with an added tool for accuracy. Thus the distraction of enemy-placed decoy TIs, or fires, and the intense glare of batteries of radar-controlled searchlights, could be eliminated by the radar confirmation of target being substituted for visual bomb-aiming. Further benefits included more accurate navigation to the target and thus better time-keeping, as well as the avoidance of heavily defended areas en route. Wing Commander Dudley Saward, later to be Sir Arthur Harris's biographer, added that blind approach and beacon facilities which would become available with H2S would obviously be denied to those aircraft without it.

The perennial problem of training was then raised with indications being given that the TRE (Telecommunications Research Establishment) had designed a synthetic trainer which would enable complete cross-country and bombing training to be carried out on the ground and 'would reduce air training to approximately 12 hours'. This meeting also heard first mention of Oboe repeater aircraft to overcome the equipment's limited range shortcomings. Mosquitoes could be fitted with the means of relaying signals from the 'Cat' and 'Mouse' stations on to more distant aircraft and the necessary black boxes were available from late 1943 onwards. For reasons that remain totally obscure, the Bomber Command reaction was lukewarm!

On 12 May, determined to build upon success and to learn from failure, the main force of 572 aircraft set out once again for Duisburg carrying 1,559 tons of bombs, greater than the total dropped by 1,000 aircraft on Cologne one year earlier. The attack was at last a spectacular success, with 85 per cent of the aircraft claiming to have bombed the target being within three miles of the aiming point. After this climax of achievement Bomber Command, no longer reliant upon the moonlight which made it – as well as its targets – so vulnerable, stood down the Main Force for the 10-day new moon period. One squadron, however, moved towards its unique place in history.

On 16/17 May, Guy Gibson led 617 Squadron to break the great dams of the Ruhr. Years later David Shannon would recall the moonlight as his lasting memory, silvering the great expanses of water and casting deep shadows in the folds of the surrounding hills and valleys. Overnight, 617 Squadron became a watchword for precision flying and accuracy of delivery. Harris decreed that it should remain so, a special unit to undertake special tasks. It was a tremendous fillip to 5 Group under whose control 617 Squadron remained, and to Air Vice-Marshal The Honourable Ralph Cochrane, who had been its A.O.C. since February. He had some very particular ideas about the place of pathfinding in the order of things, and these would have the most profound consequences for Bennett and the newly constituted 8 Group. He was also enormously respected by Harris who saw the drily academic Cochrane as his most likely successor at Bomber Command.

116

Cochrane had written to Harris after the Stuttgart raid on 14 April and the C-in-C copied the letter to Bennett asking for his comment which, when it came a few days later, ran to three closely typed and minutely argued pages. It is interesting to quote some parts of his reply to what was obviously a critical attack by Cochrane on 8 Group:

'I always feel that there is a tendency to look only at the damage done by Bomber Command and not at the potential damage wasted by our inability to hit the mark. The use of ground markers has, in my opinion, at last made it clear that without any other excuses or shortcomings, our bomb-aiming is in itself a most appalling shortcoming.'

Bennett then turned to the detail of 5 Group's complaint:

'I agree with the AOC 5 Group that there were definitely some Path Finder Force ground markers (TIs) short of the target (north north-east) but at the same time the undershooting of the Main Force and in fact the spread of the Main Force was far greater than could be linked in any way with the TI markers. The worst of the ground markers was one red four miles short of the target. Main Force crews however had been definitely ordered not to aim at the red TIs, but to ignore them and only aim at the green TIs. Although we have no photographic proof of it, there is perhaps the possibility that green TI markers might, by the end of the attack, have crept 3 miles north north-east of the aiming point. I cannot however agree with the AOC 5 Group that there were any green TI markers further away than this.'

Assuring the C-in-C that the ballistics of the marker bombs were well established he stressed:

'...if all bomb-aimers, Path Finder Force included, had been as punctilious and conscientious as the importance of their job warrants, then the raid would not have failed.'

Next the letter deals with the shortcomings of the timed-run bomb release technique, using some datum point well clear of the target as the start. Noting that this was one of his own original ideas, he records that it was a scheme which fulfilled only the purpose of avoiding completely stupid mistakes such as bombing dummies, or indeed, other towns miles from the target. Many crews had 'no idea whatever of how to make a timed run'.

Cochrane had suggested that most crews carried out their orders to the best of their ability, with which Bennett now wholeheartedly agreed this was 'absolutely right on this important point'. However, he went on to express some outspoken comment using his own operational experience, something which Cochrane lacked.

'I have, in my associations with aircrew, been of sufficiently junior rank to have learnt some of their characteristics from the inside. The term "operational accuracy" is a smug expression used by all too many of the so-called "experienced crews". These... are those brilliant young men who before the days of PFF were perfectly happy and satisfied that all was well when they were getting 3 per cent of the bombs on the built up area. They are the curse of Bomber Command... their outlook is not one of carelessness or lack of conscientiousness, but is just sheer ignorance of the extent of the inaccuracy which they advocate. So often have I heard Bombing Leaders in the Squadrons and OTU Bombing Instructors with their extensive operational experience assure the youngsters "Bomb sight! Don't be silly! You don't use a bomb sight on operations." It is not entirely their fault, [the bomb sight] cannot be used in the dark its knobs, rings and blobs have no means of illumination and, if they had, it's not stabilised.'

Later again he returned to his theme:

'I feel certain, living as I do amongst aircrews, that in general throughout the Command my accusations apply to all too many crews. I feel sure that even in PFF there are many who regard exhortations to bomb with more precision as being the "hot air" of somebody who does not know operations. I can assure you that we are doing all we can to kill such a spirit and that we shall continue on such a policy with the new crews which we receive here.'

Recognising that there were three or four bodies investigating the Stuttgart raid, Bennett submitted his own recommendations to the C-in-C:

118

'1. The fitment of Mk IV bombsights should be the highest priority of anything in the command.

'2. The entire aircrews of Bomber Command and in particular the instructors in OTUs and Heavy Conversion Units should be given a mental "kick in the pants" of the severest order. They should be given the facts concerning the percentage bombs which have gone into the target both now and before PFF days. In particular "the experienced" ones should be made to realise the extent of their inability in the business of night bombing. This should be conveyed to them as reason for revising their ideas and for improvement in the future – and not in any way as a reprimand. It should be stressed that night bombing in the fact [sic] of heavy defences is the most difficult job that aviation has ever had to face. 3. Bomb-aimers in Squadrons and in OTUs and those instructing them should be particularly selected for attention. The necessity for firm clear directions from the Bomb Aimer to his Captain during the attack should be stressed. The spirit of precision and of responsibility should be inculcated into them. Retaining this spirit in the face of defences should be advocated as their first duty.

'4. All crews should be instructed that conversation when approaching the target must be almost entirely a monotone [sic] from the bomb aimer. Only the Captain and the navigator should be permitted to add any remarks whatever. The Flight Engineer, Wireless Operator and the Gunners should keep absolutely silent except in extreme emergency.

'5. When TIs, or any other form of ground markers are used, crews should be more carefully instructed how to choose the centre of the cluster of markers seen. There is still undoubtedly a tendency to bomb on the first marker seen. It is essential that it should be pointed out to them that if there is a cluster of markers around the aiming point, then the first markers they come to must undoubtedly be short. These short markers must therefore always be overshot by all crews.

'6. The official aiming point detailed by Bomber Command should, in my opinion, be decided after the direction of approach has been chosen. The aiming point should then be ordered as a point on the far side of the area on which the main weight of bombs are required to fall. It should preferably be a factory, or some similar building which looks like a real war objective in order to induce a spirit of precision. On a place the size of Berlin it should be approximately three miles beyond the area to be blitzed. On a smaller town it should be approximately ⅔ or ¾ of the radius beyond the centre.'

Bennett concluded by expressing the belief of some progress in techniques, but there was a long way to go. 'I am sure that it can be done and that it will be done soon.'

Early in May Harris communicated his displeasure at the 'poor operational effort' shown on PFF's returns to his headquarters. In other words insufficient sorties were being flown. Bennett replied by sending the C-in-C a copy of the complex 'calculating numbers available' letter he had sent to his squadrons with its chilly final paragraph ending 'our operational effort compared with our potential strength is only a fraction of what it should be. We must revise our ideas drastically.'

Never one to miss an opportunity, Bennett concluded his letter to Harris by confirming his earlier complaint on the telephone that he had been stopped from using the Oboe Mosquitoes on nuisance raids when not engaged on other operations, and from loading his Met Mosquitoes with a bomb or two for good measure as they scanned weather over Germany. He proposed that such attacks could have a significant effect on German morale coming, as they did, quite literally from the blue, as well as proving a source of minor disruption and great irritation.

The original ban on such aggressive activity, well outside PFF's normal scope of operations, came from the senior staff echelon at High Wycombe. Obviously it emanated from a desire to keep Oboe secret and therefore to fly it over enemy territory only when absolutely necessary on major operations. Equally, one may have some great sympathy with keeping the Met flights looking at the weather. Officially, the Germans did not tolerate such flights, but then neither did they take too much trouble to intercept them. However, if they started to drop bombs it would become a different story and at the end of the day weather forecasts and therefore effective bombing could suffer. But it was always amusing to goad the staff, perceived by some as ever to be unadventurous and ageing, so one can sense even at 51 years' distance the wry smile on Bennett's fact as he dictated his letter to Harris: 'In an effort to "get on with the war" I would be very grateful if these two rulings could be reviewed.'

It is tempting to think that this was the moment of conception for one of the most successful of PFF's many spectacular achievements, the Light Night Striking Force (LNSF), which eventually comprised nine squadrons of Mosquitoes under Bennett's command. The process actually started at Marham in the spring of 1943 from where PFF operated two Oboe-equipped Mosquito squadrons (105 and 109), each comprising two flights of aircraft employed on marking duties in which they were eminently successful. A little later, in June of the same year, Bennett acquired the one and only other Mosquito bomber squadron in the RAF, 139. He decided to use this as a supporting unit, marking as necessary, but also carrying out diversionary raids to deflect nightfighters away from the Main Force.

At this point it is necessary to explain that severe doubts remained in influential parts of the Service about the Mosquito's intrinsic value as a bomber. It is difficult to make much sense of this opinion beyond saying that there were those who regarded the de Havilland aeroplane as insubstantial, perhaps a little 'flash', and not a true instrument of strategic onslaught. There was also the issue of its wooden construction and a feeling that Bomber Command would gain little by adopting yet another type of aeroplane, which was slightly maverick into the bargain! Such conservative thinking ignored the fact that a two-man crew in the early marks of the aircraft could carry 2,000lb of bombs deep into Germany at speeds that made it almost invulnerable to defences.

Within the year, on 23 February 1944, modified Mosquitoes of 692 Squadron PFF left Graveley bound for Düsseldorf, and each was carrying for the first time a 4,000lb bomb. Ahead of them flew Mosquito markers of 105 Squadron and behind them back-up aircraft, each loaded with four 500lb delayed action bombs. It was a significantly successful attack, an exclusively Mosquito operation bearing out all of Bennett's great faith in a spectacular aircraft which matched all of his expectations for rapier-precision attacks coupled with unmatched crew safety. The LNSF was entirely his concept which, as he later wrote, he 'quietly insinuated into the operations of the [8] Group without its being particularly noticed for some time. When the C-in-C did notice it he thoroughly approved of it and the idea grew.'

Bennett soon found that the rate of deliveries to the squadrons of the Mosquito were excellent. Its requirements for strategic materials were negligible and its wooden structure lent itself to quantity production in which components were widely dispersed for construction by an army of small sub-contractors. Add to that a loss rate which Bennett assessed as negligible, and he found himself able to form squadron after squadron from surplus crews and surplus aircraft. He wrote:

'The AOA would grudgingly give me a Squadron number and get it approved by the Air Ministry and I would then build that Squadron up to full strength. I kept on doing this until ultimately I had nine squadrons in addition to the Oboe Mosquitoes and the Met Mosquitoes... In ordinary nuisance raiding on Berlin, or similar cities, these aircraft each carrying a 4,000-pounder would go out in batches of up to 120 at a time or... in batches of 10 or 20 at intervals throughout the night and thus cause chaos...'

The LNSF flew 27,239 sorties between May 1943 and May 1945 and reached a record 2,950 in the month of March 1945. Their losses over the period amounted to 108 aircraft which failed to return from operations and 88 which were written off beyond repair. They dropped no less than 1,459 4,000lb bombs on Berlin in the last four months of the war. Don Bennett told the story of an American visitor, Mrs Ogden Reid of the New York *Herald Tribune*, who one evening accompanied him to watch Mosquito bombers taking off on an operation. He explained to her that the weather had led to other ops being cancelled that night, but this did not affect the Mosquitoes. As the last aircraft left she said she guessed Berlin might be the target and what bomb-load did the aircraft carry? On hearing from Don Bennett that they took a 4,000lb blockbuster to the German capital, she frowned and asked what the B-17 Flying Fortress would carry to the same destination. Bennett told her that the best they could manage with all their necessary defensive armament was 3,500lb, but in any event their bomb bays were too small to take the blockbuster. Mrs Reid replied, 'I only hope that the American public never realises these facts.' As Bennett wrote, 'the little Mosquito was a master aircraft'.

CHAPTER NINE
TRIUMPHS AND FALSE DAWNS

On 23 May 1943, at the first opportunity following the period of the full moon, the strongest attack of the Battle of the Ruhr was made against Dortmund. It was a night of records all round since the Pathfinder squadrons despatched a total of over one hundred marking aircraft for a Main Force numbering more than seven hundred. The raid discipline was exceptionally good with crews having been firmly instructed to go round again if, in the first pass over the target, they had problems in picking up the markers. As a result of this, and possibly benefiting from the freshness imparted by a long stand-down (this was often disputed), the first wave of 250 aircraft achieved an amazing 50 per cent of target photographs indicating bombing errors of less than one mile. Some 300 buildings and an important steel works were destroyed.

Even greater success was achieved on the night of 29 May when the Ruhr town of Wuppertal was attacked. Typical of the many Ruhr targets, the town was sufficiently close to the bomber bases to allow the maximum payload to be carried, with the added bonus of a comparatively brief exposure to the increasingly daunting German defences. Above all, however, Wuppertal was comfortably within Oboe range. The plan was for the Mosquitoes to mark the target at six-minute intervals, necessitating the use of a pair of 'Cat' and a pair of 'Mouse' Oboe stations at Cromer and Dover respectively. The first Mosquito approaching from the south was due to drop its markers to ignite over the target at 00.45hrs, but it was in fact some two minutes late, whereas the second was four minutes early.

The danger of this situation was that both sets of markers were likely to have burned themselves out in the 10 minutes that would have elapsed by the time the third Mosquito arrived, assuming that it was on time. However, the Pathfinders' accuracy was several orders better than their initial time-keeping and the first Oboe markers dropped their target indicators within half-a-mile of the aiming point, itself situated on the far north-eastern side of the town. This placing was designed to make maximum use of the phenomenon of creep-back by ensuring that even the most wayward of salvoes still impacted the city. As ordained by the inaccurate timing of the first Oboe Mosquitoes, there was a hiatus of 11 minutes during which no markers were burning on the ground. But then new marking was established with a similar high accuracy and, as the raid progressed, successive rings of green and red markers drew the bomb-aimers to their aiming points.

The main bomber stream comprised some 700 Lancasters, Halifaxes, Stirlings and Wellingtons in a corridor nearly 35 miles long which included further 'backer-up' Pathfinders. These would refresh the red and green target markers and the yellow indicators which were burning on the ground at a point some 25 miles south-west of Wuppertal where the bomber stream was to turn and make its run towards the town.

As the Main Force's incendiary bombs began to take hold on the ground, the huge fires became the focus for new waves of approaching bombers and negated the efforts of German ground defences to light decoy fires outside the town. The fire-fighters were rapidly overwhelmed by the scale of the attack, soon turning their main effort to escorting survivors from the developing firestorm in the town centre, which was rapidly consuming oxygen and replacing it with deadly carbon monoxide. To add to the problems of Civil Defence, the spring of 1943 had been a comparatively dry one and the river running through the town was at a low level. It was Wuppertal's misfortune that creep-back had been minimal and the bombing concentration exceptionally good. Some 700 acres had been devastated, including five out of the six major factories and the homes of over 100,000 people. Nearly 3,000 had died and a further 2,000 were injured. The bombers turned after leaving the target and flew on to a point just south of Bonn where they headed homewards on a course parallel to their original approach.

The nightfighters maintained a high rate of interception throughout the raid, but their number was limited by the Luftwaffe's still rigid rules which kept the fighters within their designated control zones. That night 33 bombers failed to return, representing a just about acceptable 5 per cent of aircraft despatched, especially when judged against the outstanding success achieved. For the Pathfinders there was a lesson to be learned. Favourable circumstances had ensured that their initial errors of timing were not material, but things could have turned out very differently. At the end of the day all the ingenuity of electronic warfare could not compensate for simple human mistakes, or downright carelessness. Bennett delivered icy reprimands to the offending Oboe crews, underlining that they had simultaneously exhausted their allowances for error and his patience.

There was also a lesson to be learned for the Main Force, in that the concentration of the attack owed as much to the paucity of the German flak defences in and around the town as to the accuracy of the marking. Wuppertal had been deemed less liable to attack than other areas of the Ruhr and had only a handful of 20mm light guns and a few searchlights to defend it. Thus the bomb-aimers and their aircraft captains unusually found themselves approaching a target with clear, almost welcoming, sky above it, devoid of bursting 88mm shells and the dazzling beams of scores of powerful searchlights. The disciplines of maintaining a straight course, delaying bomb release until precisely the right moment, and of pressing on over the target to the turning point for home, were thus that much easier to observe. Interestingly, the Pathfinders always maintained that equipment failures were primarily responsible for the timing errors of the Oboe crews.

On 26 May, King George VI and Queen Elizabeth visited Wyton and spent some hours with the new 8 Group and its commanding officer. It was a beautiful May day and even the composed, confident Australian must have thought he had come a long way from Toowoomba, Queensland.

A few days later two more squadrons joined 8 Group, 105 and 139. Both were Mosquito-equipped and had made history a few months earlier by carrying out the first daylight attacks on Berlin. No 105 had timed its attack to disrupt a broadcast by Goering to the German people, keeping him off the air for over one hour! 139 Squadron flew in later with the aim of interrupting a speech by Goebbels, but the execrable Propaganda Minister ranted on without pause. There were now nine squadrons under Bennett's command, one Stirling, one Halifax, four Lancaster and three Mosquito-equipped.

A raid on Düsseldorf on 11 June was the first on Germany that month and the second on the city in a period of just over two weeks. On the see-saw of success this was a definite downturn, although far from a failure. The first red markers were put down by the Mosquitoes directly on the aiming point, as a target photograph from a bomber in the first wave later showed. However, about half-an-hour later, another back-up aircraft put down a salvo of reds 14 miles to the north-east of the city, these being promptly attacked by 50 aircraft! There was no doubt that these were 'friendly' reds, although towards the end of May it had become clear that the Germans had developed their own red TIs and busied themselves igniting them in open country when bombing was taking place in the vicinity. A hazardous task and one that was no doubt observed with some equivocation by rural communities!

At this time Oboe was subject to many improvements and modifications to cure, for instance, malfunction of transmitters at high altitude in non-pressurised aircraft, and to anticipate enemy attempts at jamming. Interestingly, however, the next major development in the offensive came as a result of the simplest and most devastating radar-jamming counter-measure imaginable. 'Window' was a strip of aluminium foil 30cm long and 1.5cm wide. Bundles of Window comprising 2,000 such strips held together by an elastic band were released into the airstream whereupon the wind force would break the band and a large mass of fluttering strips would begin its slow descent. The enemy radars interpreted each such mass as a response from a large aircraft and would be rapidly overwhelmed by the systematic release of a host of bundles from approaching squadrons. In these circumstances there was absolutely no chance of ground controllers directing interceptors on to individual targets, and the direction of anti-aircraft guns and searchlights became impossible.

The adoption of Window was as obvious as the 40 tons of aluminium foil strip which littered the landscape approaches to Hamburg the morning after the great raid of 24 July. The Germans, from their own experiments, had concluded the value of metal strips for jamming radar, but so far had had no inclination, or overwhelming reasons, to use it against British defences. The War Cabinet had decided on 15 July 1943 to risk using the device, despite the possibility of a German response which could negate at least some of the effectiveness of Britain's radar chain which three years earlier had been her salvation. Window, as used by Bomber Command, was cut to half the length of the German 30cm radar wavelength, and fortunately this applied across a whole range of German defensive radars. The Germans never responded to this threat by widening the range of their frequencies or wavelengths.

The impact of Window was a miracle for Bomber Command, albeit a short-lived one. As over 700 bombers approached Hamburg on the night of 24 July, the German radars indicated that their airspace had been invaded by literally thousands of aircraft. Similarly the airborne sets on the Junkers and Messerschmitt nightfighters were showing a mass of aircraft which split up and multiplied like cells on the radar screens, flashing past the interceptors at horrifying speeds as if hell-bent on collision. The Pathfinder squadrons that night were beyond Oboe range and were marking on H2S. The first aircraft marked on their radars which readily picked up the distinctive outlines of Hamburg, its docks and river approaches. They released both yellow TIs and flares by the light of which the second PFF wave would release their red markers on to the aiming point. In the bomber stream were further Pathfinder aircraft whose duty was to keep the marking going, in their case with green indicators. Despite 'creep-back' causing a long corridor of incendiary fires and HE explosions miles back down the bomber stream, the raid was devastating. Some fires were still burning weeks later and the city was harder hit than any had been ever before.

Two nights later the bombers returned with more than 700 aircraft to attack the city. This time a firestorm developed when cold air was sucked into the city at twice hurricane-force, filling the void created by hot air rising from the blazing centre. Whole buildings were torn asunder by winds feeding the inferno. The temperature at its midst exceeded 1,000°C and it is estimated that 40,000 people died. Thanks to Window, Bomber Command's aircraft losses were significantly below the norm, despite some 4,000 sorties having been flown against Hamburg and two other targets in a period of four or five days. Milch, Goering's deputy, said 'the German people will give up given another five or six attacks like Hamburg, no matter how strong willed they are'. It is estimated that one million people moved out of the city to spend the summer nights in open fields. A total block was put on the reinforcement of fighter forces in Russia and the Mediterranean theatre; henceforward defence, like charity, began at home. The breeze had given birth to a whirlwind of terrifying proportions which now threatened to blow away the industrial centres of Germany and their populations.

Unfortunately, Bomber Command's efforts were switched at this time to other areas of activity and the huge advantages gained over Hamburg were not pressed home. In a period of full moon from 7 August, 8 Group led strong forces of bombers against Italian targets which included the cities of Milan, Turin and Genoa, which were concentrated into just under a fortnight. The reasoning behind these attacks was typical of what Harris referred to with some justification as diversions wasted on political targets. In this case the Allied Supreme Commander in the Mediterranean theatre, General Eisenhower, had threatened the devastation of the northern industrial cities unless Italy surrendered. Bomber Command was now charged with putting this warning into effect and the series of raids carried out in the brilliant moonlight of a southern European summer were highly successful. Whilst the Italian surrender was not, perhaps, wholly attributable to these attacks, they undoubtedly urged an already reluctant enemy to sue for peace and rid itself of Mussolini.

The second diversion was of more immediate concern to the people of Great Britain and to the slow process of building up the great armies necessary for the liberation of continental Europe. For many months persistent intelligence reports had suggested that Germany had already embarked on the production of a range of missiles, designed to saturate the British Isles with a torrent of high explosive fired from France and the Low Countries. Quite apart from the wholly indiscriminate nature of such an attack, defence against it was difficult in the case of unmanned flying bombs and virtually impossible in respect of long-range rockets and boosted super-gun shells. Clearly, the best option was either to attack the sources of such weapons' development and production, or in the final analysis their unobtrusive launch sites.

Thus it was on the night of 17 August 1943 that a force of some 600 aircraft attacked the V-weapons experimental establishment, located on the Peenemünde peninsula which jutted into the Baltic Sea due north of Berlin. The main area of the complex was spread along nearly four miles of the coastline and, although the use of 617 Squadron's precision skills was contemplated, it soon became clear that a saturation attack would be ideally suited to causing the maximum damage. The various missile test stands were situated on the northern tip of Peenemünde; to the south of them lay the experimental workshops; and further south still were various production units. Finally, the accommodation area for scientists, engineers and their families was located in woodland close to the neck of the peninsula. The inevitable forced-labour camp lay even further south at Trassenhelde. The whole target was excellently situated for positive H2S identification, being as it was a highly distinctive finger of land jutting into the surrounding Baltic. It was a far-distant target, the overland approach to which would involve prolonged exposure to nightfighter and flak defences. Therefore, it was important to try to achieve a single knock-out blow since an attack on so sensitive a target would lead immediately to the

Above: Air Vice Marshal Don Bennett escorts King George VI and Queen Elizabeth during their visit to 8 Group Headquarters at Wyton on 26 May 1943.

Below: Imperial Airways Captain D. C. T. Bennett pilot of the Mercury Seaplane with his radio operator A. T. Coster (right). The pilot of Maia, the 'mother' flying boat, Captain A. S. Wilcockson, is on the left of the picture, which was taken on the eve of Mercury's 13½-hour trans-Atlantic flight in July 1938.

Left: The Short Maia/Mercury composite aircraft. Don Bennett captained Mercury, the very long range mailplane component on its various proving flights.

Centre left: Imperial Airways conducted a series of in-flight refuelling experiments between a short C1 class flying boat and a Handley Page Harrow tanker in the spring and summer of 1939. Don Bennett was involved as the flying boat's captain on many of these trials.

Below: An early Wellington of Bomber Command flies in formation with a Hampden, while a Battle climbs away overhead. Only the Wellington and the ageing Whitley had any of the qualities necessary in a strategic bomber. The Hampden was a lightweight with many limitations, and the Battle an obsolete death trap.

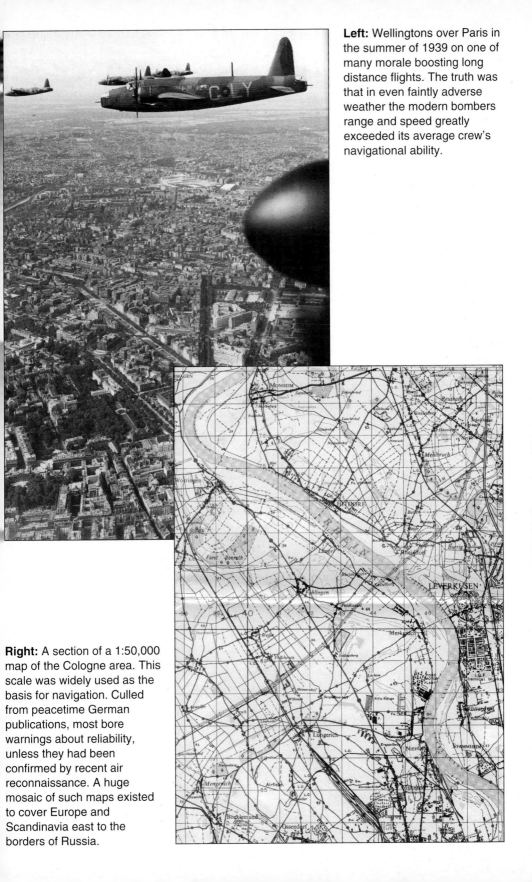

Left: Wellingtons over Paris in the summer of 1939 on one of many morale boosting long distance flights. The truth was that in even faintly adverse weather the modern bombers range and speed greatly exceeded its average crew's navigational ability.

Right: A section of a 1:50,000 map of the Cologne area. This scale was widely used as the basis for navigation. Culled from peacetime German publications, most bore warnings about reliability, unless they had been confirmed by recent air reconnaissance. A huge mosaic of such maps existed to cover Europe and Scandinavia east to the borders of Russia.

Left: The stark and vulnerable bomb aimer's position in an early Stirling bomber emphasising the rudimentary nature of bombing technology in the early stages of the war.

Centre left: Flares and the tubes down which they were hand-launched, as installed in the Short Stirling bomber. The uncertainties of this method of target illumination were numerous and it represented only a marginal refinement on techniques used in the First World War.

Below: A clutch of bombs goes down on Stavanger airfield in German-occupied Norway. An easily recognisable coastline adjacent to the target was always welcomed by aircrews. In his long operational career Hamish Mahaddie claims he is only certain of one bulls-eye – on Stavanger airfield early in the war!

Right: Sir Arthur Harris, C-in-C Bomber Command at High Wycombe in 1943.

Below: The much modified Wellington V high-altitude bomber. Flown by No. 109 Squadron under the command of one of the Bufton brothers, these aircraft contributed an enormous amount to the operational development of all Bomber Command's radars and Oboe in particular.

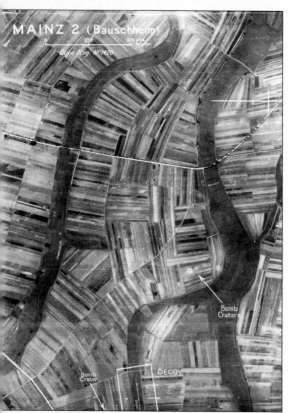

MAINZ 2 (Bauschheim)

Bomb Craters

Bomb Crater

DECOY

REGENSBURG 3 (RIEGLING)

500 0 1000 2000 FEET APPROX

DECOY

Nº 23070

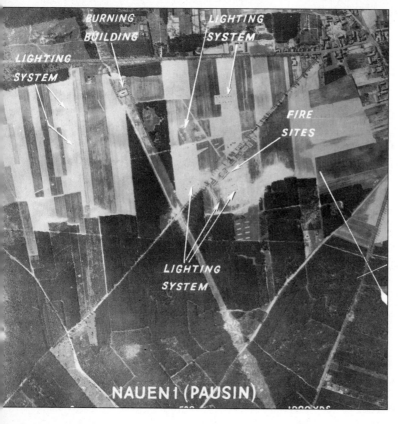

BURNING BUILDING

LIGHTING SYSTEM

LIGHTING SYSTEM

LIGHTING SYSTEM

FIRE SITES

LIGHTING SYSTEM

NAUEN 1 (PAUSIN)

Above left: A decoy at Mainz in 1942 showing so signs of success to the extent that twelve bomb craters are visible within t miles.

Above and left: Decoys discovered in 1943. High definition photographic reconnaissance pictures system at Regensburg an Nauen where lighting and burning techniques could create the illusion of a burning city area. For obvious reasons these decoys were located in remote country areas. To credit of Air Intelligence warnings, these elaborate ruses were often unsuccessful and therefor devoid of bomb craters!

Above: Capturing all the atmosphere of a Bomber station off duty, the Lancasters of No. 50 Squadron stand dispersed at Swinderby. The flat countryside and the wide sky, the scattered ground crews, the tractors and petrol bowsers and signs of the deep mud that always bordered the tarmac tracks, will evoke memories for any who served in Bomber Command.

Below: A fine portrait of the 'Queen of the Skies', an Avro Lancaster of 50 Squadron, one of Bomber Command's main force units. Based at Swinderby, this Lancaster, captained by Sergeant E. J. Morley, Royal Australian Air Force, crash-landed at Thurley on returning from a mine-laying operation on 19th September 1942. One member of the crew, a Canadian, died in the incident and is buried at Newark.

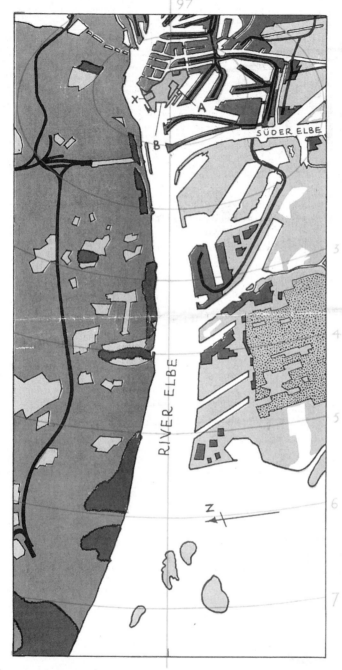

TARGET N°s 3 (e) 11 (A)   HAMBURG
              3 (a) 2 (B)
X = SUBMARINE BUILDING AREA

PLANTATIONS
SHRUBS ETC

THESE PERSPECTIVE APPROACHES ARE ALL GIVEN
ON A VISION ANGLE OF 45° TO TARGET CENTRE

ALL NORTH POINTS

A greatly simplified form of target map depicting Hamburg in this case. Some effort has now been made to depict what the bomber crew would actually see without entirely superfluous detail. With the coming of H_2S these maps could be compared with the Cathode tube images.

FACE
KINGS
PECTIVES
NLY)

TARGET

WOODS

BUILT-UP AREAS

WATER

RAILWAYS

AUTOBAHNEN

347°

ELBE

B
A
×

3

4

SÜDER ELBE

5

6

HARBURG

N

7

N

WN IN PERSPECTIVE

REFERENCE CIRCLE OF 1 MILE RADIUS AND
AT 1 MILE INTERVALS FROM TARGET MAP

Much later they were refined into transparencies which could be placed over CRTs for a perfect
target match.

Left: The marshalling Yards at Hamm, a frequent target for Bomber Command from the very start of the war. Although the railway system often suffered devastating damage, the widespread craters in the surrounding fields tell their own story of the difficulties of accurate bombing on even the most well defined defended targets.

HAMM M/Y

K. 2313 (IMM)

Below left: A typical attack photograph exemplifying the blinding confusion of flak, searchlights, flares, fires and H E bombursts. The city's streets stand out in a stark matrix.

Below: Mainz Kastel after a raid in August 1942 showing ten widely scattered areas of damage.

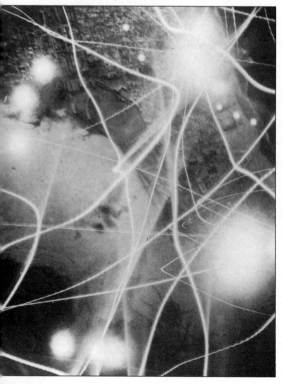

BERLIN/MITTE -
TIERGARTEN - WEDDING
K.1830
Neg.No 33536.

HAMBURG
Immediate Report
K 2838

Above: A typical picture taken at the moment of bomb release at 16,000 feet over Nuremberg on the night of 28th August 1943 at 23 minutes past midnight as one 4,000lb and two 1,000lb HE bombs left the aircraft.

Above right: The Tiergarten area of Berlin in the middle of Bomber Command's great onslaught in the winter of 1943/44. Useful damage assessment was often impossible due to the prevailing awful weather, but here on 21 December 1943 it was possible to delineate areas of major damage.

Right: Hamburg docks from 29,000 feet on 4 August 1944 – an ideally identifiable target for H_2S in the worst of conditions.

Above left: A 4,000lb 'blockbuster' and a salvo of 500lb HE bombs fall towards a cauldron of destruction covering Gelsenkirchen in daylight on 22 February 1945.

Above: Devastation at Brunswick following the attack by Bomber Command on the night of 14/15 October 1944. Brunswick received much attention from mid-1944 onwards, being raided both by the Main Force and Light Night Strike Force Mosquitoes. It was important both as a rail communication centre and for its aircraft production factories. By mid-1944 marking standards were particularly good.

Left: The platform for the very first Oboe trials installation in a Mosquito bomber. The combination of Oboe and the load carrying capability of the fast de Havilland aeroplane gave Bomber Command the means of marking targets with hitherto unimagined accuracy and reliability.

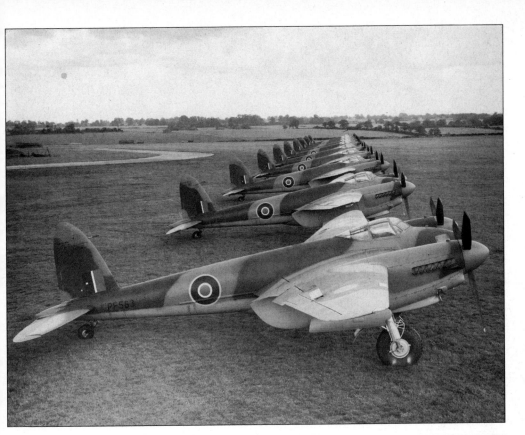

Above: Mosquitoes fresh from the Percival production line. Bennett was delighted to find he could secure Mosquito bombers in abundance mainly because his fellow Group Commanders had no real perception of how to capitalise on the aeroplane's qualities. The Pathfinders built up the Light Night Striking Force which caused disruption to German industry out of all proportion to the Force's size and at insignificant rates of loss.

Right: A Mosquito of No. 692 Squadron is loaded with its 4,000lb bomb at Graveley in the early spring of 1944. The high performance and load-carrying ability of the later marks of Mosquito made them a highly efficient weapons systems. Don Bennett rightly laid claim to having developed their spectacular operational potential to the full.

Above: A Light Night Striking Force Mosquito piloted by Johnny Turner just prior to embarking on one of the last operations of the war, against Kiel on 2 May 1945.

Left: The centre of Cologne, typifying the devastation of Nazi Germany as seen by RAF groundcrews taken on sight-seeing trips in Bomber Command aircraft after the end of the war.

Above: The first commercial flight out of Heathrow, London to Buenos Aires, New Year's Day 1946. Don Bennett in command. Obviously an event for the newsreels!

Right: Before departure from London on 1 January 1946. Don Bennett with Lord Winster, Minister of Aviation. Ly Bennett is on the far left of the picture.

Right: Don Bennett in the cockpit of a converted Avro Lancaster during post-war flight re-fuelling trials in June 1947.

Above: The Atlantic Ferry Pilot memorial, a plinth-mounted Lockheed Hudson at Gander, Newfoundland. On 25 October 1967 the memorial was unveiled by a, for once, surprised Don Bennett who had been led to believe he had been invited simply to look around the Gander Atlantic Flight Museum!

Above right: Sir Arthur Harris in 1977. The C-in-C's deep admiration for the men of his Command and his unswerving belief in what they had achieved created a great bond amongst surviving veterans. The cruel disparagement of Bomber Command by its intemperate post-war political critics remains one of the most shameful episodes of modern British history.

Right: Don and Ly Bennett at the Pathfinder Ball in 1981. After her husband's death, Ly became Patron of the Pathfinder Association and has earned the deep affection of all its members.

upgrading of its apparently low level of defences, and in the medium term to its widespread dispersal.

To 8 Group fell the responsibility of working out an attack plan, and a basis for 'moving' the markers from one target to another down the peninsula as the raid progressed. To achieve the degree of bombing discipline required, and to stage-manage the development of the operation, Bennett appointed a 'Master of Ceremonies' for the first time, Wing Commander John Searby, who was serving as commanding officer of 83 Squadron based at Wyton. Searby had had the opportunity of practising his role over the comparatively quiet skies of Turin a few nights earlier, and now set course for Peenemünde in Lancaster JA928, OL–W. The plan, which included diversionary attacks by Beaufighters and Mosquitoes on Luftwaffe nightfighter bases in Holland, also involved a spoof raid on Berlin by Mosquito aircraft of 139 Squadron to confuse and draw off enemy defences. Meanwhile the Main Force headed by Searby's Pathfinders made its way across Denmark and out over the Baltic, approaching the peninsula from the north. Nos 5 and 6 Groups would attack the experimental works, 1 Group the production factory, and 3 and 4 Groups the accommodation area to the south.

Searby arrived over the target just 30 seconds ahead of time, but shortly afterwards he was called upon to correct a major error by the first PFF aircraft which dropped their markers well to the south of the first objective, the living quarters occupied by German scientists and engineers. They were using for the first time the impregnated cotton waste markers which had a burning time of some 10 minutes and which now lay blazing in the midst of the forced labour camp. Searby managed to correct the error within two to three minutes, but unfortunately not before the leading Main Force aircraft had dropped their loads on the flimsy structures housing largely Russian and Polish workers.

The remainder of the first wave bombed to Searby's instructions and its Halifaxes and Stirlings caused severe damage and loss of life, including Dr Walter Thiel, the chief rocket engineer on von Braun's team. The first marking error was later proved to have been caused by a surprisingly indistinct H2S 'picture', within the blind marker aircraft, of the peninsula some 15,000ft below them. No 1 Group followed in to bomb the production works. The marking for this attack was better, but still far from perfect, and the busy Master of Ceremonies had his work cut out urging the bomb-aimers to concentrate on the correct markers and, most of all, to ignore the still burning TIs and huts in the labour camp.

Each phase of the attack was timed to last for some 15 minutes, so by the time 5 and 6 Groups had arrived on the scene many markers were still burning, generating smoke and further obscuring the already deteriorating visibility. To add extreme danger to the bombers' difficulties, the nightfighters were arriving in force from the Berlin area. Cochrane, 5 Group's AOC, had maintained his demands for freedom of action by relying upon the time and distance technique, although his crews were also given the option of bombing obvious markers if these seemed well placed. This was a most unfortunate piece of confusing indecision which resulted in a very patchy outcome. Although a third of the buildings were destroyed in the target area, the intended saturation failed and such structures as the wind tunnel and the highly important telemetry block survived. The arrival of the Luftwaffe wrought havoc with the precise time- and distance-running Lancasters, and the nightfighters picked off many as they turned for home.

Forty aircraft were lost that night for what, at face value, seemed only a moderate result. However, as is often the case, objective historical judgement is far away from the entirely subjective reactions of the enemy taken amidst the smoke and ruins of the morning after. Firstly, it was clear to all that Peenemünde's cover had been blown and the time-consuming disruption of moving the production of V-weapons began immediately. Plants were established in bleak inhospitable tunnels dug deep into the Hartz Mountains where 60,000 slave labourers were eventually employed, 20,000 of whom eventually died of disease and starvation brought about by the cruel indifference of their masters. The whole process cost Hitler at least 800 rockets and saved Britain some thousands of civilian dead. As for the raid itself, it resulted in the deaths of many engineers engaged on the programme and terrified surviving families in the accommodation area, many of whom clamoured for immediate evacuation. Finally, in Germany the attack on Peenemünde seemed to confirm that there was no hiding place from the bombers, no task was too precise for them, no target too difficult. For one man at least, the reckoning now being meted out to his country was intolerable and on 18 August the Luftwaffe's Chief-of-Staff, Hans Jeschonnek, put a gun to his head and shot himself.

In England there was no rejoicing over a raid which, although worthwhile, had fallen significantly short of the ideal. In 5 Group, Cochrane was particularly critical about the Pathfinders' misplaced markers. The confusion that had arisen in his own squadrons' time and distance approach, due both to conflicting bombing instructions and to the late but unwelcome attention of a host of nightfighters, further irritated him. Bennett respected Cochrane above all the other AOCs but he, like others, found the Air Vice-Marshal's patrician infallibility a little difficult to cope with, and certainly was more than usually attentive to any criticism emanating from him. Even the irreverent and irrepressible Leonard Cheshire had to suppress a frisson of alarm every time he was summoned to Cochrane's office! Bennett received a long report from 5 Group on the subject of Peenemünde and took his time over constructing a response. Cochrane had sent Harris a copy of his complaint and Bennett did the same with his reply. It was a tense moment of conflict between Bomber Command's two most outspoken and thoughtful commanders.

Bennett wrote that his own research had certainly not confirmed the 5 Group view that the case for time and distance was proved incontrovertibly over that of ground marking by the Peenemünde raid. He argued that the peninsula was perfectly suited to Cochrane's *modus operandi*, with a long approach over water from an easily discernible offshore island which provided an almost ideal starting point. On the other hand, he added, the requirement for three separate aiming points made the ground marking job more than usually complex. Arguing over the 5 Group figures, showing that their bombs had been 37 per cent useful compared to the remainder's 21 per cent figure, 8 Group re-examined the evidence and came up with figures of 37 per cent and 56 per cent respectively.

'It seems quite clear therefore, on your own figures, that visual bomb-aiming even at the end of a heavy attack would have been far more destructive than the indirect method (time/distance) even under circumstances most highly favourable to the latter. I feel myself that inherently a timed run method of releasing bombs can never achieve the same accuracy as could be obtained by direct methods. Pilotage errors over an appreciable length of time, combined with navigational errors, are all additional to the bombing error due to incorrect heading, incorrect winds, etc, which in any case is applicable at the point of release. It seems clear, in theory at any rate, that precision by such a method could never reach that obtained by the more simple direct method. On the other hand I am entirely in agreement with you that the timed run method should always be used as a matter of habit on every attack from some datum reasonably close to the target in order to ensure that no stupid Bomb Aimer mistakes occur.'

Towards the end of August, German nightfighters began a new tactic. Flares were dropped to mark the location and direction of the bomber stream so that other nightfighters could home easily on the mass of aircraft, and then switch on their short range interception radars for the kill. This coincided with a brief series of attacks on Berlin which involved a long flight over the well defended north of Germany. A most successful raid on the capital on 3 September was carried out by 316 Lancasters, with 81 more from 8 Group marking and backing-up. In addition four Mosquitoes countered the Luftwaffe's sign-posting of the bomber stream by putting down their own lines of matching flares miles away from the approach and departure routes.

German radar cover was reaching the highest standards of effectiveness from the long-range early-warning stations on the Channel coast to the sophisticated airborne interception sets in the mass of nightfighters now deployed across Europe. In the same way that Fighter Command had directed its squadrons in 1940 from operations rooms around London, so the Luftwaffe developed its own elaborate systems. Massive bunkers built of heavily reinforced concrete housed theatre-like nerve-centres. Within them, tiers of desks accommodated women plotters whose job it was to transfer raid information through miniature projectors on to a vast translucent sector map, on the other side of which the controllers sat in their communications centre. Thus the bombers' course was minutely followed and analysed, while the nightfighters circled their holding beacons and the 88mm flak batteries awaited their targets' arrival overhead.

The German home-defence fighter strength was building up towards a peak figure of nearly 1,200, which it acheived in the late spring of 1944. This was still insufficient for Goering, who demanded 2,000, adding, 'even if this means that the battle fronts get nothing at all'. Such was the undeniable impact of strategic bombing.

Certainly at this time the losses experienced by 8 Group began to mount alarmingly, although the increasing number of Mosquitoes in use continued to enjoy relative immunity. The Pathfinder 'heavies' however were faring badly, with the consequent loss of many highly experienced crews. On the night of 23 August more than 10 per cent of 8 Group's participating aircraft were lost and with them two Group

Captains, the station commanders of Graveley and Oakington. Such senior officers were not normally expected to do more than the occasional sortie, perhaps one a month, but the Pathfinders as ever were a law unto themselves.

On 5 September the Pathfinders secured a triumph with an attack on Mannheim, placing the blind and visual markers in an almost perfect group within a mile of the aiming point. Furthermore, the offsetting of this point somewhat to the east of the target made the maximum allowance for the weary problem of creep-back which still persisted, particularly over heavily defended targets. Soon a vast area of fire extended from Mannheim to adjoining Ludwigshafen and a new PFF trade, the Recenterers, blind-marked to prevent any exaggerated early release of bombs down the line of approach. A further equally successful attack on Mannheim nearly three weeks later caused Bomber Command to consider the city neutralised and not needing further attack for some time to come.

Perhaps to defer to 5 Group's ideas and test a time and distance run for themselves, 8 Group employed this tactic for a raid on Hanover on 21 September. Using a convenient and easily recognised lake as the starting point the Pathfinder aircraft began their run, but most of them immediately concluded that the wind was some 20mph stronger than forecast. This led to a significant overshoot of the target and concentrated bombing by the Main Force of the town's south-eastern outskirts. Meanwhile, the visual markers had correctly placed their flares on the aiming point with some great precision, but these were largely ignored by the remaining attackers. A second raid on 27 September again suffered from unreliable wind strength forecasts, causing markers to be released a shameful 5 miles north of the aiming point. The bombing was particularly well concentrated on these wildly misplaced indicators at an average 130 tons of explosive per square mile, which virtually eliminated one part of the city.

Harris was beside himself. He had written to Bennett after the first attack saying:

'The attack on Hanover was a complete flop, the worst failure we have ever had. The outcome of this attack shows that the majority of PFF crews must have discarded their own navigational reckoning and the indications of their aids and followed blindly, if not light-heartedly, on to misleading markers and incendiaries. If this

133

is done then the setting of dummies is only too easy for the enemy, especially on targets which have no defined landmarks. I cannot too strongly impress upon every PFF crew their individual responsibility for making as sure as possible, by their own reckoning and aids, that they are on target before blindly joining in and thus making confusion most confounded. What happened at Hanover is a lesson which you no doubt will take to heart in future in determination to preserve the name for skill and efficiency which you have achieved through much toil and bitter experience. Forget it, pull your socks up and make as sure as possible that no careless action of any one of you individually can in future serve to lead the entire force astray as on this occasion.'

The fact that two days later a worse error was committed in the same circumstances on the same town was an impossibly bitter pill for Bennett. It was said that the name Hanover was never again willingly mentioned in his presence.

In between the two attacks Bennett replied to Harris's reprimand, starting his long letter by observing that because of the Hanover fiasco it was 'advisable . . . to do a stocktaking of the Pathfinder Force for [Harris's] consideration'. Bennett began by stating that the policy declared at the point of PFF's formation of 'nothing but the best' had simply not been realised. The force had been denied the best crews – a third of them were taken with no operational experience – and manpower shortages, together with increasing demands, meant that there were less training opportunities in 8 Group than there were in the Main Force. He recounted a recent occasion when another AOC had claimed he could easily produce a dozen better crews as backers-up than the Pathfinders could muster. Bennett had enquired why, if this were so, these crews were not in PFF where they belonged? He suggested to Harris that the AOC totally misunderstood the purpose of PFF, seeing it as a rival as opposed to a facilitating organisation.

The human element caused the Hanover failure, and to overcome it AOCs would need to extend the 'nothing but the best' policy to the crews they had surrendered to 8 Group. Interestingly, he noted that whereas the average experience of his captains at February 1943 had been 32 operations, it was now down to 20. This clearly illustrated the extent to which 8 Group's experience and expertise had been diluted. Bennett went on to suggest that PFF should have the ability to select any or all crews returning to operations after resting and that no direct entry 'freshman' should join Bennett's squadrons in future ('Agree,' wrote Harris in the margin).

On the question of training, Bennett wrote that Main Force crews had the luxury of fairly long conversion courses, certainly lasting for many weeks, when converting from one aircraft type to another. In 8 Group there had been recent occasions when crews had converted from one type to another in the course of a few days during a normal run of operations! Additionally, H2S training was carried out on an *ad hoc* basis intermingled with normal sorties. Following this haphazard approach, four of 8 Group's heavy squadrons were now fully trained in the radar's operation, but remained short of 17 Lancasters fitted with the equipment.

Warming to the subject, Bennett assured his C-in-C that even Hanover was 'a paragon of success compared to the farcical raids which I can assure you from personal experience were carried out before PFF'. He added, 'on the other hand I agree with you that the results achieved with H2S have been extremely bad [but] if visual methods were employed in raids of high density and high bomb loads such as are at present applied, the result would be appalling'. Bennett observed, not for the first time, that the smoke from high explosive and from massive conflagrations was a self-inflicted obstacle 'with which a straightforward visual method [of aiming] would find it impossible to cope'. The real answer lay in better and better training and the arrival of 3cm H2S. This new version of H2S would greatly improve target identification, especially within a large town, and Bennett urged Harris to press Bomber Command's case in advance of Coastal's claims for anti-submarine use.

Turning to Oboe he suggested that Harris saw the repeater system (to extend Oboe range) as some sort of panacea ('No!' wrote Harris in the margin), but Bennett first wanted Oboe Mk II fully developed and not sidelined by the next brilliant technical breakthrough holding promise of jam tomorrow. Anyway, it was clear that Oboe was no guarantee of success, useful though it undoubtedly was.

On the subject of flares and pyrotechnics Bennett recorded that hooded flares were now months overdue, despite promises, and the production of a wider range of coloured pyrotechnics seemed too much for 'the armament fraternity'. Returning to the Hanover raid, he suggested that Main Force incendiaries were literally stealing the limelight from the Pathfinder markers and perhaps, therefore, the attack should begin with a concentration of high explosive. He concluded by asking the C-in-C to permit him to fly on operations, for 'I can never do this job as it should be done unless I am permitted to operate. I realise that this is contrary to Air Council instructions... I think the case of the AOC PFF should be regarded as an exception and I feel certain that the results would definitely improve thereby.' Whether Harris replied to this further nudge to permit Bennett to fly operationally is uncertain. Most likely he felt the official reply had been given and that now the eleventh commandment should apply.

This marked a watershed for the Pathfinders, but soon it was a question once again of 'getting on with the war', for the Battle of Berlin was about to begin.

CHAPTER TEN
A CITY TOO FAR

On 25 August 1940, 81 Wellingtons and Hampdens had carried out the first bombing raid on the city of Berlin. Their crews were strictly briefed to bomb only specified military and industrial targets such as Tempelhof airport, and various power stations and factories engaged on war production. The raid was in direct response to the Luftwaffe's night bombing of London a day earlier which has since been widely acclaimed as a 'mistake', albeit one with the most shattering long-term results. However, historical evidence suggests that the Germans were rapidly tiring of their daylight onslaught on the British Isles and the raid on London was a first, if somewhat halting, entry into the night arena. Certainly within a few weeks the night blitz on Britain was in full swing.

In the period of Bomber Command's offensive which lay between October 1940 and the late summer of 1943, many attacks were made on the German capital, but most suffered from scattered bombing results and a heavy loss rate which sometimes reached 10 per cent of sorties. The city itself represented a sprawling target, surrounded by open country dotted with residential and industrial suburbs, all of which made the recognition of targets and aiming points by eye, or by radar, exceedingly difficult. The long flight to the capital from the airfields of East Anglia significantly reduced the bombers' war load, and it was not until the advent of the Lancaster that really large high explosive bombs could be carried deep into Germany. Before this the other heavies were limited to bombs which were not wholly effective against the widely spaced and strongly built structures housing the enemy's military and civilian nerve centres.

Most telling of all, however, were the perils encountered by the attacking force approaching across some 500 miles of hostile territory, from the Dutch coast to the suburbs of Berlin. Allowing for the long range involved in the most direct approach, dog-legs and feints would involve even greater fuel consumption and therefore less war load carried. In any case such tactics were unlikely to deceive the defences due to Berlin's relatively isolated geographical position, which made it obvious as the target at a fairly early stage of a developing attack. Thus time and distance were both on the side of the Luftwaffe. As the bombers were passed from zone to zone of the German defensive radar chain they were constantly harried by nightfighters, and would finally arrive over Berlin to an alert, forewarned flak and searchlight barricade. Their journey home was, if anything, even more hazardous.

In mid-1943 several related developments seemed greatly to have changed the situation to the apparent advantage of Bomber Command. Firstly, the use of Window in the attack on Hamburg was conclusive in wrecking the German defensive radar systems and their means of controlling and positioning the nightfighter force. This tremendous coup would need to be exploited before either counter-measures to Window, or a re-organisation of defences, were put in place. Secondly, the Hamburg raids had shown what could be achieved by accurate marking by the Pathfinders, followed by a disciplined saturation attack by the Main Force. The prospect of razing Berlin by fire and high explosive, as well as securing the total demoralisation of its citizens, was vastly attractive to the Allied cause. Finally, the increasing number of H2S-equipped Lancaster squadrons available to Harris appeared to provide the means for achieving a spectacular victory. And so the detail planning for the Battle of Berlin was initiated at High Wycombe and Harris prepared to reverse the outcome of disastrous, costly raids of 1941 and 1942.

The attacks opened on 18 November when nearly 400 Lancasters went to the city. As was so often the case, at the height of the central European winter blind marking was the only means available using sky-marker flares, but these soon vanished into the thick cloud over the city and bombs inevitably scattered over a wide area.

Bennett entered the battle with a number of grave misgivings. He was concerned, as we have seen, with the quality in terms of training and experience of many of his crews. Casualty rates had become increasingly hard to bear, giving rise to a vicious circle whereby experienced but very fatigued crews were being lost, only to be replaced by less experienced men who were inadequately trained due to the urgent need for them on operations. The operational lives of such crews were likely to be even more brief and their places taken by men with still less experience and training behind them.

Attrition and campaign demands were forcing Bennett into the very position he abhorred; to him there was no substitute for perfection and quality – which were the keys to the success of the bomber offensive. If only he could achieve a general standard of excellence in his crews there would be far fewer casualties among them, and standards of marking and raid direction would improve beyond measure. For the Main Force there would be the benefit of being marshalled quickly and efficiently over clearly defined targets by seasoned Master Bombers. Not only would such well disciplined attacks confound the defences, who secured many of their victories from the pursuit of wandering stragglers and latecomers, but they would also pulverise cities by the extent of their concentration. Scattered damage was easily repaired, of only passing significance to citizens of the target town, and was unlikely to be particularly disruptive to normal life. Bennett firmly believed that half-a-dozen Hamburgs would do the trick, and he was almost certainly right.

The second main area for Pathfinder concern was that of the principal aids available to them which were beginning to demonstrate operational shortcomings. For long-range attack the basic Oboe was useless because of its range limitation, and the use of 'repeater' aircraft was still the subject of some controversy in 1943. This was principally because of the relative weakness of the vital links in the chain on which the system relied, namely, beam-repeating aircraft. One answer lay in the major efforts underway to speed up deliveries of a refined version of H2S, the 3cm system. Saundby, Harris's SASO, wrote to the Deputy Chief of the Air Staff on 16 September:

'The whole question of technical and tactical development of Oboe Repeater Systems has again been most carefully reviewed by this Command. It is agreed that experiments and trials with Oboe Mk I repeater will provide information of considerable value to the development of the Mk II repeater and three Mosquito aircraft are already engaged solely on this work and will continue to be so employed. Trials already planned include operations over enemy territory Emden and Wilhelmshaven using direct transmissions from one ground station and repeater aircraft from the other.

'The view is sometimes expressed that the operational use of Oboe Mk I repeater is desirable and worthwhile for the following reasons:

(i) The development of the apparatus is now completed; and it can be brought into operational use without interfering with other important projects;

(ii) An accurate method of marking targets at long range would be invaluable during the next few months.

'With regard to (i) above it is clear that much work remains to be done before this apparatus can be regarded as operationally reliable. There is no guarantee as yet that the system would work effectively at even 500 miles range, or that its reliability would exceed some 70 per cent. It is also considered that a decision to use it operationally on the scale proposed would inevitably interfere with the development of Oboe Mk II notwithstanding any assurances to the contrary.

'With regard to (ii) above it is certainly true that some accurate method of marking is urgently needed, particularly for Berlin, but it is not considered that Oboe Mk I repeater would be suitable for this purpose. There are many reasons for this. In the first place future attacks on Berlin and other large targets are likely to be of no longer than 15 minutes duration and operational experience with single-channel working has proved beyond all doubt that one Marker every 15 minutes, which means one marker for a main attack, would be totally inadequate. Added to this it is possible that Oboe Mk I may be jammed at any moment. Finally, a further nine Mosquito aircraft would be required for this which would mean that practically the whole of 139 Squadron would have to be devoted to this task... It is therefore strongly recommended that no development work on Oboe Mk I repeater, additional to that at present being undertaken, should be considered and no attempt should be made to use it on full scale operations...

'H2S is considered the most suitable device for marking targets beyond non-repeater Oboe range and it is felt that by hastening certain improvements to this device it would enable the Pathfinder Force to obtain a high degree of accuracy in marking targets at long range. 3cm H2S would in particular greatly assist the effective bombing of Berlin. Berlin, being a very large built-up area, presents a special problem since the definition on the existing H2S is insufficient to enable particular parts such as lakes and large parks to be picked out from the general response. With the 3cm apparatus however the definition is so improved that sufficient detail would be presented by Berlin on the cathode ray tube to enable markers to be dropped with a high degree of accuracy on the specific aiming point. It is therefore desired to re-affirm this

Command's requirement for development work to proceed in the following order of priority with all possible speed:

'(a) Improved H2S 3cm equipment with stabilised scanner for long range [operations];

'(b) Oboe Mk II non-repeater for short range [operations];

'(c) Oboe Mk II repeater, but not at the expense of Oboe Mk II non-repeater.

'There is moreover an immediate and very important requirement for 3cm H2S in the PFF at an earlier date than that already scheduled for this equipment into the first three Lancaster squadrons, ie, the end of the year. It is therefore recommended that:

'(a) A very special effort be made to install 3cm H2S equipment in six Lancaster III aircraft at the earliest possible date;

'(b) Installation of 3cm into one complete squadron of Lancaster III aircraft to be undertaken as soon as possible after the initial six aircraft have been equipped;

'(c) The roll-stabilised scanner be introduced into the above-mentioned squadron and the subsequent two 3cm squadrons at the earliest date.

'It is requested that every effort may be made to meet the above requirements with the least possible delay.'

The sense of urgency is clear even at today's distance. Berlin was widely perceived as a war-winning target and therefore worth the dangers and the costs likely to be involved. Harris would write in his autobiography:

'This then [November 1943] was, in my judgement, the right moment to begin the really heavy attack on Berlin which was so long overdue. It was of course most unfortunate that we had not been able to begin the Battle of Berlin as soon after the destruction of Hamburg as the nights were long enough. We should then have been able to strike just when everybody in Berlin and, for that matter, in Germany had been thrown into a state of panic by the news of what had happened in Hamburg. And we should also have been able to take advantage of the confusion into which the use of Window had thrown the defences. By November the fighter force had been re-organised and strongly reinforced.'

141

The Pathfinder squadrons were entering their greatest conflict well short of the state of perfection that Bennett both demanded and saw as fundamental to their success. No one could have done more than he to press for the best crews, for a force comprising Lancasters and Mosquitoes only, for absolute priority in the availability of the most ingenious bombing and navigational aids, and for a supply of pyrotechnics to meet his every need. Unfortunately the old jealousies, inter-Service, inter-Command, inter-Group, still prevailed in 1943. Resolute action by Churchill, by Portal, or by Harris could have cleared many of Bennett's problems overnight, but the sad truth was that few, apart from Harris, really believed that bombing either could, or would, win the war. High options were therefore carefully left open, commitment was sadly in short supply and the crippling impact of half-hearted compromise was imposed on Bomber Command.

Bennett the perfectionist would bear this with aggressive stoicism since, young though he was, by now he had long experience of equivocation in high places. His tactics were to keep arguing without fear or deference and to lose no opportunity for pressing his case and his demands. He never lost his wonder at the gallantry of all the bomber crews, his own and those in the increasingly hard pressed Main Force squadrons. He knew that whatever was required of them they would press on, making the best of what they had got, cursing the inadequacies of equipment and the direction of the war and hoping that they might just survive to a distant victory. Bennett later wrote of the Battle of Berlin:

'This... was indeed the bitterest part of the war for me, for not only was it gravely important that we should succeed and thereby confirm the effects of Hamburg, but also it was bitter because of the great losses which we suffered. So far as the Pathfinder Force was concerned, these losses were particularly serious because they included a large proportion of very experienced and good Pathfinder crews. I lost a number of squadron commanders and seven flight commanders and, at one stage, I thought that the backbone of the Pathfinder Force was really broken...'

And so the battle was joined. Both Churchill and Harris believed that in Berlin could be created a cauldron of destruction which would loosen the grip of Nazism on its own proud capital and thus end the war. The attacks on the German capital lasted from 18 November 1943 to the end of March 1944 and in the middle of this onslaught of almost five months' duration the Prime Minister told Parliament:

'It is true that the results of our bombing have had a noteworthy effect upon Germany's munitions production. In the people they have produced a dull apathy which also affects munition production... the honour of bombing Berlin has fallen almost entirely to us... the Anglo-American air attack upon Germany must be regarded as our chief offensive effort at the present time.'

The bad weather encountered in full measure on 18 November was to become a feature of the long winter campaign against Berlin. That night while nearly 450 Lancasters flew to the city, the remainder of Bomber Command comprising Halifaxes and the fading Stirlings went to Ludwigshafen. It was by no means an encouraging start. Only one aircraft with 3cm H2S actually left for the raid, the others having become unserviceable, and even this solitary purveyor of the new technology had to turn back with a faulty radar after jettisoning its bombs. Bennett was doing his best with 'lash-ups', rather than awaiting fully developed 3cm sets and he was paying the price. The Americans on the other hand bided their time, initially rejecting H2S despite having one of their Signal Corps officers on Bernard Lovell's team. Finally the 8th Air Force opted for British sets in their lead ships, whilst their massive home industry caught up and went straight for the 3cm equipment. The quality of the American production of British technology was indisputable and remained so.

On this dank November night even the old technology H2S Lancasters from 8 Group were in trouble. Twenty-six aircraft had been assigned to mark blind through the thick cloud which soared to 12,000ft, but 18 of them failed to do so due to problems in identifying the start point for their timed run, combined with further radar failures. To compound this confusion the winds differed widely from those which had been forecast and one PFF Lancaster dropped in error a yellow route turning-point marker, which ironically remained stubbornly visible on the target area to the total confusion of Main Force crews. Some 411 Lancasters actually attacked Berlin that night through intense flak and perhaps the only saving grace was an encouragingly low loss rate of 2 per cent. Bombs were scattered far and wide across the sprawling city.

To add to Bennett's problems and his sadness, this unsatisfactory operation cost the life of one of his finest senior flight commanders, Wing Commander John White of 156 Squadron, who had been the Deputy Master Bomber at Peenemünde.

The next attack was mounted the following Monday night, 22 November, when 764 heavy bombers loaded with almost 2,500 tons of high explosive and incendiary bombs left at dusk for the capital. No 8 Group sent 121 Pathfinder aircraft, a record number at the time. Cloud over the target was expected to be somewhat more favourable than it had been on the 18th of the month, whilst in England a near total clearance was expected. Bomber Command ordered a maximum effort to which 8 Group responded by announcing the availability of four 3cm H2S Lancasters to lead the night's marking. There must have been many fervent prayers emanating from Huntingdon that this time their faith in the radar would be justified. Air Vice-Marshal Cochrane at 5 Group had already expressed his disdain for such 'boxes of tricks' and Harris respected his judgement above all.

In fact by the time of take-off, five of the 3cm H2S Lancasters were available to Bennett. The route chosen to the 'Big City' (as the Nazi capital was known to Bomber Command crews) was an unusually direct one. By this point in the campaign it seemed to the planners that the shortest possible time spent over enemy territory conferred roughly the same benefits to their bomber crews as the possible confusion of defences by means of feints and diversions. This was particularly germane in circumstances where a route north of the Ruhr marked Berlin as the target as clearly as if it had been signposted. Furthermore, the chaos caused by Window had still not been resolved by those controlling the radar defences. Consequently, the heavy twin-engined German nightfighters continued to suffer from uncertain ground direction and confused images from their airborne radars. Their defensive place was now often taken by nimble single-seaters roving the bomber streams and searching visually for targets of opportunity. As a refinement, Focke-Wulf Fw200 four-engined maritime reconnaissance aircraft mingled with the bombers, dropping flares to mark their track for the interceptions. Bomber Command's losses began to increase alarmingly.

The planning of the raid of 22 November allowed not only for a most direct route, but also for the minimum time to be spent over the target. Berlin's flak defences were always formidable and were rapidly becoming even more so. The Mosquitoes of 139 Squadron were now utilised by Bennett to precede the Main Force, dropping Window and stream-ing off to bomb other targets causing further confusion to the defensive systems. But flak always had plenty of time to prepare for incoming attacks even if this meant thousands of soldiers standing-by, as Speer had sourly observed. The intention was to pass the force of 764 bombers over Berlin in a period of 22 minutes – a rate of over 30 air-craft a minute, or one every two seconds – the highest intensity yet achieved.

Unfortunately, to Bennett's sorrow and disgust, three of the 3cm H2S Lancaster markers had to turn back with technical failures in their sets. They bombed alternative targets visually on the way home and safely delivered their precious equipment for further repair, modification, and testing. This was an enormous frustration for 8 Group and one which bode ill for long term relationships between Bomber Command, the radar industry, and TRE. These early 3cm H2S failures were doubly infu-riating, since the crews had grown used to the better definition given in the radar picture in the course of long practice sorties over the British Isles and were positively enthusiastic at the prospect of accurately blind marking Berlin.

The Main Force and the remaining markers flew on preceded by the Window Mosquitoes. Their take-off in the late November afternoon had been into bleak low-visibility conditions, with cloud thickness and cover increasing as they penetrated western Holland and the flak con-centrations. The first markers were due over Berlin at 19.58hrs, but when they arrived almost exactly on time they found the city totally obscured by cloud which extended upwards to between 10,000 and 16,000ft. Bennett's staff had evolved a marking plan which required the joint use of both ground TIs and skymarking, which would thereafter be known as 'The Berlin Method'. The 3cm H2S aircraft, now desig-nated special markers, went in first entirely reliant on their radar pic-tures and each dropped four red and four yellow TIs, and 16 skymarkers. The first wave of ordinary H2S markers followed, again dropping both TIs and skymarkers, whilst the other half of their for-mation continued the process throughout the brief duration of the raid. The result was a most remarkable success. The direct route had lessened fighter-related casualties, the short duration of the raid meant that only four aircraft were shot down over the target. There were no collisions over the Big City and no aircraft were hit by falling bombs. Almost from take-off to landing back in England no Bomber Command crew had sighted the smallest glimpse of land beneath him. Yet Berlin had never been hit so hard and never would be again until the Russian army sacked the city at the war's end.

As the bombers left that night the city's shocked citizens looked back with horror. The RAF had arrived in force over Berlin in the midst of a night of terrible weather to deliver an accurate, concentrated attack which was over almost as soon as it had begun, leaving some 5,500 buildings destroyed or seriously damaged, and over 20,000 slightly damaged. The efficient authorities assembled a vast force of window and roof repairers to deal with the latter which turned into an endless task, and kept them constantly busy throughout the long winter. On this night, too, the few defence workers on duty outside shelters had experienced the apocalyptic sight of the clouds glowing red and green, and through them rained down a mass of bombs, high explosive, and incendiary on a confined area encompassing the central and western central districts of the city. Only the Tiergarten Park provided an oasis in the rubble of destroyed apartments and blazing office blocks. As if by some touch of benign fate Hitler's unoccupied train, parked in a siding, was totally destroyed. He had moved to Eastern Poland for the duration of the winter raids! About 180,000 people were left homeless, 1,700 died, and 7,000 were injured. The spectre of Hamburg seemed to pass over the city and all the defensive genius of the Reich would be dragooned into countering its threat.

Harris was as delighted with the result as ever he allowed himself to be. He had risked a great deal in agreeing a straight in – straight out attack which ran counter to Bennett's preference for the maximum of bluff and deception. However, it would become a totally devalued tactic four months later in the long journey to Nuremburg. Harris had also determined the briefest time possible over Berlin that was compatible with minimum standards of safety and that had paid off too. The Pathfinders had marked to near perfection and the few, unreliable, new H2S sets had held together long enough to impart accuracy to the whole great enterprise. The Pathfinders returned with pictures of the images on their cathode ray tubes to confirm that their aiming points were well marked, there were no target photographs possible through that profound depth of cloud. Next day even the high flying PR Spitfires could see nothing of Berlin, nor were they often able to in the weeks and months ahead. At Bomber Command the new science of blind bombing was recorded by cross hatching areas of destruction on

Bennett's photographs of radar images. Only when the skies cleared, perhaps in the spring, might the processes of audit begin.

On 23 November Harris ordered the Lancasters to return to Berlin, hopeful that the success of the previous night could be pressed home after the style of Hamburg. This time a few Halifaxes were involved, but the Stirlings had finally been retired from all operations over the Reich as from that morning. The decision indirectly affected the Pathfinders since Bennett had sought to offload his Halifaxes in a letter to Harris a month before at the start of the main operations against Berlin. He told the C-in-C that he withheld 35 Squadron from the Marker Force used against Munich, Stuttgart, Hanover and Leipzig because of the Halifaxes' vulnerability. Harris replied that not until all the Stirlings had been replaced in the squadrons operating them with Lancasters, would there be any chance. The attack plan on the 23rd was hardly changed from that of the previous night. Damage, attrition, and crew fatigue necessitated the smaller force which passed over the target in a remarkable 17 minutes and dropped nearly 1,400 tons of bombs, roughly half of which were high explosive and the remainder incendiary. This time the two Lancasters with working 3cm H2S took-off, but were forced back by technical failures leaving the 'unclever' set-carrying aircraft to blind mark through the still heavy cloud cover.

The enemy defences were still in some confusion and 8 Group's Oboe Mosquitoes were out and about causing further problems for the Luftwaffe. It was however a bad night for the Pathfinders, with seven aircraft lost over Germany. In one of them was the CO of 83 Squadron and two other crews lost included some of Bennett's most senior and experienced men. Thirteen more Lancasters were shot down which, with the PFF losses, amounted to a somewhat worrying 5.3 per cent of aircraft engaged.

The attack on 26 November succeeded in getting two 3cm H2S aircraft to the actual attack on the capital where the tactics employed were a masterpiece of Bennett's contribution to the planning process. Nearly 450 Lancasters were involved, making their initial approach with a strong force of Halifaxes over northern France and southern Belgium, apparently bound for Frankfurt to where the Luftwaffe directed a large number of fighters. When the stream flew over that city the German controllers assumed they were to be duped again, as they had been over Mannheim some weeks before when a raid passed over the city only to turn suddenly and come back into the attack! This time to make matters worse, after passing the raid split into two with the Halifaxes heading south for Stuttgart and the Lancasters making off to the north-east. Still convinced that an elaborate ruse was in operation, the fighters were retained in the area of Frankfurt where some were subjected to the first glimmerings of Bomber Command's fighter counter-measures. These involved the transmission of excruciating noise on German radio frequencies and false 'instructions' from German-speaking British 'controllers'. By the time it became clear that Berlin was the target it was almost too late. Short of fuel and well behind the bombers, they had no hope of reaching the city and indeed many of the Northern Sector's fighters had been despatched to meet the threat on Frankfurt. Finally, as the force reached Berlin a small force of Mosquitoes swept in releasing swathes of Window to upset the gun and searchlight radar direction, which became known as the 'Window opening'. Despite the rather clearer night all the blind marking techniques were used. Sadly, the special markers were way off target, nine miles in fact, but the standard H2S aircraft managed to mark with far greater accuracy and, although there was some scatter, this was a successful attack. However, there was fog at home, and to the 28 invaluable Lancasters and their crews lost on the attack were added a further 14 destroyed in accidents from Yorkshire down to Suffolk.

On 2 December over 450 aircraft, mainly Lancasters, set out again for Berlin but weather fronts, icing and variable winds caused a great deal of scattering which negated the impact of Window on the defences and led to the loss of 40 aircraft (8.7 per cent) and a high 9.2 per cent turning back for a variety of reasons. The route was a straight approach over northern Holland and Germany with a 20-minute attack intended, the very ingredients so successfully employed in November. Timekeeping was poor due to the bad weather and to 8 Group's mortification, the blind marking was an almost complete failure. Once again three of the four special markers suffered 3cm H2S failure and overall the bombing was up to 15 miles awry. To add to the sense of failure this raid marked the début of the 8,000lb bomb carried by Lancasters of 115 Squadron, flying out of Witchford in Cambridgeshire, south of Ely. There is no certainty where these huge missiles fell and no indication of the damage they did.

The hard truth was that events were beginning to reveal early signs of the strain that the Berlin campaign was to inflict upon Bomber Command and the Pathfinders. The lack of really conclusive proof of the accuracy being achieved or of the damage being done did nothing for morale at any level.

On 3 December the Pathfinders led the way to Leipzig, an ideal and concentrated H2S target. Since, like Berlin, this city was far-distant, the mixed force of Lancasters and Halifaxes trod the well-seared path across northern Holland as if, the Germans assumed, to the capital once again. To add to the illusion 8 Group's Mosquitoes performed a classic Bennett feint and dropped their markers on Berlin whose defences responded by calling all available fighters to the area. The force swung south to Leipzig, the Luftwaffe refused to believe the evidence before their eyes, and the 3cm sets involved for the first time outside Berlin worked and the PFF marked successfully. It was an encouraging end to the first phase of the Berlin attack and Bomber Command was stood down for the new moon phase and, as it happened, further terrible weather.

The loss rate of 8.7 per cent in the final raid on Berlin before the lull was simply not sustainable, especially when the particularly heavy losses of experienced crews were taken into account. With the exception of his increasingly large force of Mosquitoes, Bennett's other units were paying a pitifully high price. Upon the markers now depended the success of an entire night's work and, since they were responsible seasoned men, they pressed home their attacks, steady, straight and level almost regardless of the defences they encountered. The temperamental new radars in particular demanded that, when they did work, the maximum advantage was seized from the accuracy they imparted. As one ex-8 Group navigator has observed, H2S only gave a good picture of the aiming point through 10,000ft of cloud, and only if seven poor so and so's had managed to fly it there!

Bennett knew that he had rivals and enemies a-plenty, he guessed too that he could only rely on the continued support of Harris so long as he brought home a reasonable proportion of the bacon. Harris still admired him enormously, but he knew how tenuous his own position was within and beyond the RAF and how easily he could lose the support of the Prime Minister. One incident at this time illustrates the stress under which both men were operating.

Bomber Command, like any large fighting force, had its specialists with no direct involvement in the prosecution of the war. The doctors, the transport officers, the maintenance men, the trainers, and the personnel experts all made their contribution and exercised their right to the occasional attention of the various commanding officers. One of

Harris's training specialists wrote to Bennett and said that analysing the various courses he ran, Bennett's group was way down below the others in terms of the number of candidates attending. Would the AOC be kind enough to address this problem and improve his performance to the benefit of all concerned? Bennett was livid, he wrote Harris a rude and intemperate letter criticising the number of courses, their content, the motivation of all who attended them, and the virtual uselessness of the great majority! He made the fatal error of, more or less, daring Harris to support a senior member of the Command headquarters staff and he received a monumental rebuff. Harris questioned how he had concluded that 90 per cent of courses were time-wasting, since he sent few men for training anyway! He had, suggested the C-in-C, little knowledge of the difficulties of training in wartime, with all the pressures to turn very basic human raw material into an individual of real worth. Other commanders were well aware of the benefits to be gained and there was considerable competition for the few training places available. Perhaps it was because of the fact that Bennett's group skimmed the cream of fully trained and experienced men from the whole of the rest of the command that allowed him to adopt so superior an attitude. Anyway, said Harris, why complain to him and seek reassurance when the answer was plainly in the hands of 8 Group. No one was making PFF support the legitimate demands of training, but any adverse effects of not doing so would be Bennett's responsibility and his alone.

It was a disheartening exchange and no one was more conscious of the vital necessity of training than Bennett. He believed, however, that the overwhelming priorities of the war made training ideals impossible and substituted for them the rough and tumble of developing his men as and when hostilities allowed.

CHAPTER ELEVEN
A FRUSTRATED STRATEGY

Before the next series of raids on Berlin began, Harris had written to Churchill seeking his further support in persuading the Americans to enter the battle by bombing the German capital by day as the RAF's night offensive continued. In truth Harris was beginning to worry that his command would not be able to sustain the deep penetration raids, and perhaps in his heart there were doubts arising about the wisdom of what he was being called upon to do. Bennett was never off the telephone it appeared, critical of the continuing H2S failures, arguing for an exclusively Lancaster/Mosquito 8 Group, complaining of the shortage of TIs and of hooded flares, and demanding more experienced crew replacements. The Australian never shifted his ground, or his underwritten guarantee that if his demands were met fairly and squarely he would deliver the means of victory to Harris. If however he was given some of the men, some of the aircraft, and only half-effective technical back-up, then all his efforts would be compromised.

Whether Churchill ever took up the matter of bombing Berlin with Roosevelt is uncertain, the two of them had plenty more to debate in late 1943 with the master strategy for 1944 still undecided. In any event the Americans did not go to Berlin in force until 6 March 1944 when 730 bombers and 796 escorts attacked, losing 80 aircraft in the daylight pitched battle. This was the biggest numerical loss ever sustained by the Americans and, if any proof were needed, it established the hazardous reality of deep-penetration attacks into Germany.

On 16 December, the date of the next attack, Harris committed only Lancasters and Mosquitoes, nearly 500 of the former and a handful, 15, of the latter. The 8 Group Met Flight, 1409, which had been formed as an exclusive PFF unit on 1 April at Oakington, was forecasting bad weather for the night. Fog was blanketing much of northern Germany and, whilst this was in many ways a positive advantage, there was a likelihood of the same problem developing over eastern England. There was also the certainty of the waning moon putting in an appearance in the early hours of the following morning. Despite the loss of one of the Pathfinder aircraft, a Lancaster of 7 Squadron over Holland, the remainder of the marking force arrived over Berlin on time and found the surrounding skies unusually bereft of nightfighters. The enemy aircraft were being held well to the south of the city in case this was another of Bennett's tactical feints, and Leipzig turned out to be the bombers' true destination. In addition the forecast fog was having its effect upon the German inclination to get the fighters airborne. The sky markers when they went down were particularly well concentrated, but the attack, though heavy, suffered not only from creep-back but from late bombing too, so once again damage was spread in a great swathe across the city with none of the intensity that Harris so much needed.

Considering this attack and many others in the Berlin series of operations, it is easy to be critical and to disregard the great damage that was being inflicted on property and population. By this time something like a quarter of the city's pre-war accommodation had been either destroyed or damaged beyond immediate repair and industry, civil and military administration, together with the transport systems, were all critically impaired. Bomber Command's role however was perceived as shocking Germany into submission by perhaps half-a-dozen cathartic attacks on big cities, inevitably including Berlin. Bennett was marking to achieve such thunderclaps, but the Main Force seemed incapable of consistently hitting the bullseye. With all the benefit of hindsight it seems certain that bombing accuracy fell away in direct relation to the distance flown to the target. Recognising the great drain on stamina and reserves of courage imposed by 1,200-mile round trips, a new force joined the bombers on 16 December, the long range nightfighters of 141 Squadron.

Based at West Raynham from December onwards, and flying Beaufighters and Mosquitoes under the command of Wing Commander K. C. Roberts, the squadron became part of 100 Group's extensive activities to frustrate the Luftwaffe's defensive systems. It was however not the enemy fighters, but the British weather that proved the cruel killer that night. True to forecast the majority of airfields were either closed to the returning bombers or dangerously obscured by low cloud and fog. Thirty-four Lancasters were lost in a string of landing accidents including no less than 12 from Bennett's hard-pressed group. 97 Squadron at Bourn lost seven aircraft with 48 crew members being killed.

It was an appalling night which hurried the development of FIDO, the fog dispersal system which literally burned away the fog by means of jets of blazing petrol emanating from pipes extending along each side of a runway. The Main Force had apparently been equivocal about the system's value, but Bennett seized the idea with his normal enthusiasm for innovation, arranged for the installation of the system at Graveley and flew in the first aircraft, a Lancaster, when it was lit. Don Vockins, of 405 Squadron, remembers that even without FIDO Bennett was no respecter of bad visibility. 'When the squadron was grounded [at Gransden Lodge] by bad weather – fog – an aircraft would be heard edging in and everyone would say "there is only one man likely to be flying today" and, sure enough, Bennett would soon appear around the base and would talk freely to anyone, answer any question...'

As the penultimate Christmas of the war approached, the teleprinters of Bomber Command poured out the operational order for a further raid on 23 December. Again it would be Lancasters and Mosquitoes that constituted the bulk of the force, although a few Halifaxes accompanied the 400 or so aircraft in the role of incendiarists. A late take-off was planned with the flight heading along a southern route across Belgium and to the north of Frankfurt before swinging north to Berlin, leaving Leipzig to the east. Now fully engaged, the Mosquitoes of Bennett's Light Night Striking Force would at this point leave the Main Force to make a spoof attack on that city. Bad weather, coupled with the success of Bennett's elaborately planned routes and ruses, resulted in a wholly lacklustre performance by the Luftwaffe, but the marking was a disaster with two-thirds of the ordinary H2S aircraft unserviceable by the time they reached Berlin and only one of the five special markers had a 3cm set operating when they reached the target. The only good thing to emerge from a largely wasted night of scattered bombing was a loss rate of just under 4 per cent. Christmas Eve in the German capital was apparently marked by the periodic shattering explosions of delayed action bombs which provoked a particularly anti-British hatred amongst the hard-pressed population.

The markers failed completely to direct the efforts of a huge raid by 712 aircraft which attacked Berlin on 29 December. Bennett had again planned an elaborately devious attack whereby the Main Force had approached Leipzig on an absolutely direct route. As they neared the city, LNSF Mosquitoes swung off to attack Magdeburg and then as the 'heavies' swung north to Berlin more Mosquitoes spoofed south to

Leipzig. It was a copybook exercise which baffled the defences until it was too late for them to make a useful response. The attack on the capital was over in 20 minutes although well over 2,000 tons of high explosive and incendiaries were widely scattered. Again the only saving grace was a loss rate of less that 3 per cent, thanks to the elaborate plan – and the weather in equal measure.

On 1 January 1944, the opening raid of the New Year was enough even to quell the enthusiasm of Harris's most avid supporter. A change of plan took the bombers on an approach over northern Holland when the Denmark and cross-Baltic route had been intended. Eight Pathfinders were lost en route and those reaching Berlin found strong winds and cloud up to 18,000ft. The 3cm H2S brigade were spread throughout the bomber stream in an altered tactic, but their accuracy was to no avail, the sky markers blew away like so much thistledown and the TIs disappeared in the all-consuming cloud. It was snowing hard when the squadrons returned and counted the cost. The loss which approached 7 per cent included four crews from 156 Squadron at Warboys, and 8 Group as a whole suffered shattering losses amounting to over 13 per cent. Just to make matters worse, increasing photographic evidence suggested that Berlin was not being hit nearly hard enough.

For some time Pathfinder crews, flying as backers-up on the main stream of bombers, had been consistently reporting explosions on the ground some hundreds of miles from Berlin. The first thoughts were that these were either crashing aircraft or some elaborate German decoy. Although neither theory seemed likely the alternative explanation was particularly unpalatable.

Everyone appreciated that the Main Force Lancasters were setting out for Berlin at very close to their maximum weight, including a 4,000lb 'blockbuster' and a normal capacity load of incendiaries. Add to that full tanks for the long sortie and a full supply of defensive ammunition and the magnificent long-suffering aeroplane became a sluggish marginal performer, particularly at the altitudes that conferred some operational safety. The thoroughbred Lancaster was hobbled and presented a performance which left no margin for error and very little defensive manoeuvrability. Perhaps some crews rationalised that they were being asked too much. The unending trips to Berlin were bad enough, but now the odds were stacked too highly against them. Anyway, they may have reasoned, the mass of incendiaries were the really damaging agents of devastation with the blockbusters no more than terrifying big bangs. Thus at the first opportunity the big bomb was dropped, altitude and performance were regained, thus increasing the likelihood of the aircraft arriving at the target with its remaining load.

If this was a true analysis of the practice of some crews, then the results of their action were extremely prejudicial to the whole offensive. Berlin was a large and spacious city, comprising in its central districts some immensely strong and massive buildings. This was not the stuff of firestorms, even the parks and lakes and wide boulevards offered some protection against the Hamburg syndrome. Berlin needed high explosive a-plenty and it appeared somehow that the delivery was quite literally falling short. Bennett reported his concern and the observations of the Pathfinder crews to Harris. There was absolutely no suggestion of cowardice on the part of the crews concerned: they were, after all, continuing into the maelstrom of the German defences. It was as if, in an earlier war, an infantryman had cast away part of his encumbering equipment, a clip of bullets perhaps, or a grenade, in the hope that in so doing he might complete his charge through withering fire and still thrust his bayonet into the enemy's heart.

Harris considered that Bennett's hesitant analysis of what might be happening had the most appalling implications, and its possible truth was something he was simply not prepared to even contemplate. It had been Bennett's intention to persuade the C-in-C that it was better to send self-confident, unstressed crews with fewer bombs to the target than to have men struggling towards Berlin with full bomb-bays and a motivation to be rid of their burden at the first faintly acceptable opportunity. This surely was a further manifestation of all the problems of creep-back and scatter which bedevilled most attacks, but particularly those on the German capital.

The C-in-C had more than enough with which to concern himself, the onslaught on Berlin was something to which Churchill was deeply committed, but Portal and the Air Ministry tacticians did not share the enthusiasm. Other demands, including one calling for the destruction of enemy transport systems in advance of the invasion of Europe, were gaining enthusiastic support to which Harris would ultimately have to respond. In the meantime however his belief in what he was doing never wavered, although he was realistic enough to appreciate that the time he had left to deliver victory through bombing alone was rapidly running out. It is not surprising that he should have begun again to consider the fundamentals, including the whole concept of an independent pathfinding force.

These were desperate times and perhaps other options needed to be tested. Unfortunately Harris's relationship with Bennett was at a temporary low ebb and the C-in-C was undoubtedly irritated by his subordinate's aura of infallibility. The undesirable truth was that Bennett, generally, was right, his thinking and his analysis of problems was as immaculate as his appearance, but this did not make him any easier to manage. Whatever conclusion Harris might ultimately arrive at would be in Bomber Command's vital interests and to further its war-winning capability. This might mean some compromise over pathfinding which would be profoundly unacceptable to Bennett. However, as Harris knew more than most, no one was irreplaceable.

It should be remembered that Harris had been against the formation of the Pathfinders as a separate force in the first place, but once this had been forced upon him he had diligently supported the concept. However, the pressures on him to modify the idea so that target marking was devolved back on to the Groups themselves, were never really relaxed. In a way the disappointing performance of H2S and 3cm H2S in 8 Group's hands heightened these pressures. There were those who argued that all the radar eggs should not be in the Pathfinder Force basket, and that a widening of operating experience with these irritatingly temperamental black boxes might help to solve the problems. The point was also made that perhaps more pressure could be put on German defences, and more use made of the increasing variety of bombing aids, especially Oboe, if the Bombers did not operate in a single strategic mass each night with only a few minor raids on the fringes of the main attack. Proponents of this philosophy could point to the immense impact of Bennett's own Light Night Striking Force on Germany which was completely out of proportion to its modest size. In particular Cochrane, AOC of 5 Group which included the undoubted skills of 617 Squadron, scarcely used since the Dams raid, chivvied Harris on every possible occasion for a change in policy.

By January 1944 the criticism of H2S was reaching a crescendo in Bomber Command. The scientific lobby joined forces with the radar industry in criticism of the Pathfinders' and the Main Force's operating and maintenance procedures. It was the old problem of delicate apparatus working magically well in the laboratory and in controlled field tests, only to fail too often in what its creators saw as the 'hammer and hobnail boot' regime of the squadrons. One shocked boffin reported having seen a muddy footprint on the back of an H2S scanner dish!

Harris, for his part, reacted by damning all the boffins in the same terms as he damned the 'panacea merchants': he called them 'a bunch of pimply prima donnas, struggling to get into the limelight'. Inevitably it fell to others to forge a deeper understanding between science and soldiering skills, embodying commendable patience on both sides. Whilst commanders, ministers and civilian managers impacted one another like meteorites, all sound and fury, their subordinates got on with it and laid the foundations for a lasting good relationship between Britain's defence industry and her armed services. It must be said that Harris did little to help cultivate this situation and on the whole that was his loss.

Bomber Command flew again to Berlin on 2 January, straight in and out on a night of rotten weather with no diversionary attacks. The Pathfinders suffered badly before ever reaching Berlin and those returning with radar faults further depleted numbers. One of the 3cm aircraft with a highly experienced crew was shot down over the city by one of the nightfighters, which were up in force to capitalise on better weather in eastern central Germany. A total of 26 Lancasters was lost that night, 7 per cent of the force despatched.

The period of the full moon induced another lull in the bombing which ended on 14 January with an attack on Brunswick, resulting in heavy casualties among the bomber force. The fact was that the Luftwaffe, in an almost superhuman piece of organisation, had equipped a large number of its heavy nightfighters with the new SN-2 radar. This equipment was proof to the effects of Window and enabled the heavy Junkers Ju88 nightfighters in particular to be homed onto the bombers and to intercept at will, using their lethal upward-firing cannon installation. Dreadful casualties would be inflicted in the weeks ahead by the revitalised defences which came as a costly shock to Bomber Command.

As a first reaction the bombing tactics reverted to elaborately complicated routing. On 20 January this involved an oval flightpath approaching Berlin across the south of the Danish peninsula and returning in a great arc reaching the North Sea at the northern coastline of Holland. The LNSF went for Kiel and Hanover, but since only 10 aircraft were involved, five to each target, they were dismissed by the defences for what they were. Meanwhile the SN-2-equipped nightfighters harried the 700 or so bombers for some 500 miles. The Pathfinders achieved good skymarking and the subsequent bombing was reasonably concentrated in an eight-mile line north-east to south-west across the city. On the next night, 55 bombers were lost in a raid on Magdeburg which included 35 Halifaxes, amounting to over 15 per cent of the Halifax force operating that night! The next Berlin attacks on 27 and 28 January involved the now usual circuitous routes, heavy diversionary attacks rather than the Mosquito spoofs, and using the latter aircraft to put down lanes of flares well clear of the attack route to lure the fighters away from the stream. In addition non-Pathfinder squadron aircraft were used as support markers. This was an exceptionally bad period for everyone under Harris's command, including the planners. Berlin remained obstinately cloud covered and there was no real evidence of bombing effectiveness beyond H2S images photographed at the point of bomb release. Such as they were these seemed to be encouraging, but it was for all the world like firing bullets into a thick fog against an elusive and unresponsive enemy.

In the elaborate ploy of bluff and counter-bluff the bombers followed what appeared to be a diversionary attack of minelaying on 30 January, following a northerly track almost along the Danish frontier. This was the seventeenth raid of the campaign and taken with the immediately previous attack it was amongst the most damaging of all. Berlin was beginning, but only beginning, to come apart. There was a sense of the deepest gloom caused by the bombers' apparently unrelenting return to the city, whilst also managing smaller-scale attacks on other targets. If the citizens were cheered by stories of crashing aircraft and the heroics of the high scoring fighter aces, there was also the sight of the mountainous piles of rubble in public open spaces, dumped there by the army of men employed on clearing the streets. Power supplies were at best intermittent and the city's transport system was in chaos. As had been wryly observed at High Wycombe, Berlin's saving grace was that it appeared to be non-inflammable.

After the final raid in January the Command was rested for two weeks in a spirit of some optimism on the part of 8 Group. The H2S failures were apparently becoming less frequent and blind marking seemed to be attracting a useful tonnage of well placed bombs. The tactics were certainly becoming increasingly complex to meet the revitalised fighter opposition and Bennett had his work cut out evolving ever-new ruses.

The raid on 15 February was set to break records when nearly 900 aircraft, well over half of which were Lancasters, were despatched on a raid calculated to saturate Berlin in a period of 22 minutes. Whilst this massive force struck the capital mines were to be laid in German waters, the LNSF was up bombing fighter airfields in Holland and other Mosquitoes were hunting the Luftwaffe in the bomber stream. As if all this were not enough Bennett sent some of his H2S Lancasters to 'open' a raid on Frankfurt which in fact was a total hoax. However, this did not really lead to any lessening in the intensity of the free ranging nightfighter attacks. A two-corridor withdrawal from the target back over central Germany became a vast wide mass of bombers which increased their vulnerability and gave the interceptors a huge margin for success in searching out their targets. The majority of aircraft that were lost fell before they reached Berlin, in yet another shift of fighter tactics which would soon bring the Germans far out over the North Sea to meet the incoming aircraft! This largest raid of the series, in which 2,700 tonnes of bombs rained down, was only a limited success due to the spread of bombs with 40 aircraft per minute hurrying to release their loads on some well-placed markers. The daunting balance sheet had brought another quirk of accounting: speed over target not only reduced losses, it increased crew tension and inevitably reduced accuracy substantially.

Terrible weather forced another pause upon Bomber Command and there followed, on 19 February, a highly unsuccessful and expensive raid on Leipzig. The failure was caused largely by the confusion on timing brought about by exceptionally strong tailwinds which created an altogether new problem. The more expert Pathfinder crews soon realised by visual and radar checks that the forecast winds were hopelessly wrong, and accordingly indulged in a series of dog-legs and other manoeuvres designed to lose time despite the dangers that this implied. However, many other crews arrived at the target well ahead of schedule and understandably were in no mood to hang around. Accordingly, bombs were dropped ahead of the Pathfinders' arrival. When the markers did go down on time, aircraft approached from all directions and there were undoubtedly several collisions that contributed to the loss rate of 9.6 per cent of the 830 aircraft despatched.

Harris made a number of decisions in the days surrounding this raid, if not in the 24 hours that followed it. He concluded with all honesty and realism, which he possessed in full measure, that he had overstepped what was achievable by the force under his command. Whatever the reasons for relative failure, the standards of dedication and courage displayed by his crews were not amongst them. Short of a miracle he would not now be able to secure the surrender of Germany as he had promised to Churchill in November 1943: 'We can wreck Berlin from end to end if the USAAF will come in on it. It will cost us between 400 and 500 aircraft. It will cost Germany the war.'

By the end of the final raid in the long campaign, 625 aircraft had been lost and within them almost 2,700 Bomber Command aircrew had died. Harris had lost the Battle of Berlin, it was a city too far, too widespread, too substantial in its architecture, and as much a symbol for heroic defence in Germany as it was a focus for unforgiving detestation in Britain. If the Nazis could not rely upon the perverted patriotism of the population of Berlin, then they were lost everywhere. Bennett's Pathfinders had spearheaded a long offensive which elevated the spectre of defeat for all Germans to see. Whatever Hitler's propagandists might say, their war had become one of desperate defence, not glorious conquest, and the resources committed to protecting the Reich were now all-absorbing. Bomber Command might not have won the Battle of Berlin, but Germany had already lost the war.

One more attack was mounted before the end of March and it included all the elements that had so frustrated the bombers from the outset of the campaign. Long preparation led to a technically competent attack plan while new techniques, including the use of a Master Bomber, spoke of lessons learned. Spoofs were planned, including a LNSF Mosquito attack on Kiel and a large number of aircraft from the OTUs were detailed to fly off over central France as if heading for southern Germany.

It was hoped that before they turned for home they would have lured at least some of Berlin's defending fighters away from their bases. The weather, which had so cruelly frustrated Harris's attempts to judge his success, appeared to offer clearing skies over Berlin and 1409's Met Mosquitoes were up over the Baltic in the morning sniffing out the prospects for the bombers' approach. This time they were to cross central Denmark which would provide a couple of coastline crossings for more precise navigation. The distrusted H2S sets were to play a lesser role, with the Pathfinders marking visually.

No one had anticipated the winds which were blowing from the north at unprecedented strength so far as most navigators were concerned, often exceeding 100mph. The defending fighters were hampered both by this alarming weather and the northerly route taken by the attacking force. As a result losses before the raid had begun were relatively minor, a change from the Luftwaffe's recent tactics of downing bombers while still fully laden. The start of the bombing was hopelessly disrupted, the Pathfinders found broken cloud moving at high speed across the aiming point – a confusing new phenomenon – and sky-markers were blown away before they could serve any useful purpose. The now normally concentrated bombing period, due to be 20 minutes for over 800 aircraft, was hopelessly extended with some crews arriving over 10 minutes early, while others were blown past the capital and had to find their way back from unfamiliar territory.

The bombs fell that night over an immense area around Berlin and most parts of the city received hits. German casualties on the ground were so small as to be insignificant, but the scattered returning bombers now flew into a German fighter defence of unprecedented ferocity and strength. Some crews faced the additional hazard of being blown into the Ruhr flak, which had been reorganised and regrouped during the long lull in the attacks on industrial targets. The figures speak for them-selves since, of the 72 aircraft lost that night, no less than 57 were felled after leaving Berlin.

Even disregarding the evidence of failure in the Battle of Berlin, Har-ris had the added problem of husbanding both aircraft – and, more vitally, crews – for the support of the forthcoming invasion of Europe. In essence he began to turn away from large-scale unified attacks and to reconsider the views of many, including the formidable Cochrane, that better results could be achieved by well-disciplined smaller attacks. This would imply a rejection of Bennett's long-argued philosophy of a central expert force of Pathfinders able to set and maintain high stan-dards of training and marking.

Cochrane was undoubtedly a most successful commander and 5 Group was regarded by even the most cynical of Bomber Command's 'old lags' as having some magic. Obviously this was helped by such luminaries as Gibson and the now legendary 617 Squadron, by this time led by the indestructible Leonard Cheshire. Before Cheshire's time, however, Cochrane had been convinced by 617's temporary squadron commander, Micky Martin, that even a precision squadron needed Pathfinders and that ideally these should be home-grown. By February 1944 Cheshire had convinced him that the answer lay not so much in Bennett's science, professionalism and electronics, but rather in low level marking where TIs were almost placed on factory roofs by hand! He demonstrated this with spectacular effect in an attack on Limoges where it was obviously necessary to avoid French casualties as far as possible. Cheshire flew his Lancaster at exceptionally low level back and forth over the factory until even the most absorbed worker would have gathered that something unpleasant was afoot and left. Cheshire then placed the markers precisely and 617 demolished the premises before the cameras of the RAF Film Production Unit.

This was quite enough for Cochrane who went to Harris with the suggestion that low-level marking techniques be used on Berlin to overcome the burgeoning problems from faulty radars, rotten weather and diminishing expertise. The C-in-C was in the market for new suggestions from his fighting AOCs at this stage, he had had more than enough from the scientific fraternity to last him a lifetime, and he outlined the proposal in a telephone conversation with Bennett who immediately rejected it. There was no substitute, the latter suggested, for the application of precise, careful skill to marking targets, and high speed low level flight allowed none of this. He told Harris that he had tried flying low over densely built up areas at night and it was almost impossible to identify even the most prominent features before they flashed past underneath, let alone individual buildings or factories. He conceded that such tactics might be useful in some circumstances, but certainly not generally. Considering the pressures on Harris at this time it is probable that Bennett's reaction was something of a last straw for the C-in-C. Here was Cochrane doing his best to be positive and helpful whatever personal motivation he might have, and here was Bennett dismissing the proposition more or less out of hand.

The conversation ended abruptly and with a minimum of courtesy. Bennett replaced the receiver convinced that he had defended his group well and had persuaded Harris by the incontrovertible nature of his argument. If there was any conceit in his assessment of the outcome it must have evaporated almost immediately. The C-in-C summoned him to High Wycombe a few moments later and Bennett flew quickly over from Huntingdon in his 'hack' Hurricane, landing at Halton and driving down to the headquarters. Harris did not waste time on any niceties. He had decided, he said, to transfer two of Bennett's Lancaster squadrons, 83 and 97, to Cochrane in 5 Group forthwith, together with the Mosquitoes of 627 Squadron which had been formed at Oakington the previous November. The Lancasters moved up to Coningsby and 627 went to join 617 in residence at Woodhall Spa.

There was no disguising the enormity of this setback to Bennett and the Pathfinders. The 8 Group squadrons, like those of the Main Force, had more demanded of them than they could possibly have hoped to deliver; at the same time they were short-changed in almost all their requirements. Inevitably in war, time and chance were both in short supply and there were few occasions when more of either could be expected. Bennett retained one small consolation. Wherever they might be, 'his' squadrons continued in their loyalty to him, to wear 'his' badge, to retain the proud name Pathfinder. The sadness was that at this stage of the war most people were too busy, or too tired, to even notice.

Harris had decided to go for the other cities in Germany in advance of D-Day, and must have fervently wished that he had never allowed himself to offer to deliver Berlin to the Prime Minister. As a last, largely political gesture, he decided to open his Southern Reich campaign with a devastating attack on Nuremberg.

CHAPTER TWELVE
VINDICATION AND FINALE

It soon occurred to Bennett that Cochrane, in winning over Harris, had secured two aces. Not only had he gained direct control of three squadrons of experienced Pathfinders, he had also found ample reason to allow the supply of seasoned crews from his own group to 8 Group to dry up completely. Thus Bennett had lost some of his very best men and seemed likely to be denied the opportunity of making this good, a least from 5 Group. Even more worrying was the blow which had been struck against the Pathfinders' morale. Whatever assurances might be given there was bound to be concern that the whole of 8 Group might be broken up and distributed unit by unit throughout the command. Certainly any Main Force crews considering the wisdom of volunteering for Pathfinders at the end of their tours would, perhaps, be well advised to bide their time and see what happened next. Finally, there was real anger at Pathfinder headquarters that somehow they were shouldering the blame for the failure of an ill-conceived campaign against Berlin, which they had spearheaded at great cost and which the other groups had clearly failed to exploit. As ever, it was the unfortunate pianist who was being shot!

On the morning of 30 March there was little time in Pathfinder country for harbouring resentment or for licking wounds. Clearly Harris was on the move again. For those in the know a start was to be made in re-sighting the bombing offensive to cover targets that had so far largely escaped the full thunder of Bomber Command. The weather was not prepossessing as March neared its end and spring edged its way into East Anglia. Thick cloud lingered over most of the airfields and the 1409 Flight Met Mosquito which left after breakfast to penetrate deep into Germany vanished into the overcast almost as soon as it had left the ground. It returned at about mid-day and the meteorologists pieced together a forecast which projected extensive layered cloud over southern Germany, including the target city Nuremberg.

A maximum effort raid was signalled from High Wycombe, and work began immediately on route planning and the organisation of such diversionary attacks as were to take place. On this subject of diversions Bennett's own memory and a very few contemporary accounts must suffice. He always maintained that he was vehemently opposed to the direct routing of the raid, but was over-ruled. One turning point was involved over Charleroi followed by an easterly track of 250 miles to the target. The LNSF was only marginally involved with an attack on Kassel. Saundby, Harris's SASO, subsequently expressed his personal surprise at the simplicity and obvious nature of the attack plan. Cochrane recalled no great arguments between the AOCs that day and no particular disavowal of the plan from Bennett.

It was, Cochrane observed, a long attack and the type of dog-leg or feint favoured by PFF could have increased the dangers by lengthening the sortie towards daybreak. Lastly, there was undoubtedly a measure of double-bluff in the hope that the Germans would assume that so obvious an approach could not possibly define the true target. Thus fighters would be kept in reserve in the north to meet an anticipated change of course. One thing is certain, if Bennett had misgivings he would have expressed them strongly, but he was over-ruled. It is unthinkable that, piqued by Harris's recent decision, he would have remained silent and let the rest of them get on with it. Such a reaction would have been utterly foreign to him.

The selection of Nuremberg for this very heavy raid remains the final element of the mystery. The city had been on the target list for many months but with the temporary reprieve of Berlin, Churchill was likely to have nudged Harris towards a saturation attack on Nuremberg, long recognised as the showcase of Nazism. Saundby always believed this to have been the case and could imagine the Prime Minister's enthusiasm for a grand gesture before the bombers were fully committed to supporting the forthcoming invasion. The outcome was to be a sad culmination of the great endeavour which seemed to diminish all that Bomber Command had achieved.

To begin with, the weather forecast had been hopelessly wrong. Bright moonlight and strong winds ravaged the huge stream of aircraft and, combined with navigation and timing errors, these factors facilitated enemy interception of the many straggling and heavily laden bombers. Ninety-four were shot down, representing 11.8 per cent of the force despatched, a rate never exceeded before or since. The marking by 8 Group was significantly below standard and the bombing was, frankly, chaotic. On the ground, 133 Germans died in Nuremberg, and in Schweinfurt and Bamberg, both of which were bombed in error. This was but a small fraction of RAF aircrew losses. The crew reports of the raid were so dismal that no one had the heart to order a post-attack photographic reconnaissance of the city.

Apart from the spoof attack on Kassel, 8 Group sent its Mosquitoes that night to Aachen, Cologne, and to the fighter airfields at Twente, Vokel, Deelen, Juvincourt, and Julianadorf. The 32 aircraft involved and the 19 despatched to Kassel all returned safely. Whilst this must have undoubtedly cheered Bennett, he faced the loss of almost 10 per cent of the 119 Lancasters which had gone to Nuremberg. His criticism of his fellow AOCs over the routing of the raid was firm within the constraints of his overall loyalty to Harris and to Bomber Command, but he did write: 'Why the Main Force group commanders should be so critical and intolerant of the [PFF] methods which had saved so many lives I could never quite make out, beyond the fact that it seemed merely human weakness that they should revolt against the loss of their power to a youngster...'

Bennett's setback was another 'youngster's' opportunity and Leonard Cheshire spent much of April perfecting his ultra low level marking techniques using the ubiquitous Mosquito, supported by other 617 Squadron stalwarts such as David Shannon and Joe McCarthy. When they were good and ready 5 Group set out for Munich with 617 operating at low level, and with the ex-8 Group Lancaster squadrons putting down back-up markers and incendiaries to emphasise the aiming points illuminated by Cheshire. They proved that low level tactics were a practical proposition even against well defended targets, for Munich was hit hard that night.

As the terrible memory of Nuremberg began to fade, the spirits of Harris's crews were uplifted by the obvious signs that the invasion of continental Europe was imminent. The most clear indication of this was the radical shift of targeting both in terms of location and nature, with the emphasis lifted from the strategic destruction of Germany and German industry.

The aim of the Transportation Plan, as it was called, was to wreck road and rail communication throughout northern France. Allied success in the landings on the Normandy beaches, which were relatively less well defended than those of the Pas de Calais, depended on surprise in the first instance and the denial to the Germans of a means of reinforcing the area thereafter. The direction of the bombing campaign was transferred to the Supreme Allied Commander, General Eisenhower, from whom Harris would receive both strategic and tactical orders. Harris was unhappy about the massive scaling down of attacks on Germany, since it clearly indicated the War Directorate's loss of faith in his ability to deliver victory. However there was much more to it than this very personal reaction, since Harris now recognised that his chances of ever again amassing the number of aircraft he needed to secure a bombing victory were now negligible. What he did not perhaps appreciate was the extent of the victory that he, Bennett and the Command at large, had already won.

The truth was that regardless of their desperate need for air support in France and the Low Countries, the Germans never reduced the number of fighters committed to the defence of their homeland. Thus whilst a comparative handful of such aircraft sought to influence the outcome of the battle of Normandy, over 1,000 first-line fighters were held in Germany. Furthermore there were virtually no bombers to commit against the advancing Allies because the whole emphasis of Luftwaffe's aircraft production and development effort had been on fighters.

Even at this distance in time it is possible to imagine the lightening of tension in Bomber Command which must have accompanied the switch away from deep penetration raids. However, the targets now selected for destruction were in the midst of friendly towns and cities populated by hard pressed and enslaved allies. Accuracy was at a premium, not only for such considerations of humanity, but also to minimise peripheral damage which might ultimately impede the advancing armies.

Late in April the Oboe Mosquitoes led attacks on marshalling yards and rail junctions at Rouen, Tergnier, and Noisy-le-Sec, their first markers being backed up by other aircraft throughout the duration of the raid. The technique of using Master Bombers was now widely used and the running commentaries and exhortations of these brave men circling the target did much to impose bombing discipline. However at Rouen, despite superb marking, there was creep-back which led to French civilian casualties.

Another technique developed at this time was to have the Oboe Mosquitoes each drop different coloured markers, leaving it to the Master Bomber to select the most accurate from his observations and instruct the Main Force accordingly. On 30 April attacks on Somain and Achères were turned from an inaccurate marking fiasco into overwhelmingly accurate bombing successes by the Master Bomber. At Achères in particular the bombing result was 48 per cent better than forecast.

Cochrane's new-found freedom was serving him well at this time and there was the same sort of determination in 5 Group to 'support the boss' as existed among Bennett's squadrons. One subtle point of difference was of course that Cochrane's Pathfinders were doing their job for their own 5 Group Main Force, and this allowed a happy coincidence of interests and mutual support. Bennett, on the other hand, was working for the great amorphous Main Force which had an unhappy tendency to embark on self-serving denigration of the target marking if things went badly wrong.

Bennett was determined not to let the 5 Group experiment be taken as having succeeded because no one had argued otherwise. A week before D-Day and six weeks after losing his squadrons he wrote to Harris drawing his attention to the dangers and inefficiencies of the dissipation of the pathfinding effort. He suggested a unified command was the only way in which several different sized attacks could be allocated the support they justified. Under the present regime 5 Group always had two Lancaster and one Mosquito pathfinding squadrons, while 8 Group now struggled to cover all the rest. He continued by reporting the unhappiness of the detached squadrons:

'They complain that operational planning is so confused and so often left to the last minute that they are quite unable to give of their best. There is little knowledge of the principles of pathfinding in their direction and they are at times placed in an extremely awkward position in endeavouring to plan their attacks in the face of the lack of understanding of their methods... they are controlled by people who, on their own admission, know nothing whatever about pathfinding and are not in any case specialist navigators.'

Bennett continued by returning to the argument against Cheshire's low level marking:

'Their method is suitable only for very good weather conditions... it seems that the only difference between the method they purport to use and that normally employed by PFF proper is the use of Mosquitoes for low level shallow dive-bombing for marking purposes. The fact that they have been "selling" this method on the grounds that they never get errors greater than 30 yards is somewhat difficult to understand in view of their captain's reports... it is agreed that sometimes they will be able to achieve fairly good accuracy but [pre-war trials] showed that shallow dive-bombing was one of the least satisfactory methods when used at night from aircraft with no dive brakes and no form of dive-bombing sight.

'In view of the fact that the AOC 5 Group has himself told me that it has always been his policy to shout the loudest in order to get what he wants, I would most respectfully urge you to judge this experiment and the question of its termination in the light of what is right and wrong in actual fact and not merely on vague claims, or loud assertions, I feel sure that on the results achieved you will agree that the experiment has not been so far a success... results on German targets can be summarised as two failures, one partial, and one in which the raid was a success, but the 5 Group marking a failure... It is felt in any case that if the Pathfinder Force had been marking for 5 Group the results achieved by that force might perhaps have been at least as good, if not better than, those which they have in fact achieved and their losses might have been lower. I would ask you not to regard this appeal as a symptom of "sour grapes" on my part, but rather as something for the good of the Command as a whole.'

Harris discussed the letter with Saundby who by this time was his Deputy (a promotion given in the light of Saundby's loyal refusal to leave his boss and enjoy further promotion). Between them they determined that Bennett's outspoken comment was only to be expected and that he must be told that there would be no change for the time being. The letter bears Saundby's comment 'Answered verbally'; Bennett was told kindly to shut up and get on with it!

There was a great deal to get on with and this was no time for intellectual debate, for the scent of battle was in the air. Bomber Command moved on from the Transportation Plan to pulverising attacks on military installations, ranging from the Belgian border along the sweeping coastline to Cherbourg and for miles inland. The Mosquitoes went for airfields, the bombers went for the coastal radars and gun batteries, the majority of the latter being scrupulously marked. On the night after D-

Day 8 Group led elements of the Main Force to a saturation attack on Rennes airfield whilst other crews maintained pressure on the railways and the road network.

Just after 04.00hrs on 13 June, seven days after D-Day, two Royal Observer Corps men, A. M. Wraight and E. E. Woodland, sighted the first incoming flying bomb from their post atop a Martello tower near Dymchurch. Peenemünde had spawned its first weapon of indiscriminate attack which crossed Kent to explode on farmland near Swanscombe. A second bomb also landed in a field, but the third killed six and injured 30 more at Bethnal Green. The attacks would peter out by early September as the last launching site was overwhelmed, although by that time 9,251 had been plotted in their approach to Britain.

Often led by Oboe Mosquitoes, 2nd Tactical Air Force squadrons had been attacking launch sites under construction since the New Year. Now with the threat against Britain translated into reality Bomber Command joined this new and complex battle. Needless to say the number and separation of targets strained 8 Group's resources to the full, despite the fact that two full squadrons of Oboe aircraft were now available. No 109 Squadron moved to Little Staughton and 105 to Bourn, thereby widening the spread of Pathfinder country. Bennett, deeply hurt by Harris's apparent betrayal, nevertheless maintained a rigid business as usual attitude, reducing neither his demands on the C-in-C nor his criticism of his peers whenever he felt so justified. In mid-June, as some small recompense, he was appointed CB, his highest honour, but he deserved so much more.

The attacks on the V1 sites meanwhile intensified as indeed did those in support of the ground forces' still tenuous continental foothold. Heavy raids on the Pas de Calais were directed at pulverising the small – but vital – buildings and ramps necessary to assemble and fire the flying bombs. The Germans had deliberately designed the weapon system to be highly mobile and difficult to hit making the job of their location and destruction incredibly difficult. Although the early 'ski-sites' (so called because of their distinctive shape) were more substantial structures with an air of formidable permanence, Allied bombing soon drove the enemy to ground. The Oboe Mosquitoes had their work cut out marking accurately and, although many attacks were made in daylight using sky smoke markers in quantity for the first time, results were disappointing. For once it began to seem that attempts to destroy the source of menace from the enemy were less effective than destroying the missiles themselves. Indeed it was finally calculated that an incredible 44,000 tons of bombs had demolished only 25 per cent of the launch sites. It must also be remembered that, like some virulent cancer, the elimination of one launch ramp merely spawned another more cunningly disguised elsewhere.

However, the other two V-weapons revealed by Allied intelligence and Resistance movements in occupied Europe at least a year earlier, simply did not present the option for the interception of the missiles themselves. One, the V2, was an early intermediate range ballistic missile whilst the other, the V3, was a so-called supergun capable of firing 300lb shells at London at a rate of 10 per minute. The only immediate possibility of dealing with these two threats was to bomb the rocket manufacturing, storage and transportation systems and to destroy the supergun itself, buried deep under huge amounts of concrete at Mimoyecques near Calais. The long term solution was of course the advance of the Allied armies out of the Normandy beach-head to capture the sites themselves.

Bennett found himself drawn deeply into the land battle from the middle of June until the breakout into northern France some six weeks later. The tactical problems for the Pathfinders were no fewer despite the fact that the majority of these attacks were carried out in daylight and in a situation of near total air superiority. The proximity of Allied forces to the enemy frontline due to be bombed was obvious enough and represented considerable risks of 'own goals', especially if the phenomena of creep-back and poor bombing discipline again manifested themselves. Bennett took great care to plan such raids so that the route across the target area was such that either creep-back or overshoot would still result in bombs falling clear of Allied ground forces. Generally this worked well, so well in fact that the armies next complained that when the time came for them to advance they were impeded by the enormous devastation that had been caused to roads and landscape alike! However, serious incidents occurred.

On and around 14 August Operation 'Tractable' was launched by the British and Canadian armies against a German defensive line across the Caen–Falaise road. The plan involved the heaviest air support to help break the stalemate and for once the air-to-ground liaison fell well short of ideal. Bennett later wrote that the army, having suffered a near miss from a salvo of bombs, lit smoke flares the colour of which was identical to that being used by the target markers. To the army their signal was no more than the Allied identification colour of the day, but no one had thought to check if it coincided with the colour of the TIs that the Pathfinders would use. Very many British and Canadian soldiers died through this 1944 example of 'friendly fire' and several units were put out of action for weeks. To make matters worse American bombers had earlier subjected the area to some wildly inaccurate attacks which killed yet more Canadians and a distressing number of Polish troops. Far more successful was an attack by over 100 bombers led by blind markers of PFF to shut the main routes out of the closing Falaise Gap encirclement of the German 7th Army.

During this period Leonard Cheshire had led 617 Squadron and 5 Group's activities against the V3 sites. Through heavy flak and in daylight he dived the single-seat Mustang fighter to which he now aspired, and released from it the smoke markers which would guide the bomb-aimers on to the great 16ft-thick concrete dome covering the multiple gun barrels at Mimoyecques. As the 12,000lb bombs struck home the huge structure collapsed down on itself, entombing the whole complex arsenal and all who were working within it. It was almost Cheshire's last operation before Harris grounded him 'without the option'.

From August 1944 through to mid-September the Pathfinders led some spectacular attacks on military targets and airfields in northern France and the Low Countries, as the Allied ground advance gained momentum. With minimal fighter opposition but a great deal of flak, there was some spectacularly accurate marking and bombing in the brilliant summer days. At night Oboe Mosquitoes guided the Main Force to continuing somewhat smaller scale attacks on targets in Germany which remained stubbornly well defended. No 156 Squadron sent 13 Lancasters to attack Gelsenkirchen on 11 September and, although only one aircraft was lost, no less than 11 were very severely damaged. No 8 Group crew losses were still tragically high and numbers of veteran Pathfinders died as the odds against survival lengthened.

At the end of August Bennett celebrated the approach of PFF's second birthday by writing to Harris to complain again that he was being short-changed on crews from the other groups. He wrote:

'The Pathfinder Force... has, I believe, proved to be a very vital factor in making the bomber offensive successful. It changed night bombing from something very doubtful into a concrete and most powerful weapon. It is still however far from perfect. Mistakes still sometimes happen. It is my belief that many of the imperfections which still exist in the Pathfinder Force can and should be cured. I feel that we have never been 100 per cent Pathfinder minded and, although much progress has been made in the past two years, there are still very many who fail to support the policy whole-heartedly... Over the past few months the numbers of aircrew coming to us have been adequate in quantity but have still varied in quality.'

He went on to propose two new alternative means of selection. His preference was for the first a 'Travelling Selection Board' which would be fathered by Harris's HQ and roam the groups choosing the best volunteers, thereby absolving the group commanders from this self-damaging task. Alternatively, Bennett suggested 4 Group's system be adopted whereby a sort of 'seal of quality' was imparted on each new volunteer for PFF endorsed by the appropriate squadron, station, base and group commanders who would therefore be 'more careful to send people who are of a reasonably high standard'. The truth was that originally Bennett had to accept more or less whosoever volunteered for 8 Group, such were the demands made upon him and the losses sustained. At the same time the volunteers were almost by definition of a high standard, mostly well experienced battle-proven men. No one but a total idiot could consider target marking a cushy number, or that it was more readily survivable than a Main Force tour. In any case a condition of acceptance by Bennett was an understanding that a Pathfinder tour comprised 45 operations, which to many seemed (and sadly became) an unattainable target.

Bennett's problem was that he wanted the best, all the best. While he would never have argued that great courage was not required by Main Force crews, he did tend to regard them as the hardworking lorry drivers who needed brains only to follow the sign-posts and deliver their cargoes to the right address. Provided that the Pathfinders were without exception professional and expert, bombing should improve to unparalleled levels of perfection.

In fairness, Harris was by now operating almost on a different planet, beginning to be cold-shouldered and suffering from acute competition for the Prime Minister's favour against the suddenly prominent generals of the new land war. He was advised by his staff officers that Bennett's

'Travelling Selection Board' would be seen as a formalisation of Hamish Mahaddie's horse-thieving activities. Although they said there was no doubt that Hamish had only been doing what he was told (by Bennett), the system was not the best way of getting results! Capel, Harris's Air Officer (Training), also grimly noted that Mahaddie was now station commander of Warboys, the location of the PFF Navigation Training Unit. This, he suggested, meant an extension of his powers of skimming off the cream even though his propensity for prowling round the other groups was now slightly curtailed. Hamish in fact enjoyed good relations with most of the AOCs, although he wrote that two would have nothing to do with him!

Capel concluded his report back to Harris by suggesting that since 5 Group was now a closed book to Bennett, 1 Group was notably supportive of PFF, and no whisper of complaint about 4 Group or 3 Group had emerged from Huntingdon, thus only 6 Group, the Canadian formation was left. There had certainly been no complaints about them, so perhaps Bennett's concern was still based upon the lingering memory of battles with Cochrane. There seemed to Harris no need to impose Bennett's second suggestion on the groups, since the implication of multi-signature recommendations was surely that they were not to be trusted. It was not a good time for Bennett and relationships cooled a little further.

Attacks on Germany, always maintained during the first critical weeks of the Allied invasion of Europe now began to gather strength again, especially against industrial targets, and on the long-running onslaught against oil production which had been initiated on 12 June when a plant near Gelsenkirchen had been targeted. Before the end of July Stuttgart and Hamburg were bombed on the same night against a mass of nightfighters, which accounted for some 30 of the 62 aircraft lost. However the bombers were now having some success in fighting back and that night the Luftwaffe lost 10 per cent of the force of 300 it had committed.

Another most significant factor came into play. Oboe, that vital but range-limited bombing aid, was now suddenly in France, run from mobile stations following the armies as they 'rushed forward', as Bennett himself wrote. Although H2S was getting better all the time it was, and would remain, difficult to interpret. No 8 Group noted, with no pleasure, that the experimental widespread use of H2S in Main Force aircraft had produced a raid on Brunswick as ineffective as anything in the early days of the bombing war.

The first tentative signs of a shift in bombing fortunes were breaking through as the long and historic summer faded. There was Oboe stretching its guiding presence deep into Germany, and the multi-faceted jamming activities of 100 Group were beginning to pay great dividends. German defending fighters found their radio reception destroyed by cacophonous noise, often emanating from microphones installed within the engine cowlings of the jamming Lancasters! Hysterical 'controllers' screamed at Luftwaffe pilots to return home as they closed in for an interception, or to climb away as they came in on finals to their home bases. The RAF's German speakers had found a new and dramatic role within 100 Group aircraft as they crossed Germany transmitting false information and great bursts of Wagner's music at ear-splitting volume.

Bomber Command's various defensive radars were working better too and there were few shortages of flares and TIs, although poor Bennett complained that Cochrane was making unreasonable demands. He had written to the C-in-C, 'for weeks past we have had to contend with the varying whims of 5 Group with regard to colour, fusing, timing, etc. of the initial markers which they might or might not require. Every day we have really had more work in trying to satisfy 5 Group's unknown requirements than we have had with all the other Groups in the Command!' Things were clearly not getting any better in this particular arena.

The other entirely new possibility was that of close fighter escort for the bombers, with increasing numbers of over-run French airfields becoming available to the RAF and USAAF. Bennett told Harris that the Pathfinders had neither noticed much advantage, nor too many friendly fighters in their lonely task of leadership. Harris wrote a bland reply quoting the other group commanders: 'Effective', 'Very Satisfactory', 'No Complaints', 'Extremely well done'. Harris wrote the complaint off as a problem of perception.

September saw Bennett proposing that Oboe aircraft be used to sky mark for supply drops to the beleaguered airborne forces at Arnhem, and his fertile mind was forever active in pursuit of solutions to overcome various setbacks in the Allied land campaign. In particular he deplored the Army's tendency to sit and do nothing around centres of continuing German occupation, such as the northern Channel ports and Antwerp, which put great strain on the supply lines as the offensive moved further east. Noting the need to restrict casualties as much as possible, he suggested that lives lost in the capture of these vital ports would mean many lives saved later on.

Eisenhower relinquished his overall strategic control of Bomber Command as the autumn began and Harris resumed his attacks on the Ruhr with three-quarters of the total tonnage dropped falling in the main on Duisburg, Dortmund, Essen, Cologne and Düsseldorf. Vast damage was done with loads comprising in the main of high explosive. Duisburg in particular suffered two consecutive attacks by over 1,000 aircraft on each occasion on 14 and 15 October, the first of the two raids being in daylight. The Oboe Mosquitoes provided five superb aiming points for this raid and the quality of marking on the second, made in clear weather in the early hours of the morning, was impeccable. It was the Command's all-time peak effort within any period of 24 hours. Duisburg was visited again on three occasions before the war ended and was entirely laid waste.

Essen, Cologne, and Düsseldorf joined the list of shattered cities as the winter progressed and in early November Bochum was 83 per cent destroyed in two raids marked by the Oboe Mosquitoes. Loss rates in all these attacks became lower and, accordingly, crews began to build their experiences from the natural extension of their operational lives. At the same time the sweet smell of victory had at last begun to permeate the skies whilst the defenders of the Reich saw their nation literally dissolving into dust before their eyes.

Two new Pathfinder Lancaster squadrons had been formed, 635 at Downham Market and 582 at Little Staughton, in March and April 1944 respectively. This had been achieved by taking one flight each from the other four Lancaster units, thus leaving PFF with six two-flight heavy squadrons and making more room to accommodate the increasingly valued Light Night Striking Force formations at each airfield. Early in October 1944 the Lancasters took off from Downham Market for Norway to mark submarine pens under construction by the German occupation forces in Bergen. The accuracy of the attack was especially important to the avoidance of civilian casualties among a population which had contributed so many of its young men to the Allied cause generally, and to the RAF in particular. The planned attack involved the use of a Master Bomber and a Deputy as well as primary visual markers and backers up. Typically, at this stage of the war the marking was exemplary under the clear early morning northern skies. The Main Force inflicted very heavy damage and as a bonus four submarines were sunk at their moorings.

Perhaps inspired by this exercise, Bennett suggested to the C-in-C in a letter dated 4 November that some of his Mosquitoes should move to northern Scotland to mount a series of attacks on the German battleship *Tirpitz* moored in Tromsö Fjord. Each aircraft would carry a pair of 2,000lb armour-piercing bombs and use the newly fitted Mk XIV bombsights from 24,000 ft. Bennett had an old score to settle with the *Tirpitz*, but Harris turned him down writing:

'On the whole therefore I much prefer to allow the 12,000-pounder experts to waste such effort as has to be wasted on this useless war machine [the *Tirpitz*]. Admiralties being what they are, something has to be done about it. One or two more hits with a 12,000-pounder will put her under for good.'

He was right. A week later Cochrane carried off the honours when 617 Squadron capsized the *Tirpitz* at her moorings.

From 1 October until the end of hostilities Bomber Command dropped over 150,000 tonnes of bombs to support the advancing Allied armies. No 8 Group was kept exceptionally busy. General Montgomery called for heavy bombing to eliminate strong German resistance at Kleve and Emmerich and the Main Force duly obliged. Markers were now being particularly well placed and when the Americans asked for bomber support against Düren and Julich, 800 aircraft destroyed the towns; it was 16 December, the day that von Rundstedt started his great offensive through the Ardennes taking the Allies completely by surprise.

Overnight there was a desperate need to cut the supply lines to the enemy advance and Eisenhower asked Harris to concentrate on the rail network in Western Germany. Accordingly, in the midst of the dreadful weather which was helping the enemy advance by denying close air support and ground attack to the Allies, major attacks were developed against railway marshalling yards at Bonn, Cologne and Koblenz. On 23 December Pathfinder aircraft mounted a raid on Cologne's railyards against very heavy flak and a mass of fighters operating in the clearing weather conditions which prevailed over the target. The marking was well executed but one 582 Squadron Lancaster, the Oboe lead aircraft, was badly damaged by flak. Disregarding the obvious course of jettisoning his bombs and turning for home, its pilot from 109 Squadron, Squadron Leader R. A. M. Palmer, continued to the aiming point. Only when he saw his own bombs fall on to the target area, and that the rest of the formation had bombed at the same time, did he turn for home. Almost immediately the Lancaster spun to earth enveloped in flames. The first Pathfinder Victoria Cross was awarded to Squadron Leader Palmer, posthumously as Bennett had predicted.

As the German Ardennes offensive was slowly checked Bennett was called upon to attack a vital crossroads at St Vith. Thick fog covered the target when the Pathfinders arrived to put down markers under Oboe control. The area was reduced to a cratered moonscape through which it was impossible for the enemy to pass either supplies or reinforcements.

Tactical air support once more became a possibility as the weather began to clear and Bomber Command's attention returned to the destruction of Germany, its communications, and its oil production facilities. Pforzheim was heavily bombed on 23 February and a spectacularly good piece of marking was observed by the Master Bomber, Captain E. Swales of the South African Air Force. Under his direction the bombing was as good as the marking, but towards the end of the raid his Lancaster was intercepted by a nightfighter. Despite considerable damage, including the loss of both inboard engines, Swales decided to attempt a return to England, or at least the nearest friendly territory. However matters worsened as the weather closed in and he ordered his crew to take to their parachutes, which they did. Shortly afterwards he attempted a forced landing but was killed when the Lancaster stalled and spun into the ground. Swales was 8 Group's second posthumous VC.

Harris had a new list of targets from the DCAS, Sir Norman Bottomley, which included Dresden, Chemnitz, Leipzig and Berlin, all of which were considered of some great importance in support of the Russian advance from the east. Dresden was selected for further attack on 13 February, the Americans having bombed it extensively on 16 January. No 5 Group attacked first, but their bombing was not well concentrated due to a cloud bank which moved away as the second phase of the raid commenced. There was enough smoke about by this time to prevent visual marking, but the blind markers put down an excellent pattern and the Master Bomber ordered the Main Force in.

The effect was almost beyond imagination and represented the culmination of the bombing strategy which made even Hamburg pale into insignificance. The death of Dresden – for that is what befell the city –

would have been the subject of near universal celebration a mere six months earlier, but now generally mischievous elements seized upon it to question the whole morality of bombing in the light of Germany's prospect of imminent defeat. This prospect, however did not stop the Germans from continuing to develop an awesome range of weapons, working fanatically to perfect them in what was left of their industry; neither did it for a single second damp down the greedy fires within the still multiplying concentration camp crematoria.

For Germany Dresden was a Nemesis and this terrible raid caused the whole edifice of the Nazi state – morale, defiance and the pursuit of its disgusting philosophy – to begin to crumble out of control. On the following night the Main Force and 8 Group went to Chemnitz while Cochrane's squadrons conducted a mass diversion on Rositz, and the LNSF Mosquitoes flew at will everywhere, causing air-raid alerts to the immense distress of populations who now lived in fear of the end. The Pathfinders now had a mass of techniques, markers, spoofs, diversions and radio counter-measures to call upon. Blind skymarking, Wanganui, was achieving a near complete concentration of bombing by the Main Force, Oboe reached everywhere that Harris needed to attack, British nightfighters roamed free in the bomber stream making the Luftwaffe's job one of mortal danger. Daylight raids became more frequent as the defences dwindled and finally dried up. Wuppertal in particular was demolished all over again under the coloured smoke sky markers, as 354 bombers returned on 13 March to destroy all that had been repaired since May 1944.

On 6 April Harris was ordered to end the bombing of cities unless requested by the military authorities, but fuel, power, communications, and war industry were still to be hit as hard as might prove necessary. Accordingly the shipyards of Hamburg were attacked on 8 April and at Kiel three capital ships, the *Admiral Scheer*, the *Admiral Hipper* and the *Emden* were either capsized or burned out. There were still fighters about, but fuel and communication shortages were making them less and less effective.

On 25 April 1945, 375 Lancasters and Mosquitoes attacked Hitler's villa and the SS barracks at Berchtesgaden in the Bavarian Alps. No fighters flew to intercept them on their journey across 250 miles of territory still held by the Germans, although there was some flak over the target. Despite the lingering Alpine mists the attack was made visually with the Deputy Master Bomber, Flight Lieutenant G. G. Hitchcock, dropping his TIs on the main cluster of buildings. High above were the Oboe Mosquitoes, their equipment somewhat compromised by the soaring mountains. It was a deeply symbolic raid, even though the Führer of the 'Thousand-Year Reich' was actually in Berlin, by now insane and summoning non-existent battalions to his aid while the Russian guns reduced his capital city to rubble. Later that same night the glorious 'heavies' made their final attack on a Norwegian oil refinery; after this they would never again go to war.

It fell to the Light Night Striking Force to deliver one of the final blows on 2 May when airfields and naval dockyards were attacked at Kiel, the place where it had all begun in 1939.

It is almost impossible to imagine Bennett's feelings as hostilities ended in Europe. At the start of the war he had been well known only in the exclusive circles of civil air transport, now he commanded 16 squadrons (19 counting the three exiled to 5 Group) which occupied 11 operational stations and were served by thousands of airmen and airwomen. On 19 April 1945, 8 Group operated 369 aircraft and had proudly achieved most of what had been demanded of it. Indeed if Harris, Bennett, and Bomber Command had received the unequivocal support that once had been promised they might well have brought Germany to her knees in 1944, single-handed. However other pressures had prevailed and Bennett was not a man predisposed to resentment or recrimination. He realistically assessed the likely role of Bomber Command in the Japanese war as being a mere footnote in comparison to the mighty presence of American air power in the Pacific, and accordingly prepared for the early dissolution of his command. In the meantime there were other vital tasks to be performed.

Early in April evidence emerged of instructions being given by Berlin to the effect that prisoners of war were to be shot once it became impossible to move them deeper into Germany as the Allied armies advanced. Pathfinder aircraft were despatched to drop leaflets over major camps making it clear to guards that they would be held individually responsible for any such action before war crimes tribunals.

More positive still was Bomber Command's alleviation of the plight of the civilian population of a large area of northern Holland, by-passed by the British Army and stubbornly held in occupation by the despicable Arthur Seyss-Inquart, Austrian-born *Reichskommissar* of the country. Some three-and-a-half million people were literally starving to death and, acting on the suggestion of the Dutch Queen in exile, the Allied governments authorised a truce being offered to the Germans in the area so that an air drop of food could be made. Accordingly negotiations were quickly put in hand and by 29 April agreement was reached. On that day over 200 Lancasters and 18 Mosquitoes made the first drop on red TIs dropped by the Pathfinders near the Hague and Rotterdam. Thus 500 tons of flour, dehydrated foods, soup powder, fats, tea and chocolate were flown in and released, free-fall, over the marked zones. Most sacks and packages survived the experience and were collected for distribution by the civilian police authorities while, it must be said, most German soldiers honourably looked on. Two days later a record drop was made by 500 aircraft of Bomber Command and on 1 May the US 8th Air Force joined the operation, flying in with nearly 700 tons of their famed and greatly appreciated 'K' rations! By the end of the war some 10,000 tons of vital foodstuffs had been dropped, two-thirds by Bomber Command and the rest by the Americans. On 5 May the port of Rotterdam was opened to shipping and the tired young men of 8 Group and Bomber Command could finally rest.

The teleprinters fell quiet, the briefing rooms were empty and the great wall maps hung festooned with the coloured ribbons marking the routes of the final operations. On the silent airfields the great bombers stood unwanted at dispersal and the long runways shimmered in the late spring sunshine.

With the whole world finally at peace, by the end of August 1945 the last, posthumous, Pathfinder VC was awarded to Squadron Leader I. W. Bazalgette. A year earlier he had stayed at the controls of his fatally damaged aircraft, holding it steady whilst most members of his crew baled out. He then attempted an emergency landing with the remaining two wounded and disabled crew members. The Lancaster exploded on touchdown.

The moment was surely approaching for a grateful nation to bring honour to all who had flown with Bomber Command in its great endeavour but, in the event it never came.

CHAPTER THIRTEEN
THE CRUELLEST BETRAYAL

On VE-Day, 8 May 1945, Bennett sent his victory message to the Pathfinder Force from his headquarters at Huntingdon. He wrote:

'Great Britain and the Commonwealth have made a contribution to the civilised world so magnificent that history alone will be able to appreciate it fully. Through disaster and triumph, sometimes supported, and sometimes alone, the British race have steadfastly and energetically over many long years flung their forces against the international criminals. They have fought the war from end to end without a moments respite, in all theatres, and with all arms land, sea and air.'

'Bomber Command's share in this great effort has been a major one. You, each one of you, have made that possible. The Pathfinder Force has shouldered a grave responsibility. It has led Bomber Command, the greatest striking force ever known. That we have been successful can be seen in the far reaching effects which the bomber offensive has achieved. That is the greatest reward the Pathfinder Force ever hopes to receive; for those results have benefited all law abiding peoples.

'Whilst you have been hard at work through these vital years, I have not interrupted you, as I would like to have done, with messages of praise and congratulation. You were too busy; but now that your great contribution to the world has been made, I want to thank you each man and woman of you personally and to congratulate you on your unrelenting spirit and energy and on the results you have achieved.

'Happiness to you all – always Keep Pressing On along the Path of Peace.

Don Bennett.'

With the war drawing to an obvious close Bennett had begun thinking about ways in which Britain's vast force of bombers might be used when they were no longer required for operations. He had written to Harris as early as 9 November 1944 suggesting that the Lancasters would serve well as transports to bring home the prisoners of war, as soon as the advancing Allied armies secured their release. Since many had been held captive for up to five years Bennett reasoned that they deserved the speediest of all homecomings. Bennett told his C-in-C that he had carried out a number of air tests from which he had established that 23 minimally encumbered passengers could be accommodated in the aircraft with its five-man crew 'in comfort'! In the final days of the European war his proposal was followed and with the RAF's fleet of Dakotas still needed for flying bulky supplies to the army and to the advanced landing grounds, the Lancasters assumed a transport role, actually with up to 25 passengers and a six-man crew. In a 24-day period from 2 May 1945, the aircraft flew almost 3,000 round trips and transported 74,000 released prisoners of war home to England. Sadly, one Lancaster crashed whilst trying to make an emergency landing at Juvincourt in northern France on 9 May, killing all on board.

Meanwhile, Harris confirmed that Bomber Command's role in the Pacific would be a small one and any involvement of the Pathfinder squadrons in their designated role was very unlikely. Therefore he concluded that if Bennett was determined now to leave the RAF and pursue some new career he might as well plan to go sooner, rather than later.

Bennett had two possible career choices which were not necessarily mutually exclusive. Most obvious was for him to return to civil aviation, where his relative youth, immense span of experience and knowledge coupled with his reputation for incisive leadership, made him an ideal candidate for a top job. At the same time he was not in the least well disposed to the close involvement of government in airline operations, and all the indications suggested that a Labour administration would make air transport a veritable flagship of public ownership.

In fact Bennett had been offered the job of chief executive of an airline in January 1944 by a consortium of shipping concerns anxious to open up air routes to South America, a destination largely ignored by BOAC. He accepted the post of Operational Director, indicating bluntly that they would see nothing of him until after the war was won. The new airline was to be called British Latin American Airways (BLAA) and the new director, who was unique within the Board in having aviation experience, let it be known that he would only be happy operating

British-made aircraft along its routes. The choice lay between the hastily converted Lancaster bombers, known as Lancastrians, and the more sophisticated Avro Yorks, which incorporated a new transport fuselage on Lancaster wings, tail surfaces, and powerplants. Both types were ordered by BLAA which, as the war ended, set about recruiting air-crews and engineers, the majority of whom were interviewed person-ally by Bennett. Not surprisingly the new organisation experienced little difficulty in attracting job applications. It seemed set to become an immensely happy organisation full of promise and enthusiasm. Its tragedy was borne of the attractive innocence which marked so many airlines in the immediate post-war years. Civil aviation would become an unprincipled jungle where government policy, often ill-advised, dis-placed sound commercial judgements and dynamic management.

Don Bennett was also an ideal Parliamentary candidate and his active, questioning mind lost no time in addressing the immense prob-lems facing the post-war world. He had written a book setting out his manifesto for the establishment and preservation of world peace. This involved the application of the rule of law to whole nations in precisely the same way as it was applied to individual citizens, making use of an internationally controlled force to ensure compliance.

The slim volume comprised a well argued manifesto for the avoidance of future international conflict and was quite unlike the anarchic ideal-istic moonshine of the peace movements in the years ahead. Bennett wanted law and order on a world scale, promoted and preserved by an international armed force to which all nations were subordinate. He wrote that pacifists represented a wishful, hopeful need which was totally impractical, that Communists were happy to blame all conflict on capitalism in support of their own socialist views and that national-ism, though perhaps laudable in the short-term, inevitably led to war and rivalry. 'All nations', he declared, 'should take part in all the activi-ties concerned with applying international law in a just and logical pro-portion. The troops of any one nation must be distributed throughout the rest of the world and merged so as to form an International Law Force in which no national interest shall be predominant in any one place.' He foresaw huge opposition born of 'pride and prejudice, those two impostors who dog the human race and are perhaps the greatest enemies of peace'; he drew up a proposed Agreement of Nations, con-structed an international organisation chart, and even evolved a system of control and a structure of ranks for the World Security Force.

Months before the dawn of the nuclear age he declared, 'I am no pessimist, but I know a little about war and I say quite openly that the present indications show that another war would probably employ weapons and methods capable of destroying a very large part of the human race... such insanity cannot – must not – happen. This time we are going to make certain. This must be the last time.'

With publication imminent he sent the manuscript to Portal who found it impossible to give Bennett even the slightest nod of approval. On the one hand, one must be fair in acknowledging the difficulty that any Service chief on the brink of victory might face in contemplating the future internationalisation of his command; on the other hand Portal was even then of a vanishing generation and his own world would change beyond recognition within months. He told Bennett bluntly, but kindly, that he must not and indeed could not publish the book while still serving in the RAF. Bennett ignored the warning but, appreciating the consequences, took the first steps towards his political career.

The various political parties were busy recruiting candidates for the inevitable forthcoming election and Bennett received a number of approaches. His personal beliefs came closest to those of the Liberal Party and it was therefore to Sir Archibald Sinclair that he turned for advice and support. Sinclair, who had been Secretary of State for Air in the wartime coalition, suggested that Bennett should stand for the vacant seat at Middlesbrough which had been held by a Liberal, and by wartime convention any seat could be filled unopposed by the incumbent party. Thus, in a remarkably short time after his tense interview with Portal, he became a Member of Parliament. Professor Bernard Lovell, then with the TRE, recorded in his journal: '8 Group is scarcely any more and the Air Vice-Marshal who caused us so much trouble, but who was nevertheless one of our staunchest friends, has grown into an MP'.

Air Vice-Marshal J. R. Whitley assumed command of 8 Group at Huntingdon on 21 May and saw the Pathfinders through to their final disbandment on 15 December 1945. The Force, whose genesis had attracted so much debate and fury, faded from the scene almost unnoticed. Only those who had flown in the 19 squadrons and remained in uniform continued to wear, with consummate pride, the small gold eagle below their medal ribbons.

For Don Bennett there was no recognition in the wide sweep of victory honours and awards. He alone among the group commanders was not knighted and yet in his brief period of high office his active contribution to victory had been greater than most. Typically he carried no grudge into civilian life and any distress he felt arose from the implied slight to his gallant Pathfinders. Much later too, in the closing years of his life, he once said to his wife Ly, 'I really didn't mind for myself, but I would have liked to have made you a Lady!'.

It fell to the Germans to pay 8 Group its greatest compliment. In March 1944 after the great campaign against Berlin had ended a Luftwaffe report on the Pathfinders concluded:

> 'The success of a large scale night raid by the RAF is in increasing measure dependent on the conscientious flying of the Pathfinder crews... The grouping of the Pathfinders into a bombing group of their own made it possible to standardise the equipment and the training, to put new ideas into operation and immediately to evaluate all experiences... The [British] assumption that the majority of bomber crews would be less careful in their navigation once they had become used to the help of the Pathfinders and that therefore the total efficiency and success of raids would diminish, has hitherto not been confirmed. The navigation training and equipment of the ordinary British bomber crews has been improved.'

There is surely a no more objective endorsement than that of the enemy, and the Luftwaffe's words might just as well have been written by Don Bennett or Syd Bufton.

Scarcely had he begun to find his way around bombed Westminster when a General Election was called. On 5 July a Labour Government was returned with a massive 158 majority over all the other parties combined, and amongst the very large number of MPs who lost their seats in the socialist landslide was Don Bennett. With the Attlee government in power, changes in all aspects of national life followed in profusion. In air transport a Minister of Civil Aviation, Lord Winster, was appointed and the favoured national airline was split to allow the formation of British European Airways (BEA) to operate alongside BOAC, which shortly decided to 'survey' the South American routes operated by BLAA. The suggestion was made, not unreasonably, that Bennett should accompany the survey team in his capacity as BLAA's Operations Director, but this was dismissed out of hand. Undiminished by this boorish treatment Bennett argued his case with Winster, pointing out that it was patently absurd to set up a second organisation to compete on a pioneering and still largely unused route network. He also stressed the care with which he had developed his embryo organisation and the quality of its crews. All captains held First Class Navigator's Licences for instance, and his original intention had been to dispense with navigators as such. He even required the new generation of co-pilots to obtain a navigator's licence. By now exasperated by BOAC, he turned down a tentative olive-branch offer of places for his crews at its Training School writing, 'I would stress that our own requirements are higher than those of BOAC, not lower'. In the end Bennett won the day and although the South American routes were moved into the public domain the process involved the complete nationalisation of BLAA to become British South American Airways, with Don Bennett appointed Chief Executive.

During 1946, Lancastrians and an increasing number of Yorks were delivered to the new airline, all bearing names prefixed 'Star' to match the company callsign 'Starline'. On 1 January 1946 Bennett commanded the first commercial flight out of the newly opened Heathrow Airport, flying Lancastrian G-AGWG, *Star Light*, en route to Buenos Aires. For this proving flight he arrived impeccable as ever, attired in black homburg and civilianised RAF greatcoat. The flight staged through Lisbon, Bathurst, Natal, Rio de Janeiro and Montevideo. Just over two months later a twice-weekly service was inaugurated and when the Yorks were introduced to operations they took over this route, leaving the Lancastrians to ply the route to Bermuda and beyond, down to Argentina and Chile via Nassau, Jamaica, Venezuela and Peru.

By 1947 the limitations of the airline's equipment were becoming clear. Two Yorks had crashed – one in the course of take-off in the tropics, the other attempting an emergency landing at night near Dakar. The cramped Lancastrians, although doing a worthy job, were totally eclipsed by the growing number of Lockheed Constellations and other modern American aircraft entering service with other airlines. Even if the parlous state of the British economy had allowed the purchase of such aircraft, Bennett's sense of patriotic duty would not have countenanced it. Instead, he turned again to Avro who had suffered a disastrous experience with BOAC over their Tudor airliner. The Tudor was another interim type which utilised the wing of Avro's successor to the Lancaster, the Lincoln, and incorporated a modern, pressurised circular section fuselage. Certainly, the aeroplane had inherent problems and the simplicity of its evolution from a well tried bomber belied the aerodynamic difficulties that were encountered but eventually overcome.

However, far greater problems were caused by BOAC and the Ministry of Civil Aviation who between them devised a list of special requirements and inane modification demands which would have caused Lockheed or Douglas to suggest they should take their business elsewhere! Avro were not in this happy position of choice and desperately tried to meet the customer's requirements as the programme slipped further behind. The truth was that BOAC did not want the aeroplane and had their eyes fixed on American purchase, thus avoiding a great deal of the trouble involved in introducing a wholly new aeroplane and pioneering its engineering and spares support.

Bennett watched the fiasco of the Tudor with increasing impatience and took matters into his own hands by flying a Tudor to Jamaica for hot weather performance trials. He spent some days putting the aircraft through its paces. There had been an emergency over the Atlantic en route caused by a shut fuel cock, but at the end of the test programme Bennett pronounced himself more than satisfied. In a bland statement, similar to the occasion when he asked Harris if he might please 'get on with the war', he let it be know that he found the Tudor superior to the Constellation and wondered what BOAC was playing at!

However, BSAA's crews did not quite share in their Chief Executive's declared enthusiasm. One problem with the Tudor was a distinctly unreliable heating system, critical to any high-altitude operation. Then there was the lack of the new and much admired tricycle undercarriage configuration which featured on all post-war American airliners. Finally, the massive fin and rudder, made necessary to cure the earlier aerodynamic difficulties, caused very hard work on the flightdeck in a crosswind. That said, in its simple but attractive BSAA livery the Tudor looked good and deserved a little encouragement. Bennett provided it in full measure. He took on the rejected BOAC Tudor Mk Is and his version was known as the Tudor Mk IV. This new mark had its forward fuselage lengthened by 6ft, there was no provision for a flight engineer, and it could carry 32 passengers. The IVB's were upgraded Mk Is, retaining the engineer's station and carrying 28 passengers in the shorter fuselage. BSAA ordered four Mk IVs and two Mk IVB's.

Early in October 1947 the Tudor fleet began operating on the London–Bermuda route with Bennett as its delighted and enthusiastic supporter. Tragically this situation was not to last long, for during the night of 29 January 1948 Tudor G-AHNP, *Star Tiger*, vanished without a trace over the sea north-east of Bermuda. A normal radio signal had been received when the aircraft was 200 miles from the island, but no wreckage was ever recovered, or even sighted in the course of an extensive search. The Air Registration Board recommended to Lord Nathan, then Minister of Civil Aviation, that the Tudor be grounded in advance of an investigation which was unlikely to be particularly fruitful given the circumstances. Bennett was infuriated by this apparently spineless suggestion. There was absolutely no evidence against the Tudor. He was invited to comment by the *Daily Express* and was quoted by that paper as saying: 'There are two outstanding forces at work in civil aviation today . . . those who are openly anti-British . . . and those who entered it either for selfish reasons, or for other reasons – but are totally ignorant of aviation.' Bennett received scant support from BSAA's Board who required him to publicly withdraw his comments or resign. He did neither and was sacked.

The aviation world, and particularly those people with a love and admiration for the British industry, were saddened by his going, particularly if this spelt the end of his connection with commercial air transport. His aircrews in BSAA, many of whom had served him in war and peace, felt the loss deeply and this anger was openly expressed. Almost to a man they regarded BOAC as a mundane and tedious lot, unexciting bus drivers devoid of spirit. It was not an edifying situation and when in January 1949 a second Tudor, G-AGRE, *Star Ariel*, vanished without trace between Bermuda and Nassau, the airline virtually folded and its routes were taken over by BOAC.

It is interesting to record Bennett's view that *Star Tiger* had suffered an act of sabotage. Certainly, the enquiry set up to investigate the accident found nothing to which the disaster could be attributed and services were resumed. The second crash in near identical circumstances made his theory either more difficult or, it must be said, easier to swallow, depending upon the investigators' point of view. Another less credible theory is regularly proposed, namely that both aircraft fell victim to the mysterious forces said to abound within the so-called 'Bermuda Triangle'.

Perhaps the cause was more mundane in that both aircraft were fitted with troublesome petrol-burning heaters whose tendency to unserviceability was matched only by their lethal characteristics. Carbon monoxide which they produced in volumes could prove an odourless and rapid killer, especially when flooding into an early and unsophisticated pressurisation system. At night with most passengers already asleep, perhaps there would be no warning to alert any member of the crew before they too were overcome. A steep high-speed dive into the ocean characteristically leaves little surface wreckage and at the end of a long flight the remaining fuel spillage and resultant slick would both be minimal.

Furious with the socialism which he now perceived as the ruination of his country, Bennett searched for a means of fighting back through Parliament. In March 1948 he stood as a Liberal Parliamentary candidate for North Croydon – appropriately so in view of its air transport connections – but although he fought a tough outspoken campaign, the Conservatives held the seat with Bennett coming third. Harold Nicholson for Labour was second.

Events on an international scale brought Bennett back into aviation and could indeed have easily caused him to put on the uniform of an Air Vice-Marshal once again. The Russians imposed a total land blockade on the city of Berlin situated deep in the Russian-occupied zone of East Germany. The city had been jointly occupied by agreement since the end of the war by the four victorious powers of Britain, America, France and Russia. The Western Allies briefly considered fighting their way through and the prospects of a full scale nuclear war seemed close. However, calmer minds prevailed and it was decided that the city could be supplied, at least at a basic level, by an airlift. The RAF and the US Air Force embarked on Operation 'Plainfare' and soon civil operators in the shape of charter companies were encouraged to join the lift, against reasonable contract rewards from their respective governments. Bennett responded almost immediately and bought two long-fuselage Tudors, a Mk 2 and a Mk 5, lying unsold at Langley airfield and began operations down the dangerous air corridors to the beleaguered city. The ARB, no doubt nervously, responded to the re-emergence of their arch critic and certificated the aircraft for cargo-carrying, unpressurised. With one other pilot employed the new company, Airflight Ltd, commenced operations with its owner, managing director, and chief pilot flying in 10 tons of potatoes to the city that he had so recently caused to be devastated! Ly Bennett filled the vital post of operations manager.

Bennett's pilot employee was licensed for daylight operations only and obviously the great airlift was a round-the-clock affair. Accordingly, the boss undertook three round trips to Berlin on most nights and in October moved into the specialised area of fuel transport by having both his aircraft equipped to carry 10 tons of diesel in flexible bags. By the end of the emergency, Airflight's Tudors had made nearly 1,000 round trips to Berlin, between them earning the small company a handsome reward to match the unbelievable effort put in by its owner and his small band of employees. It also opened a new lease of life for the unfortunate unwanted Tudor.

Bennett converted the aircraft back to civilian passenger transports, incorporated modifications suggested by a more co-operative ARB, and obtained certification for the carriage of up to 78 passengers on them. Both machines operated on charter worldwide until 12 March 1950 when the Mk 5, G-AKBY, on charter to a party of 75 rugby supporters home from Dublin, stalled on final approach to the too-small airfield at Llandon in Wales. All 80 on board were killed in this air disaster, the worst to date, and which would remain so for many years to come. No blame attached to the aircraft.

Don Bennett was profoundly shocked and saddened by this terrible accident. It was difficult to avoid the conclusion that its cause lay in the dismissal of many of the principles of airmanship which he held so dear. He questioned in his mind again and again the wisdom of taking such a large and heavily laden aircraft into so small an airfield. He considered the Tudor's low-speed performance characteristics and was satisfied, as ever, that there was no fundamental flaw in these. Indeed, some of his own airlift experiences, which included one take-off with the starboard elevators accidentally locked, had encompassed a number of most difficult approaches without a hint of trouble. Now for some reason the Tudor's speed had been allowed to decay to a dangerous point and it appeared that power had been applied too rapidly and too late causing the nose to rise and initiating a full stall. Yet the pilot, Captain Parsons, was an experienced man who had worked for Bennett on the Berlin Airlift. No cause of the accident was ever established and Bennett continued to operate the other aeroplane in Airflight's inventory, undertaking a great deal of profitable freight and passenger business from the company base at Blackbushe in Hampshire.

The Tudor even found work transporting supplies to Korea for British forces involved in the United Nations action against the Chinese and North Koreans in that war-torn peninsula. It was an idealistic situation which appealed to Bennett's abiding belief that the strong application of international law was the only means of securing peace. He abhorred the new pacifism, by then a growing trend, and the concept that nothing was so valuable as to be worth fighting for, least of all love of country. He tried once again for Parliament, contesting the Norwich North seat in 1950, but Labour won and he decided that enough was enough.

By the end of 1951 it was clear that Airflight had either to grow or to go, and Bennett felt that at the age of 41 he wanted more out of life than the directorship of his own airline in a world hostile to small enterprise. He found another Tudor enthusiast, a struggling entrepreneur whose small company, Air Charter, operated out of Luton. Air Charter was interested in Bennett's freight contract to Berlin and set about purchasing all available Tudors to build up a uniform fleet. Soon it assembled four Mk 1s, two Mk 3s, and four Mk 4s, converting all of them to the highest freight standards which included the incorporation of a generously sized loading door on the starboard side just aft of the wing fillet. Air Charter's owner re-named the Tudors 'Super Tudors' and, being somewhat of a patriot himself, named the first *El Alamein*. The Tudors – so vilified by BOAC, so hastily grounded by the ARB – passed the most comprehensive Certificate of Airworthiness requirements with an authorised maximum all-up weight of 83,600lb. The owner of Air Charter was Freddie Laker who operated the Tudors safely and profitably until 1959.

After the sale of Airflight Bennett pursued many interests in the course of his remaining years. He tried to purchase the huge Princess flying-boats, which had been of interest to him in BSAA days and which in 1960 lay unwanted at Calshot. BOAC had decided that flying-boats were of no use to them, but Bennett saw the possibility of completing them for profitable operation. It all came to nothing chiefly because yet another Minister, Conservative by this time, found it impossible to make up his mind and the interest of the financial backers dwindled despite Bennett's enthusiasm. He bought most of Blackbushe airfield only to find himself locked in conflict with Yately Council who owned a part of it, including a section of runway. The Council was determined not to sell out to Bennett, rightly fearing that he would seek to fly large aeroplanes from the aerodrome. For the 16 years that he was owner only light aircraft were permitted to use it. The Council rejoiced in the establishment of a massive retail market on their ground with all the compelling attractiveness of a permanent car-boot sale.

Bennett wrote his memoirs, was an active member of the United Nations Association, and kept up with his friends, his one-time colleagues, and with those who had fought alongside him. He was proud of 'his' Pathfinders and their Association which he so enthusiastically supported. Harris was right, of course, all those years ago. If there was to be a Pathfinder Force there was really only one man to command it. Bennett's overwhelming professionalism defied criticism and fostered a degree of self-confidence which many regarded as reason enough to follow him to the gates of Hell.

Perhaps the last word should be left to a Pathfinder. Don Vockins served as a signaller on Wellingtons in the Middle East supporting the ground battle, before returning to join 405 (Vancouver) Squadron, RCAF, at Gransden Lodge for the last months of the war. With the squadron he packed in 26 operations principally against German targets. He writes:

'The only time during my operational flying (63 ops) when I felt I was doing something worthwhile was with the Pathfinders. The rest of the time seemed of no consequence, we were just making up numbers... It is a long, long time ago, 50 years, but I cannot recall ever hearing anything disparaging about Bennett. If he had said we were going to the moon – we would have gone...'

CHAPTER FOURTEEN
COURAGE AND ACHIEVEMENT – A FINAL ANALYSIS

Perhaps the ordinary British people did not at first forget Bomber Command; memories of the great night raids on their cities by the Luftwaffe were etched too deep in the minds of the wartime generations and the mighty revenge wrought in their name was sweet indeed. Any lingering doubts about the intensity of that revenge were swept away in the war's closing weeks by the disclosure of the full extent of Nazi bestiality in Germany's sprawling death camps. Thus there was little concern that many thousands of civilians had died in the enemy's devastated cities, and certainly no suggestion that those victims were somehow "innocent". The only innocents were seen as the world's enslaved peoples to whom finally freedom had been returned. If justification were needed for the total war that had been pursued against Germany it was not hard to find.

The Observer caught the mood a week after VE-Day: 'modern war is national, total, plebeian and unrestricted. It is fought for ideas and ethics and philosophies. It has nothing to do with the old football match campaigns conducted by a few dynasts and their specialists with some forced or hired levies. And the old inter-officer codes now look absurd and infuriating.' In the same edition the paper records, 'tributes to the RAF in finishing the war continue to abound. Kesselring joins von Rundstedt in regarding Bomber Command's tremendous and sustained hammering of German factories, supplies and communications as a chief cause of the Reich's collapse. Nobody is better qualified than the beaten German generals to know what smashed "Fortress Europe" and so powerfully assisted the passage of the seemingly impassable.' At the time there was a proud certainty that the Allies could have been blamed for one crime only in all the six years of war – to have lost it and allowed the triumph of Germany.

Bombing alone did not win the war, it required the actual invasion and conquest of Germany to achieve this, which was a source of great frustration to Sir Arthur Harris. There is not the slightest doubt however that strategic bombing was the single factor that made victory attain-

194

able. Without it the enormous strength and energy of the enemy would have contrived the eventual conquest of Russia and the defence of the European western seaboard to the extent of making Allied invasion impossible. There would also have been sufficient unimpeded time to allow for the evolution of a German nuclear weapon. A means of delivery for such a weapon was being prepared at the Letov Works in Prague as early as 1942, in the shape of a heavily modified Heinkel He177.

Germany was forced by Bomber Command and the US 8th Air Force to concentrate on the manufacture of defensive equipment to the exclusion of much else. The undoubted genius of Albert Speer, Reich Munitions Minister, was wasted as he recognised the need to disperse and reorganise shattered industries. The Reich's massive reservoir of skills was drained to produce and man the radars, the nightfighters, and the guns, whilst unskilled manpower was spent on the clearance of rubble and the patching up of millions of homes to make them more or less habitable. As a single example recorded by Speer's Ministry, 10,000 civil engineering workers were taken off their work on Hitler's Atlantic Wall for six months to repair the damage to the German dams, power stations, railways and services, caused by Guy Gibson and his 132 men of 617 Squadron. Then, too, there were the firemen, the wardens, the rescue teams, and the hospitals, doctors and nurses, all committed to stemming the tide of destruction. The ordinary civilians, the war workers, the civil servants and administrators, the grass-root support upon whom the ghastly edifice of Nazism depended, were demoralised, deprived of sleep, of warmth and shelter, and of easy transport. Despite subsequent protestations to the contrary they deserted workplaces, towns and cities in droves, either for the temporary shelter of the countryside, or on more permanent evacuation, if they managed to persuade the reluctant authorities to permit them to leave. Unlike Britain, Germany organised no general evacuation of women and children in anticipation of bombing.

Germany's increasing productivity, which was a feature of the war years, was born of the vital necessity to build on her remarkably low level of military output at the commencement of hostilities. Quite contrary to Britain, she did not commit her womenfolk to war work, even when final defeat was looming. Instead, the mass of slave workers dragooned from the populations of occupied Europe were forced to even greater efforts, particularly in the cold gloom of underground factories in the mountains of southern Germany.

After Hamburg, Albert Speer concluded that six similar attacks would 'end Germany's capacity to continue the struggle'. Later he wrote a more measured reaction whilst he was in prison after the war:

'The real importance of the air war consisted in the fact that it opened a second front long before the invasion of Europe. That front was in German skies... Defence against air attacks required the production of thousands of anti-aircraft guns, the stockpiling of tremendous quantities of ammunition all over the country and holding in readiness hundreds of thousands of soldiers doing nothing.'

Harris achieved all that he did with less than half of the 4,000 bombers he believed necessary to ensure victory. Neither was he even allowed to sustain his attacks, being constantly diverted by the 'panacea merchants' among his superiors. As early as 21 October 1942 he wrote to Portal:

'I am worried about the ever increasing dispersion of our bombing effort by piecemeal instructions which reach me from day to day to do this, that, or the other thing, rather than concentrate on what we have been doing.

'You will recall my submission that the effect of a Certain Operation [Torch] would inevitably end for the foreseeable future Bomber Command's pressure on Germany.'

After referring to the 'futile purpose of bombing impenetrable submarine pens' he continues:

'...in addition the "Oily boys" choose this moment yet again to emerge with their fairy stories about oil... a year or so ago we were told that Germany was at her wits end for oil; but in spite of that she has subsequently run the whole Russian campaign which must have made fantastic drafts on oil reserves and resources which she was then loudly asserted not to possess.

'...additional mining is required of us on the West Coast ports [of France]. This I am willing to do because in any circumstances it is effective... then Schweinfurt [ball bearings]. Another panacea target in which I know you have faith... my information is by no means as enthusiastic as yours and is indeed very far from reaching that level of the Schweinfurt fans... And now on top of all this comes the request for a Lancaster squadron for the initial convoy work. I fear that more than the initial convoys will require special protection once the precedent is set.

'Pardon me therefore if I feel depressed. I write this mainly to draw your attention to the fact that these varied demands frequently arise from different and disconnected sources of origin and parochial enthusiasm, only you can save us from again becoming victims of wide and disastrous dispersion of an already inadequate force... Individually and generally the above projects, like the proverbial housemaid's baby, are only little ones... In sum they spell the end of our effective bomber offensive against Germany proper... I know I shall have your support in sticking to the bombing of Germans in Germany.'

Unfortunately he didn't and those opposed to him kept up the pressure with persuasive words in high places.

Almost as the war ended, with high morale and goodwill burgeoning throughout the nation, the assassins were at work against Harris and his command. A steady intellectual pressure, mainly left wing, began to paint the victims of Allied bombing as doubly persecuted, firstly by the regime that governed them and, secondly, by the relentless attack to which they had been subjected. The true dimensions of the damage inflicted on German towns were now visible for all to see and paradoxically what would have been hailed as a triumph of British might only weeks before, became suddenly shameful evidence of indiscriminate attack! The politicians, the sociologists, the analysts, and the statisticians swarmed in to construct their own pet theories on how the war was won and how much better its direction might have been.

Their sterile arguments have raged ever since, in and out of the hasty history and destructive fiction. To their efforts has been added the hindsight of politicians, sadly including Churchill who was a probably reluctant, but highly influential, early betrayer of Bomber Command. Sensing the immediate post-war softening in public mood he said: 'The destruction of Dresden remains a serious query against the conduct of Allied bombing'. Since he had authorised the operation he should have found it possible to answer his own question and this was a sad reflection on a great Englishman. A little later in his victory broadcast to the nation Churchill paid fitting tribute to all the major elements of the armed forces one by one. He even praised the small Southern Irish contingent who fought for the Allied cause. He made no mention of Bomber Command whatsoever.

Left wing politicians were similarly seeking to distance themselves from the wartime coalition, and from Churchill and all his policies, as the inevitable General Election approached. There was much mileage to be had from adopting the philosophy of worldwide reconciliation and building on the grand alliance with Soviet Russia. Thus the 'ordinary' German was increasingly portrayed as the victim of misapplied violence, whilst the might of Soviet Russia was applauded as the true instrument of Hitler's downfall. Subtly the distinction was drawn between Nazism and Germany, terms which had so recently been indivisible.

In the middle years of the war certain churchmen had voiced their protests against Allied bombing, including Bishop Bell of Chichester who had spoken up in the House of Lords, but the Archbishop of York reflected the views of the overwhelming majority when he replied: 'Frequently a choice has to be made between two evils, and it is a lesser evil to bomb the war-loving Germans than to sacrifice the lives of our fellow countrymen who long for peace, or to delay the delivery of many now held in slavery.' Undoubtedly York spoke for the nation at the time and perhaps even the gentle Chichester would have modified his views had he anticipated the dreadful fate that awaited a German he greatly admired. Pastor Bonnhoeffer was executed by the Gestapo for exercising the self-same right of dissent that Bishop Bell was left free to proclaim.

Latterly, at High Wycombe, Harris was forced to tolerate an irritant he could well have done without in the shape of the Headquarters Padre, John Collins, who would later become a leader of CND, the Campaign for Nuclear Disarmament. The C-in-C made a number of attempts to rid himself of his 'turbulent priest', but some perverse and authoritative Air Ministry official stubbornly kept Collins in office. Perhaps it was to demonstrate some sort of lunatic even-handedness that a vituperative critic of Harris's war should have been left in spiritual office over his headquarters. Perhaps the church itself felt happy to let the matter stand.

If Collins was an irritant, a truly malevolent cancer existed within the Air Ministry Directorate of Bombing Operations in the unprepossessing shape of a 41-year-old non-aircrew wartime Squadron Leader, John Strachey. If Harris previously had experienced doubts about the sanity of elements within the Air Ministry, then their placing of Strachey in such a sensitive job confirmed his worst misgivings. Strachey was a member of a respected and honoured family and it would be tempting to dub him its black sheep. However, his inconsistencies went well beyond definition by a single hue. This discreditable man, Eton and Magdalen educated, entered Parliament as a socialist in 1929. Two years later he resigned and in the next few years embraced variously the Communist Party and the British Union of Fascists. By 1939 he had undergone some unexplained remedial self-appraisal which left him a socialist once again. Unreliable, unpleasant, and politically eccentric he had no right to any position of influence, let alone the one he held. However, he had friends in very high places who were obviously blinded by his arrogant, wafer-thin intellect, and conformed to the strange British admiration for eccentrics no matter how perverse and unprepossessing they may be.

The effect of such a man on Harris was electric and entirely pre-dictable. Strachey represented just about everything that he despised and he would have made no secret of the fact to the man himself and to his superiors. He was appalled and hurt that the service he loved could employ Strachey in any capacity, let alone as an officer in a mar-ginally influential position. He ignored the man to the extent of scarcely recognising his existence and constantly complained that Strachey should be ejected as an obvious security risk. He was totally ignored and not for the first time Harris resigned himself to the situa-tion and got on with his job. It was not in Strachey's make-up to forget such treatment and his moment for political retribution was not to be long delayed. Elected again to Parliament in the 1945 General Election Strachey was appointed by the Prime Minister, Clement Attlee, to the post of Under Secretary of State for Air. Effectively therefore he became one of Harris's political masters and set about destroying the reputation of Bomber Command and its leader. In this he had enthusiastic support from certain of his government colleagues who were entranced by the fact that electoral victory gave them the power to re-write the past and dispose of uncomfortable critics.

The war was increasingly depicted by the left as a conflict of capital-ism in which the working masses were manipulated into abject suffer-ing. Harris was singled out and denied a peerage, although all the other great commanders were so honoured. He weathered this personal insult, but fought a hard and increasingly bitter battle for a campaign medal to be awarded to all who had served Bomber Command. This would have provided general recognition for the deeds of 120,000 aircrew and for the stoic work of countless thousands of ground staff on the great airfields. Other awards for the war's campaigns were announced including the Burma Star, the Africa Star, the Atlantic Star and so on, but nothing was done for the bombers. There should have been a public outcry, but so deep was the euphoria of peace, so enchanting was the prospect of life without danger that nobody thought it mattered much. Harris never forgot, nor forgave, what had been done to his men.

He left for South Africa in 1946 and stayed there for many years. In 1951 he was offered a peerage by the newly re-elected Conservative Government led by Churchill. He declined gracefully saying that it did not now suit his life as an ordinary businessman. Brendan Bracken did however persuade him to accept a baronetcy.

Strachey became Minister of Food in 1946. He was widely held responsible for continuing food crises and for the continuation of rationing well past the time that other nations had returned to normality. He also masterminded a groundnut growing scheme in Tanganyika, pouring into it huge sums of taxpayers' money. All it achieved was a bonanza for scrap dealers who cleared tons of rusting agricultural equipment which had proved useless in the harsh climate and stony fields of Africa. Still, his weird predominance held and he became Minister of War as the United Nations faced up to the developing conflict of Korea. Fortunately the American influence in this new war zone was supreme and it is doubtful whether Strachey's existence was noticed, let alone recognised. He was swept away in the 1951 General Election and died in obscurity 10 years later.

The arguments over the bombing of Germany and, indeed, bombing in general have raged on for half-a-century in intellectual and political circles, particularly among those unlikely ever to face a military decision. Hiroshima and Dresden have become pacifist icons paraded to define what is and is not acceptable in the fundamentally dreadful process of waging war. Perhaps only those actually involved in the fighting should be allowed to determine what may be done to shorten or ameliorate conflict. Perhaps only those earmarked to invade the Japanese mainland, or to fight inch by inch through a virile and largely undamaged Germany should retain the right to express a view on Hiroshima, or Hamburg, or Dresden.

Don Bennett died on 14 September 1986, his 76th birthday. Air Chief Marshal Sir Arthur Harris had died at his home in England just over two years earlier, on 5 April 1984, at the age of almost 92 years. Bomber Command's other great leaders, the group AOCs who saw the mighty offensive through to its victorious conclusion are no more. 'The parties in Valhalla', about which Harris once wrote in his preface to Guy Gibson's posthumous autobiography, must now be filled with the eternal company of Bomber Command now sadly including many who survived long enough to enjoy their hard won peace. Cheshire and Shannon, Martin and Searby, Embry, Edwards and Tait, are all no more. Only a handful remain to tell of this unique campaign waged against Germany on German soil until the consuming obscenity that beset her finally began to wilt. Half-a-century earlier Kipling had written:

> Oh, it's Tommy this an' Tommy that
> an' 'Tommy go away'
> But it's 'Thank you Mr Atkins'
> When the band begins to play
> It's Tommy this an' Tommy that
> an' 'Chuck him out the brute'
> But it's 'Saviour of 'is country'
> When the guns begin to shoot
> Then it's Tommy this an' Tommy that
> an' 'Tommy 'ows yer soul?'
> But it's 'thin red line of 'eroes'
> When the drums begin to roll.

He might as well have been writing about Harris and his 'old lags'.

There can be no finer tribute to Harris, Bennett and the 120,000 who flew with Bomber Command than that paid by an elderly Dutch lady attending the funeral of a Lancaster crew, found still in their aircraft when part of the Ijsselmeer was recently drained. As the service ended she approached an Englishman who was there to represent the squadron to which the Lancaster crew had belonged. She thanked him for all that had been done for Holland during the war and for the sacrifice of so many young airmen. He welcomed her sentiments but demurred saying, 'I often wonder if we did enough, after all you had to tolerate occupation and to maintain your courage and hope for five years'.

'Just to hear you night after night', she said, 'flying to bomb Germany – that was enough...'

EPILOGUE

In 1989 Ly Bennett went on holiday to Norway, determined to explore the area where her husband's Halifax had crashed and the starting point for his escape to neutral Sweden. The crash site is now marked by a cairn of stones on top of which is one of the Halifax's engines. A suitably engraved metal panel taken from the aircraft records for visitors the events of April 1942. While in Norway she met Olaf Horten who had witnessed the raid on the *Tirpitz* and had made a number of clandestine visits to the wreckage of W1041 before it was cleared away by the Germans. Almost as an after-thought he said, 'Of course, I have the propeller'.

'The propeller?' said Ly.

'Yes, not the whole propeller, you understand, just one part. It is difficult to store in my loft. You wish to see it?'

Scarcely believing what was happening, Ly Bennett said she would very much like to see it and off went the old Norwegian to retrieve it. When he eventually returned bearing his souvenir Ly saw that the blade was almost complete, although the extreme tip was gone and the protective covering had broken away here and there to reveal the beautiful laminated wood structure of the Schwartz blades with which the Halifax's Rotol constant speed propellers were fitted. She was delighted to see how well this last fragment of Don's aeroplane had survived the intervening years and, sensing her thoughts, Olaf Horten said 'I have tried to look after it, but it is not an easy thing to display well in the house'.

'Perhaps the Norwegian War Museum would take it?' suggested Ly.

'They have no interest I think, there are so many relics of the war,' replied the Norwegian.

Ly says that at this point she said nothing, praying and willing him in the long silence to say the words he finally spoke. 'I don't suppose you would like to have it, Mrs Bennett, would you?' A little later it was in her car fitting almost exactly between the firewall in front and the rear window. 'Very efficient,' she thought, 'Don must have had a hand in all this!' Ly was also given Don's Mae West found near the crash site and this is now displayed with other Bennett memorabilia in the Queensland Australia Air Museum.

Back in England she presented the blade to the RAF Museum. There it remains on permanent display in a case beside the preserved wreck of another Halifax, shot down in the same raid as Don Bennett's 'B' Baker and salvaged long after the war by the RAF from a Norwegian fjord. Close by another display is devoted to 8 Group and the Pathfinders. It includes the impeccable uniform of an Air Vice-Marshal belonging to that 'most efficient airman'.

APPENDIX A

LUFTWAFFE INTELLIGENCE EVALUATION OF PATHFINDER FORCE OPERATIONS

No: 61008 Secret Ic/Foreign Air Forces West.
A/Evaluation West

Great Britain: British Pathfinder Operations as at March 1944, Issued by Luftwaffenführungsstab Ic/Fremde Luftwaffen West.

British Pathfinder Operations
Contents
Preface
A. Development
B. Organisation and equipment
    I.   Organisation and aircraft types
    II. Personnel
C. Pathfinder operations
    I.   General
    II. Markers
    III. Execution of Pathfinder operations
        i)   Dividing of the Pathfinder crews
        ii) Route markers
        iii) Target markers
        iv) Release of markers
        v) Navigation
    IV. Mosquito Pathfinder operations
D. Conclusions

PREFACE

The success of a large-scale night raid by the RAF is in increasing measure dependent on the conscientious flying of the Pathfinder crews. The frictionless functioning of the attack is only possible when the turning points on the inward and outward courses, as well as the target itself, are properly marked.

Lately, these attacks have been compressed into about four minutes for each wave averaging 120–150 aircraft.

Dense and high reaching clouds, which hide the sky markers over the target, and exceptionally strong winds which blow the markers away quickly, represent an unpredictable barrier to Pathfinder operations and can often appreciably decrease the efficiency of an attack.

Another reason for the failure of a raid may lie in the partial failure of the first Pathfinders, the 'Initial Markers', to arrive, since experience has shown that succeeding Pathfinders, in spite of being equipped with H2S and blind marking equipment, have allowed themselves to be influenced, to a certain extent by the initial markers.

A. DEVELOPMENT

1. The concentrated large-scale RAF raid on Cologne on 30/31 May 1942, during a full-moon night and with an alleged strength of more than 900 aircraft, was the first attempt to imitate the 'focal point' raids initiated by the German Air Force during this strategic air war against the British Isles during the years 1940 and 1941.

The lessons taught by this first large-scale raid, the increasingly high losses and the fact that the Hyperbola (Gee) navigation system could only be used in certain conditions, forced the AOC-in-C of Bomber Command to develop new systems of attack.

Using the German system of 'Illuminators' and 'Fire Raisers' as a model, the use of Pathfinders was developed towards the middle of August 1942, in order to bring on to the target all the aircraft, some with inexperienced, others with only medium-trained crews, and to allow of the dropping of the bombs without loss of time.

2. Air Vice-Marshal BENNETT, at present still in command of these special units, was appointed Chief of the Pathfinder formations.

This 35 year old Australian – known as one of the most resourceful officers of the RAF – had distinguished himself as long ago as 1938 by a record long-range flight to South Africa in a four-engined seaplane which was launched in the air from a Sunderland flying boat (composite aircraft). In 1940, BENNETT established the Transatlantic Ferry Command with aircraft of the Hudson type. As an example of his personal operational capabilities, an attack may be cited which he made on the German fleet base at Trondheim.

BENNETT's appointment as commander of the Pathfinder formations is also based on the fact that he has written two standard books on astro-navigation.

3. The use of Pathfinders in the first large-scale raids was comparatively primitive. Several particularly experienced crews were sent out first as 'Fire Raisers' ahead of the main bomber force, and, in order to facilitate and ensure the location of the target, moonlit nights were especially favoured. Shortly after the formation of these Pathfinder groups, however, the principle of raids during moonlit nights was dropped and raids in dark cloudless periods began to take place.

BENNETT strove to render the raids independent of the weather and at the same time to make it easier for the less experienced crews to locate the target.

4. At first there were only four bomber squadrons, equipped with Stirlings, Halifaxes, Lancasters and Wellingtons, and in January 1943 these units were organised into 8 Bomber Group, the Pathfinder group.

The grouping of the Pathfinders into a bomber group of their own made it possible to standardise the equipment and the training, to put new ideas into operation and immediately to evaluate all experiences.

During the course of 1943, the number of Pathfinder squadrons was increased to meet the increased demands and among others, several Mosquito squadrons were detailed to the Pathfinder group.

B. ORGANISATION AND EQUIPMENT

I. ORGANISATION AND AIRCRAFT TYPES

1. 8 Bomber Group at present consists of:
   Five Lancaster squadrons;
   One Halifax squadron;
   Four Mosquito squadrons (including two special bomber squadrons with
      Bumerang (Oboe) equipment);
   One Mosquito Met. Flight.

For further information concerning the organisation of these units see 'Blue Book Series' Book I: 'The British Heavy Bomber Squadrons'.

2. In addition to the normal navigational aids (see also 'Blue Book Series' Book 7: 'British Navigation Systems') the aircraft carry the following special equipment:

a) Four-engined aircraft (Lancaster and Halifax): Rotterdam (H2S) for
   location of target and bombing without ground visibility.
   Hyperbola navigation instrument (Gee).
   Identification Friend-Foe (IFF).
   Acoustic nightfighter warning instrument 'Monica'.
   Visual nightfighter warning instrument (cathode ray oscilloscope) 'Fish
   Pond'.
   Provision for bomb release in the cabin as well as in the navigation
   room.

b) Twin-engined aircraft (Mosquitoes).
   Hyperbola navigation instrument (Gee).
   Special equipment according to mission, for example 'Bumerang'
   (Oboe).

The existence of Mosquitoes equipped with H2S has not as yet been definitely established. According to latest information available, this special equipment does not yet seem to have been installed in the Mosquito.

II. Personnel

1. The crews are no longer composed mainly of volunteers as was formerly the case. Owing to the great demand and the heavy losses, crews are either posted to Pathfinder units immediately after completing their training, or are transferred from ordinary bomber squadrons. As in the past, however, special promotion and the golden eagle badge are big inducements to the crews.

At first Pathfinder crews had to commit themselves to 60 operational flights, but because, due to this high number there were not sufficient volunteers, the figure was decreased to 45.

After transfer to a Pathfinder squadron, a certain probationary period is undergone. The crews are not appointed Pathfinders and awarded the golden eagle until they have proved themselves capable of fulfilling the equipments by flying several operations (about fourteen) over Germany. Before the award of the golden eagle each member of a crew has to pass a special examination to show that he is fully capable of performing two functions on board, for example gunner and mechanic, or mechanic and bomb-aimer, etc.

2. There is a special Pathfinder school (NTU Upwood Special School). All new crews, however are sent on a special navigational course lasting 8-14 days at a navigation training unit, where particularly experienced instructors, who have already completed their Pathfinder tours, train the crews in the operation of the special equipment and put the final polish on their already good navigational training.

New Pathfinder crews fly training flights over Great Britain. These are usually made south-west from the Cambridge area, course then being set for the Isle of Man. On the return flight a large city, such as Birmingham or Manchester is approached, dummy bombing using H2S is carried out, and target photographs are brought back to the home base. Flights of this kind are flown to a strict time schedule, just as in the case of a large-scale raid on Germany or the Occupied Western Territories and are taken into consideration in the assessment of the crews as Pathfinders. If on several occasions, the schedule is not adhered to the crew is transferred to an ordinary bomber squadron.

C. PATHFINDER OPERATIONS

I. General

The operational tactics of the Pathfinders have been under constant development ever since the earliest days, and even now cannot be considered as firmly established or completed. New methods of target location and marking, as well as extensive deceptive and diversionary measures against the German defences are evident in almost every operation.

Whereas the attacks of the British heavy bombers during the years lasted over an hour, the duration of the attack has been progressively shortened so that today, a raid of 800–900 aircraft is compressed into 20 minutes at the most. (According to captured enemy information, the plan for the raid on Berlin on 15/16 February 1944 called for 900 aircraft in five waves of four minutes each.)

In spite of the increased danger of collision or of dropping bombs on other aircraft which must be taken into account, the aim has been achieved of allowing the German defences, the commands as well as the defence weapons themselves, only a fraction of the time available to them during the raids in the past.

The realisation of these aims was made possible by the conscientious work of the Pathfinder group and by the high training standard (especially regarding navigation) of the crews.

The markers over the approach and withdrawal courses serve as navigational aids for all aircraft and above all they help them to keep to the exact schedule of times and positions along the briefed course. Over the target, the markers of the Pathfinders enable all aircraft to bomb accurately without loss of time.

II. MARKERS
Up to date, the following markers have been identified:

i) <u>Target</u> <u>Markers</u>
a) <u>Ground</u> <u>Markers</u>, also called cascade bombs, are red, green and yellow. Weather conditions govern the setting of the barometric fuse, whereby the ground marker container is detonated at a height varying from 800 to 5,000 metres, thereby releasing 60 flares which fall burning and burn out on the ground.

Ground markers are mainly dropped in the target area, but they are also sometimes used as route markers. Ground markers are also dropped in 10/10-th clouds in order to illuminate the cloud base from below. When the clouds are thin, the crew can see the glare without difficulty. The average duration of burning a ground marker is 3–4 minutes.
b) <u>Sky</u> <u>Markers</u> are parachute flares, of which several are usually placed simultaneously. As a rule the flares used are red ones from which at regular intervals quick burning green flares ('dripping green stars') drop out. Besides these, green sky markers with red stars and although comparatively seldom, green sky markers with yellow stars are also used.

The bomb-aimers are for the most part briefed to drop their bombs into the middle of a group of sky markers. This corrects the opinion held until now that two sky markers are set, one to indicate the point of bomb release and the other to indicate the target.

c) <u>White</u> and <u>Yellowish</u> <u>Flares</u> are used chiefly to illuminate the target. They are also sometimes used as dummy markers.

During raids in the autumn of 1943, the enemy attempted to mark a target approach corridor by setting numerous flares. It may be assumed that he dropped this system because of the heavy losses inflicted by German single-engined nightfighters in the target area.

ii) <u>Route</u> <u>Markers</u>
a) <u>As</u> <u>Track</u> <u>Markers</u> or indicators, sky markers are used in 10/10ths cloud.
b) <u>Ground</u> <u>Markers</u> (Spotfires) are red, green or yellow; red and yellow are mainly used.

A ground marker does not split up into different traces, but burns with a single bright light for three to eight minutes.

iii) <u>New</u> <u>kinds</u> <u>of</u> <u>markers,</u> <u>as</u> <u>yet</u> <u>not</u> <u>clearly</u> <u>identified</u>
The enemy has often tried to introduce new kinds of markers with varying lighting effects.
a) Among others, a quick falling flare bomb was observed lately. After it hit the ground a 90-metre high column of sparkle was observed, which slowly descended in many colours. Confirmation however, is not yet available.
b) To designate the beginning and the end of the attack, a large reddish-yellow 'Fireball' has often been observed. Red flares fall from the fireball and at low heights these again split up into green stars. The light intensity of these bombs is unusually high.
c) The so-called red 'Multi-Flashes' are apparently used as route markers. They have been observed sparkling to the ground at intervals of 2–3 seconds.
d) The enemy seem to have stopped using enormous 1,800kg size flare bombs. The reason for this could not be determined.

III. EXECUTION OF PATHFINDER OPERATIONS

i) <u>Dividing</u> <u>of</u> <u>the</u> <u>Pathfinder</u> <u>crews</u>
a) At present, Pathfinder crews are divided into the following categories:
  Blind Markers;
  Blind Backers-up;
  Visual Backers-up;
  Visual Markers;
  Supporters and Pathfinder Main Force.
About 15% of the bombers used for a large-scale operation are Pathfinders. For example, out of a total strength of 900 aircraft, 120 would be Pathfinder.
  20 to 25 would be Blind Markers
  30 to 45 would be Blind and Visual Backers-up

60 to 70 would be Pathfinder Main Force

b) <u>Blind Markers</u>. It is the duty of the blind markers to locate the target using H2S and to set ground or sky markers, or both according to weather conditions, at zero hour minus 2 to 5 minutes.

The blind marker crews alone are responsible for the success or the failure of the raid. They are more strictly bound to the time schedule than all the other aircraft taking part in the raid. They are not allowed to drop their markers if the schedule is deviated from by more than one or two minutes, or if the instruments fail, or fail to indicate accurately. In such cases the blind marker aircraft automatically becomes part of the Pathfinder Main Force and must drop its HE bomb load exactly at zero hour.

With smaller targets, it is the duty of the blind markers to set flares over the target area, in order to illuminate it.

Another duty of good blind marker crews during the initial stages of the attack is not only to set new markers, but also to re-centre the attack. Experience has shown that the first aircraft of the Main Force drop their bombs near the markers but that succeeding aircraft tend to drop them short of the target area during the progress of the attack. It is the duty of the blind markers detailed for this purpose to bring the bombing back to the original target by re-setting the markers past the first aiming point in the direction of the withdrawal.

For several months past, the blind markers have had a further duty. In several operations it was repeatedly shown that errors in the navigation of the Main Force occurred owing to inaccurate wind forecasts. Experienced Pathfinders were therefore instructed to transmit their established wind calculations to England by W/T. Each group picks up these reports and transmits them every half hour to the airborne bombers.

c) <u>Blind Backers-up</u>. The duties of the blind backer-up are similar to those of the blind markers, except that they fly in the bomber stream. Thus, they drop their markers during the attack, also in accordance with a strict previously laid down time schedule. Blind backers-up are used to set ground markers and, above all, sky markers, which are always renewed by means of the H2S and never visually.

d) <u>Visual Backers-up</u>. In order to give new Pathfinder crews a chance to gain experience for future operations as visual or blind markers, they are allowed to set new markers visually; these, however, are always of a different colour. Theoretically, these markers should be on or very near to the original markers, but as in practice this is very seldom the case, the impression given is that of the target being framed by markers. The bomb-aimers of the succeeding bombers are therefore briefed to release their bombs in the centre of the markers dropped by the backers-up.

e) <u>Visual Markers</u>. An attack on a small or pin-point target (definite industrial installations, dockyards, etc.) necessitates still more accurate marking than is possible by the blind markers. The visual markers, therefore locate the target visually from medium heights, sometimes from as low as 1,500 metres, and then release their ground markers on the centre of the target, in order to concentrate the attack of the high-flying bombers. The visual markers are aided by the illumination of the target are aided by several blind markers (Newhaven attack) [sic].

f) Supporters. New crews who come from training units or other squadrons and who are to be trained as Pathfinders fly their first operations in the Pathfinder Main Force. They carry only mines or HE bombs, arrive exactly at zero hour and try, at the first concentric bombing, to create the conditions necessary to allow the incendiary bombs of the succeeding waves to take full effect.

ii) Route Markers
Route markers are set by good blind marker crews and are renewed during the approach of the bomber stream by further good blind marker crews. Ground markers (spotfires) are sometimes set visually, and sometimes by instruments, but sky markers used as track markers or indicators are set only by means of H2S.

The routes of approach and withdrawal are generally identified by three markers set at especially prominent points or turning points. The colours of these markers for any single night raid are usually the same, either red, green, yellow or white. It has often been observed that the route markers do not always lie exactly on course. They are set somewhat to one side so that the approaching bombers are not unnecessarily exposed to the danger of German nightfighters.

iii) Target Markers
The target markers used will differ according to weather conditions. More sky or ground markers are set, according to the visibility and cloud conditions prevailing.

To date, the following methods of attack and target marking have been recognised:

a) The 'Paramata' attack under a clear sky and with good visibility. Ground markers are used only.

b) The 'Wanganui' attack with 8–10/10ths cloud cover. Sky markers only.

c) The 'Musical Paramata' attack with 5–8/10ths cloud cover. Mainly ground markers, but some sky markers.

d) The 'Newhaven' attack, in which the target area is illuminated by means of parachute flares coupled with several ground markers.

e) The 'Musical Wanganui' attack with 8-10/10ths cloud cover. Mainly sky markers, but some ground markers. This system of target marking has been used to a great extent lately during bad weather operations.

iv) Dropping the Markers

The setting of the Pathfinder markers requires a great deal of experience. For this reason, training flights with markers of all kinds are often carried out over Great Britain, serving for practical experiments with flares as well as for training purposes.

When the target area is already illuminated by previously dropped flares, the ground markers are released visually by means of the ordinary bomb-sight.

In cases where 10/10ths cloud or dark conditions are found over the target area, H2S is used for dropping all markers.

A great deal of experience is required for the setting of blind markers. Close co-operation between the navigator and the H2S operator (*see 'Blue Book' Series Book 7: 'British Navigations Systems' for the difference between the two*), who sit side by side in the navigation room, is the first essential for the precise setting of markers by means of H2S. Above all, drift must be calculated before the markers are set, so that the main attacking force only has to navigate on the markers themselves.

v) Navigation

The basis for all Pathfinder navigation is dead reckoning, and all other systems are only aids to check and supplement this. H2S equipment is valueless without dead reckoning because the ground is not shown on the cathode ray-tube screen as it is on a map.

To facilitate the location of the target, an auxiliary target, which experience shows to give a clear picture on the cathode ray tube, is given during the briefing. This auxiliary target should be as close to the actual target as possible, in order to eliminate all sources of error. Cities, large lakes, or even the coastline features are used as auxiliary targets.

The course and the time of flight from the auxiliary target to the actual target are calculated in advance, taking the wind into consideration. The H2S operator then knows that the main target will appear on the screen a given number of seconds after the auxiliary target has been identified.

IV MOSQUITO PATHFINDER OPERATIONS

The Mosquito aircraft have special duties as Pathfinders, concerning which the following information is available:

i) Setting ordinary Markers 15 to 20 minutes before the beginning of the actual attack, in conjunction with other Lancaster Pathfinders, over an auxiliary target.

ii) Setting dummy Markers, along the coast and at other places to indicate a false course and a false target.

iii) Dropping so-called 'Fighter Flares', which are imitations of the white and yellow flares dropped by German flare-carrying aircraft, to attract and divert German nightfighters.

These dummy markers are often three to five minutes flight from the target, or are sometimes placed at points off the approach and withdrawal courses, although always in some sort of relationship to these.

iv) <u>Dropping</u> 'Window' <u>from</u> <u>great</u> <u>heights</u>. This is so timed, after taking wind conditions into consideration, that a cloud of Window will be over the target when the first four-engined Pathfinders get there. This is made necessary by the fact that the target must be approached in straight and level flight, without evasive action, in order to get a good H2S picture. It is supposed to eliminate to a great extent aimed fire by the flak.

v) <u>Release</u> <u>of</u> <u>single</u> <u>HE</u> <u>bombs</u> 20 to 30 minutes after the main attack and observation of the results of the main attack.

vi) <u>Identification</u> <u>of</u> <u>pin-point</u> <u>targets</u> for succeeding Mosquito waves by setting ground markers with the aid of 'Bumerang' (Oboe). The succeeding Mosquitoes then drop their bombs visually on the marked target.

D. CONCLUSIONS

1. Strong criticism from amongst their own units was at first levelled against the British Pathfinder operations, but they were able to prevail because of the successes achieved during the years 1943/44.

2. The original assumption that the majority of bomber crews would be less careful in their navigation once they became used to the help of the Pathfinders, and that therefore the total efficiency and success of raids would diminish, has hitherto not been confirmed.

The navigation, training and equipment of the ordinary British bomber crews has been improved.

3. The operational tactics of the Pathfinders cannot be considered as complete even today. There are in particular continual changes of all markers and marking systems.

4. The trend of development will be towards making possible on one and the same night two or more large raids on the present scale, each with the usual Pathfinder accompaniment.

Distribution
Units of the R.d.L. and Ob.d.l.
Luftflotten down to operational Gruppen.
Flakabteilungen and Ln. Regiments.

[Translated post-war from Luftwaffe records]

PORTAL'S LETTER TO HARRIS, 14 JUNE 1942

AIR MINISTRY (Dept. OA),
KING CHARLES STREET
WHITEHALL S.W.1.

SECRET

14th June, 1942

My dear Harris,

This is in answer to your letter ATH/DO/6 of the 12th June giving your latest views on our proposal for forming a Target Finding Force. As I read your letter, both you and those of your Command with whom you have discussed the scheme, agree on the urgent need for finding some method of using the best of your crews to identify and mark the target so as to enable the remainder to concentrate their attack on it and thus to avoid the present waste of effort which results from the majority of your attacks being dissipated over a wide area. I take it that you also agree that something must be done to prevent less expert crews from lighting fires in the wrong places during the first stage of an attack.

2. In the third para. of your letter you say that all the Command representatives were utterly opposed to the formation of a Target Finding Force on the lines proposed by the Air Staff. Yet the suggestions which follow all seem to me to imply an admission of the need for such a force and present no reasonable argument against the Air Staff proposal. In fact they seem to me to include those earlier proposals for singling out the best crews and giving them distinctive badges etc. to which you formerly objected so strongly on the grounds that this would involve the creation of a "corps d'élite." Please do not think that I fail to understand the objections to the "corps d'élite' idea. To pack one unit with experts at the expense of other units which have to do the same job is most unsound and bad for morale. This is emphatically not what we are proposing. The T.F.F. would have an entirely different and far more difficult task than the ordinary "follow up" squadrons and this creates both the need and the justification for having a formation containing none but expert crews.

3. Over a period of three months your attitude seems to have progressed from the complete rejection of the Target Finding Force proposal, through a Target Finding Squadron phase to this present raid leader suggestion. I

cannot feel it is logical that you should now reject the final and essential step of welding the selected crews into one closely knit organisation which, as I see it, is the only way to make their leadership and direction effective.

4. I cannot believe that your compromise will give equal results. You say that there is nothing particular to be gained from bringing the selected crews into one unit and locating them together on one aerodrome. As we see it, this is the essence of the problem. Without this close association there could be no continuity of technique; there could be no day to day improvement of method; and we could not ensure that the plans and briefing for each individual operation were similarly and clearly interpreted and acted upon by the force as a whole. In effect it would mean perpetuating the present rule-of-thumb tactical methods by segregated crews rather than introducing the finesse and polish which one would expect from a well trained and co-ordinated Target Finding Force. The problem confronting us is clearly so great that nothing less than the best will do.

5. There is one further point which I particularly desire to emphasize. Your Raid Leader scheme would depend for such success as it might achieve largely upon the assistance of T.R.1335. We have already had this equipment in use three months. We cannot expect immunity from interference much longer. When it is denied to us as a target locating device, it is clear that your proposal could not ensure to the bomber force the leadership which they must have if the average crews are to overcome their great and increasing difficulties.

6. The new objection which you now advance in connection with the manning of the Target Finding Squadrons is not, in my opinion, a sufficiently serious one to be given much weight. There is little reason why foreign or Dominion crews should not be included in these squadrons if they are good enough, and I should expect little difficulty in convincing their Governments of the need for their co-operation. In fact, the close association of specially selected crews in such a force might well be an excellent thing in balancing the main disadvantage underlying our present policy of segregating Dominion and foreign personnel within their own homogeneous units.

7. The varying types of equipment which we have in our squadrons do create a difficulty which we would have to face. It would of course be possible for a crew from any Wellington Squadron, of which there are at present 13, to be incorporated within the three Wellington III Target Finding Squadrons. it might be worth considering whether the three heavy squadrons should not be established on one of each type and thus give their respective Groups a stake in the force which would enliven their interest in manning and maintaining it at the highest pitch of efficiency.

8. The admission in para. 5 of your letter of the difficulty of seeing the target on a dark night, is a convincing indication that the methods which we have employed up to now are not equal to the occasion. It is perhaps sig-

nificant that our more ineffective raids have often been characterised in the past by the phrase "intensive darkness and haze". I had not previously seen the reports which you forwarded with your letter but in Appendix "A" to B.109 it is clearly brought out that this "haze" factor diminishes with more effective illumination and that in fact flares do make it possible to see these built-up areas in the Ruhr. What we need to aim at is an effective degree of illumination and incendiarism in the right place and only in the right place. It is our opinion that this admittedly difficult task can only be done by a force which concentrates upon it as a specialised role, and which excludes those less expert crews whose less discriminating use of flares or incendiaries in the vicinity of the target have recently led so many of our attacks astray.

9. The Air Staff receive only your night raid reports which go into statistical rather than tactical details. I attach extracts from those received to date of your raids on Germany since you began operations with the T.R.1335 equipment. If you glance through these you will, perhaps, understand why I feel so reluctant to accept any compromise in introducing new tactical methods to improve the results being obtained. While the efficiency of our attacks remains on the average so low, the expansion of the Bomber force is clearly of secondary importance to improving its efficiency and effectiveness even though this may require the taking of most drastic measures. It is the opinion of the Air Staff that the formation of a special force with a role analogous to that of the Reconnaissance Battalion of an Army Division would immediately open up a new field for improvement, raising the standard and thus the morale which could not fail to be reflected throughout the whole force.

10. At the same time, I fully recognise the practical difficulties, and, although I do not consider the proposals which you have so far made go nearly far enough, I am reluctant to impose the Air Staff proposal upon you while you object so strongly to it. I would therefore like to discuss the subject with you tomorrow as a preliminary to holding the conference arranged for next Thursday, and I hope we shall be able to formulate an agreed scheme.

11. The need for early action is increased by the Singleton report which is now before the Chiefs of Staff. It brings out very clearly the urgent need for an increase in the percentage of bombs on the target, and any failure on our part to effect a radical improvement may well endanger the whole of our bomber policy.

[*signed: Yours ever, Charles*]

Air Marshal A. T. Harris, K.C.B., O.B.E., A.F.C.,
Headquarters, Bomber Command,
c/o G.P.O., High Wycombe,
BUCKS

PATHFINDER SQUADRONS, AUGUST 1942 TO MAY 1945

Unit	To PFF/8 Group (date)	Equipment
7 Squadron	T/F Aug 42	Stirling Lancaster (from Jul 43)
35 Squadron	T/F Aug 42	Halifax Lancaster (from Mar 44)
83 Squadron	T/F Aug 42	Lancaster
97 Squadron	T/F Apr 43	Lancaster
105 Squadron	T/F Jun 43	Mosquito
109 Squadron	T/F Aug 42	Wellington Mosquito (from Aug 42)
128 Squadron – Re-formed Sept 44		Mosquito
139 Squadron	T/F Jun 43	Mosquito
142 Squadron – Re-formed Oct 44		Mosquito
156 Squadron	T/F Aug 42	Wellington Lancaster (from Jan 43)
162 Squadron – Re-formed Dec 44		Mosquito
163 Squadron – Re-formed Jan 45		Mosquito
405 Squadron	T/F Apr 1943	Halifax Lancaster (from Aug 43)
571 Squadron – Formed Nov 43		Mosquito
582 Squadron – Formed Apr 44		Lancaster
608 Squadron – Re-formed Aug 44		Mosquito
627 Squadron – Formed Nov 43		Mosquito
635 Squadron – Formed Mar 44		Lancaster
692 Squadron – Formed Jan 44		Mosquito

(*Note*: 97, 83 and 627 Squadrons were 'loaned' to 5 Group in April 1944.)

PATHFINDER STATIONS AND SQUADRONS, AUGUST 1942 TO MAY 1945

Station	Squadrons	
Bourn	97	(to 5 Group Apr 44)
	105	
	162	
Downham Market	635	
	571	(to Graveley Apr 44)
	608	
Graveley	35	
	692	
	571	(to Oakington Apr 44)
Gransden Lodge	405	
	142	
Little Staughton	582	
	109	
Marham	105	(to Bourn Apr 44)
	139	(to Wyton Jul 43)
	109	(to Little Staughton Apr 44)
Oakington	7	
	627	(to 5 Group Apr 44)
	571	
	1409 Flight	(to Wyton Jan 44)
Upwood	156	
	139	
Warboys	156	(to Upwood Mar 44)
Wyton	83	(to 5 Group Apr 44)
	139	(to Upwood Feb 44)
	1409 Flight	
	128	
	163	

APPENDIX E
SUMMARY OF BOMBER COMMAND REPORTS ON RAIDS ON GERMANY, 1 MARCH 1942 TO 1 MAY 1942

Date	Target	Sorties	Night Raid Report No.	Photographic Evidence
8/9 Mar	Essen	211	22	Altogether 43 aircraft took night photographs with bombing ground detail. Although none of these shows the target, 12 are within 5 miles of the aiming point. A number of photographs were, however, in the vicinity of the Margareten-höne decoy, and it is therefore uncertain whether or not all the large fires reported were genuine. The photographs show that a large proportion of the main striking force bombed the southern outskirts of Essen. 7 other photographs plotted between 5 and 7 miles from the aiming point show that bombs were dropped in built up areas near Hamborn, Duisburg and Oberhausen. Subsequent PRU's revealed no damage to the target, but several incidents are apparent south of the target in the suburbs of Essen.
9/10 Mar	Essen	185	23	43 aircraft obtained succesful night photographs. None could be plotted within 5 miles of the target, and there was no evidence that any attack was delivered on the primary target etc.
10/11 Mar	Essen	126	24	Although 22 photographs were obtained on this night very few of

Date	Target	Sorties	Night Raid Report No.	Photographic Evidence
				them have been plotted. One aircraft however has been plotted at Essen, and as this crew reported fires and activity in the vicinity it appears that others may also have attacked near the target. One aircraft plotted over Dortmund may also have achieved useful results.
12/13 Mar	Kiel	68	25	Altogether 26 photographs were obtained, 3 of which were of the docks and a further 14 within 5 miles of the target. All but one of the plotted photographs lie within 3 miles of the Deutsche-Werke yards. About six aircraft appear to have attacked the neighbourhood of Elschenhagen, a village 2½ miles SE of the docks.
13/14 Mar	Cologne	135	26	Of 31 night photographs obtained, 11 were of the target area and a further 7 within 5 miles of it. It is estimated that at least 50% of the force which claimed to have attacked Cologne reached the target and a large proportion of these aircraft bombed the city. There is no evidence that the many decoys in the Cologne area diverted any considerable proportion of the effort.
25/26 Mar	Essen	254	30	The photographic evidence obtained gives no indication that the attack on Essen achieved any success. Although 46 photographs were taken with bombing, none of them has been plotted within 5 miles of the target. 15 aircraft took

Date	Target	Sorties	Night Raid Report No.	Photographic Evidence
				photographs in the vicinity of Rheinberg, and several of these show large fires burning in the open country to the north of this town. It is certain that a decoy attracted a large part of the attack. The other photographs show widely scattered areas, and some of those which remain unplotted show features suggesting they were taken over Holland.
26/27 Mar	Essen	115	31	The photographic evidence of the results of this raid is comparatively small. 13 photographs showing ground detail were obtained with bombing. One of these has been plotted in the SE part of Essen and 3 in Duisburg-Rhurort, but the others show widely scattered points. There is no indication that any useful concentration was achieved over the target or over any other built-up area.
28/29 Mar	Lübeck	234	33	32 photographs were obtained with bombing. 17 of these show parts of the island town, and a further 11 are within 2 miles of it.
5/6 Apr	Cologne	263	39	There is no photographic evidence to show that any success was achieved in this raid. 17 photographs were taken but none was within 5 miles of the target.
6/7 Apr	Essen	157	40	This is very meagre, and does not indicate that much success was achieved. 4 photographs were obtained of which only 1 is within 5 miles of the target.

Date	Target	Sorties	Night Raid Report No.	Photographic Evidence
8/9 Apr	Hamburg	272	41	There is no photographic evidence to suggest that this raid achieved any success. None of the 7 photographs taken are within 5 miles of the target and three of those have been plotted between 30 and 75 miles from it.
10/11 Apr	Essen	254	42	8 photographs were taken. Only 1 of these was of the target, but it showed no fires or bursts.
12/13 Apr	Essen	251	43	31 photographs were taken with bombing. Only 2 of these show Essen and a further 4 were within 5 miles of it, but none of these shows any steady fires burning. The attack appears to have been scattered over the Ruhr.
14/15 Apr	Dort-mund	208	45	Although 39 photograph were taken with bombing, none shows the target, and only 7 are within 5 miles of it. The attack seems to have been scattered, and those photographs which show fires burning are all of open country.
15/16 Apr	Dort-mund	152	46	12 photographs were taken with bombing. None of these was within 5 miles of the target and there is nothing to show that any success was achieved. The 4 photographs which have been plotted were at distances of from 12 to 51 miles from the target. A daylight reconnaissance has tended to confirm the evidence of the night photographs.

Date	Target	Sorties	Night Raid Report No.	Photographic Evidence
17/18 Apr	Hamburg	173	48	Of 22 night photographs obtained, 2 were of the target area and a further 2 within 5 miles of it. Daylight reconnaissance after the raid provided no evidence of new damage.
22/23 Apr	Cologne	69	50	5 photographs taken with bombing. None of these shows the target but 2 are within 5 miles, 2 more lie just outside the limit, and another aircraft took a photograph 2 minutes after bombing which suggests that it bombed within 5 miles.
23/24 Apr	Rostock	143	51	Ample photographic evidence was obtained, 58 photographs being taken with bombing. 9 of these were of Rostock itself, and 28 were within 5 miles of it. However, most of the photographs lie from 2 to 6 miles SE of the old town, and the brunt of the attack appears to have fallen on suburbs, villages, and some of it in open country. There is evidence of small fires in scattered areas in the town. No photographs of the Heinkel factory were obtained.
24/25 Apr	Rostock	91	52	59 photographs showing ground detail were taken with bombing in the raid on Rostock. 21 of these showed the target area in the town, and 3 the Heinkel factory. A further 27 were within 5 miles of the target.
25/26 Apr	Rostock	128	53	71 successful photographs were taken with bombing, 30 show the

Date	Target	Sorties	Night Raid Report No.	Photographic Evidence
				centre of the town, and a further 34 show points within 5 miles of it. A further 3 show the Heinkel factory.
26/27 Apr	Rostock	107	54	The photographs obtained on this night were most successful, since all the 52 taken proved to be of the target area, including 18 of Rostock and 13 of the Heinkel works.
27/28 Apr	Cologne	92	55	Only 2 of the eighteen photographs taken with bombing by aircraft attacking Cologne actually show the town. A further 3 are within 5 miles of it. It appears from this that only a small proportion of the force despatched attacked the target. Large fires could, however be seen burning and a reconnaissance on the next day confirmed that there was considerable fresh damage to the city.
28/29 Apr	Kiel	88	56	This raid seems to have been fairly successful. 19 photographs were taken with bombing of which 6 were of the target and 5 were within 5 miles of it... A subsequent daylight reconnaissance revealed only a few new points of damage, but they were significant.

[*Harris Papers, RAF Museum, Hendon*]

NOTES ON THE EFFECTIVENESS OF PFF OPERATIONS, 18/19 AUGUST TO 21/22 NOVEMBER 1942

Introduction
1. These notes are intended to give preliminary rough figures as to the results achieved against German targets since the formation of the PFF and to make a first attempt at estimating the probable effect of the introduction of H2S (a) into the PFF only and (b) into the whole force. The results quoted are those achieved by the whole force as evidenced by night photographs and are expressed as a percentage within 3 miles of the aiming point of sorties claiming attack.

General
2. No. of nights in period considered   94
     No. of opertions against Italian targets   9
     No. of operations against German targets   21

		Weather	
		Good	15
		Moderate	10
		Bad	5

Details of all attacks are given in tabular form in Appendix G.

The Effect of Weather on Execution of the Pathfinder Technique

Execution		*Weather*		*Average percentage within 3 miles*
Successful	7	Good	5	44%
		Moderate	2	40%
		Bad	0	
Partially successful	6	Good	2	
		Moderate	4	
		Bad	0	
Failed	5	Good	1	
		Moderate	3	
		Bad	2	
Wrong Target	3	Good	1	
		Moderate	1	
		Bad	1	

4. The PFF have never succeeded in bad weather and have never failed in good. Diversions are equally divided between the three classes of weather.

The Effect of the Success of the PFF on the Results of the Main Force
5. The percentage of night photographs within 3 miles actually achieved has been compared with the expectation based on pre-PFF results. When the raid shows a noticeable increase on expectation, and crews of the Main Force have reported that they have been assisted by the PFF, the results are stated to be 'improved'.

Effect on Main Force Results		*Execution of Pathfinder Technique*	
Improved	8	Successful	6
		Partial	2
		Failed	0
		Wrong Target	0
No measurable effect	10	Successful	1
		Partial	4
		Failed	5
		Wrong Target	0
Diverted	3	Wrong Target	3

6. Success by the PFF in executing their planned technique has almost always resulted in an improvement in the results achieved by the Main Force.

7. When the PFF have failed, the Main Force has never been able, by its own efforts, to improve upon expectation.

8. The Main Force has invariably been diverted when the PFF have marked the wrong target.

9. Judging by night photographs:

The greatest percentage of a/c bombing within 3 miles	58%	(Bremen 4/5 Sept.)
Average percentage of a/c bombing within 3 miles of raids improved	40%	
Overall average percentage of a/c bombing within 3 miles	24%	
Overall average of expectation	21%	

10. The approximate degrees of improvement over expectation based on pre-PFF results have been as follows:

Maximum improvement	3 times (Osnabrück 6/7 Oct.)
Average improvement of raids improved	2 times
Overall average improvement	1.2 times

Estimate of Future Possibilities

11. The average of 24% within 3 miles so far achieved on PFF Operations, gives much scope for improvement, as it represents only about 5% within 1 mile. Improvements in the near future are to be expected from the introduction of H2S. into the PFF and from the use of marker bombs.

12. An estimate of the improvement to be expected from the use of H2S by the PFF can be made on the assumption (a) that H2S would enable the PFF to mark the target successfully under all weather conditions, (b) that the average percentage within 3 miles achieved in good and moderate (para. 3) are representative of those which would be achieved if all attacks were successful and (c) that in bad weather conditions marking would be ineffective. From the figures given in paragraph 3:

Estimated average percentage within 3 miles with PFF using H2S	=	36%
Estimated average percentage within 2 miles with PFF using H2S	=	20–25%

Hence the use of H2S by the PFF is likely to improve the present average bombing results of the Main Force by a factor of 50%.

Blind Bombing

13. Having regard to the fact that bad weather forecasting is likely to lead to a failure of the marking technique, even if the PFF employs H2S, and to the fact that operations were rendered impracticable by weather over targets on about 30% of nights within the period, it would seem that considerable further improvements could be obtained by equipping the whole bomber force with H2S since this would permit blind bombing when the weather is bad as well as being of great assistance as an aid to visual location when the weather is more favourable.

14. *The BDU trials* indicate that when blind bombing with H2S, almost 100% of bombs fall within 1 mile of AP (the accuracy against large cities is smaller, but most of the bombs still fall on the city).

Taking into account the lower standard of the average navigator working under opertional conditions and the fact that about 30% of sets are likely to fail before reaching the target, it is estimated that

About 70% of bombs will fall within 2 miles of AP.

Hence, it is estimated that the effectiveness of bombing with the aid of H2S by the whole bomber force (70%) would be about three times the effectiveness obtained if the PFF only has H2S (20-25%). Moreover, this opens up the possibility of operating under bad weather conditions, when target marking would be impracticable and the defences are seriously handicapped.

15. The conclusion in the previous paragraph depends upon the possibility of training the average navigator in the use of H2S Information on this point is urgently required.

GAR/RR.IV
BC/S.28153/ORS

[*Harris Papers, RAF Museum, Hendon*]

DETAILS OF RAIDS LED BY PATHFINDER FORCE, 18 AUGUST TO 21 NOVEMBER 1942

	┌─── Planned Pathfinder Technique ───┐					
Attacks on Germany					**Weather**	
				Marker	**and Moon**	
Date and Target 1	**'F** 2	**Illuminators** 3	**Ground Markers** 4	**Flares** 5	6	**Execution of Pathfinder Technique** 7
18/19 Aug Flensburg	6	–	17 aircraft, 192, 120, 72 x 30lb, 14 x 250lb	–	Moderate None	Target not located. Blobs scattered over wide area mainly to N of target.
24/25 Aug Frankfurt	–	–	20 aircraft, 192, 120, 112 x 30lb, 24, 14 x 250lb	–	Bad Bright	Target not located. Blobs scattered over wide area but some together 5 mls N of target.
27/28 Aug Kassel	4	–	17 aircraft, 192, 112, 72 x 30lb, 24, 14 x 250lb	–	Moderate Bright	1 finder dropped flares across target at Zero hour. Most 'Blobs' on Kassel, but scattered in S part of town.
28/29 Aug Nurnberg	5	–	15 aircraft, 192, 120, 112, 72 x 30lb, 24, 15, 14 x 150lb	Target	Good Bright	Finders dropped flares across target. 'Blobs' were well placed. Marker flares dropped over target.
1/2 Sept Saarbrücken	3	–	13 aircraft 23, 14, 13, 8 x 250lb	Target	Good Medium	Finders did not reach target. First blob dropped on Saarlautern and all others followed suit. Marker flares dropped there also.
2/3 Sept Karlsruhe	4	(2 finders) ➡	13 aircraft 23, 14, 13, 8 x 250lb	Target	Good Medium	3 finders dropped flares across target. Blobs and marker flares well placed.
4/5 Sept Bremen	–	19 aircraft 19 ➡ at zero hour	19 aircraft 11, 8, 7, 6 x 250lb in sticks	Target	Good Medium	Flares well concentrated and dropped low over target. Sticks of I.B. & marker flares dropped close to aiming point.
6/7 Sept Duisburg	–	21 aircraft 10 at Zero hour 2 at Zero +3, +6, +9, +12 1 at Zero +15, +18, +21	–	Target	Good Medium	Flares somewhat scattered but a number of sticks across aiming point. Some of the aircraft detailed for Zero hour were late. Some marker flares dropped to aiming point.
8/9 Sept Frankfurt	–	22 aircraft 22 ➡ at Zero hour	22 aircraft 22, 9, 8 x 250lb	–	Moderate None	Target not located. Flares very scattered. A number of blobs dropped close to Russelsheim.
10/11 Sept Düsseldorf	–	18 aircraft at Zero hour	6 aircraft 15 x 250lb 1 x 4000 lb(2)	Target	Good None	Early flares rather scattered but later ones and marker flares well placed. Blobs and 1x4000lb I.B. dropped on aiming point.
13/14 Sept Bremen	–	19 aircraft 13 ➡ at Zero hour	17 aircraft 15, 8, 6 x 250lb 1 x 4000lb(2)	–	Moderate None	Early flares scattered but later ones well placed and most of blobs and 1x4000lb IB dropped near aiming point. 2 blobs dropped near decoy 13 mls WSW of target.
14/15 Sept Wilhelmshaven	–	14 aircraft 10 ➡ at Zero hour	15 aircraft 15, 8, 6 x 250lb	–	Moderate None	Early flares scattered but target well illuminated from Zero + 10 mins. Most blobs dropped close to aiming point.
16/17 Sept Essen	3	12 aircraft at Zero hour	4 aircraft 4 x 250lb	Target	Moderate None	One finder dropped stick on Gee over S Essen and river and then marker flare over target. 3 illuminators then dropped flares over aiming point and the 3 blobs were dropped on target. 2 other sticks of flares dropped but wide of target.
19/20 Sept Munich	–	11 aircraft at Zero hour 11 ➡	11 aircraft 6 x 250lb	Last Turning Point	Good Medium	All aircraft late but target illuminated from Zero + 10 mins. Some early flares about 5 mls SW of target. Most blobs scattered over built-up area of city but 1 dropped 4mls W in open country.

For explanation of columns see page 234.

...rce Reports on ...er Technique	Attack of Main Force 10	Photographs Expected 11	Photographs Obtained 12	Effect on Main Force Results 13	Reason for Failure or Partial Failure 14	P.R.U. Results 15
	Scattered	(10%)	0%	None	Weather. Inexperience of Pathfinder crews. Finder flares not well enough placed.	–
	Mainly scattered but some concentrated about 5 mls N of target. At least 1 aircraft bombed target.	0%	0%	None	Weather.	Area of 4 acres devastated by fire.
...t very distinctive	Moderate concentration of bombing centred 1½ mls S of aiming point. Much scatter by remainder with some on decoys.	(25%)	24%	None	Probably too few finders	Scattered damage chiefly in S half of city.
...tinctive and useful. ...ares very useful.	Heavy attack centred about 1½ mls S of aiming point.	(30%)	53%	Improved	–	Considerable scattered damage throughout city.
...d marker flares very	Very heavy attack on Saarlautern.	40%	0%	Diverted	Too few flares. Error of judgement by one crew.	Many scattered incidents on edge of town and in Fraulautern. Rest of town not covered.
...d marker flares very	Very heavy attack but centred about 2mls W of aiming point. Some aircraft up to 4 mls W of aiming point on inland port.	35%	44%	Improved	–	Very heavy damage particularly in indutrial district and docks W of town. 260 acres devastated.
...specially markers very Sticks of I.B. not effec-	Main weight of attack around aiming point, but some scatter to SW and SE up to 5 mls away.	40%	58%	Improved	–	Very heavy damage throughout city.
...uite useful but scatter ...effectiveness.	Attack rather scattered to S and W of aiming point up to 5 mls. distance.	35%	32%	None	Too few flares at any one time.	Scattered items of damage some important, chiefly in S half of town.
	Considerable proportion of main force bombed near Russelsheim. Remainder scattered.	20%	1%	Diverted	Weather. Early flares not well enough placed.	Number of incidents at Russelsheim some in town and some in Opel Works.
...fective. Blobs not very ...e. Burst of 1000lb I.B. ...e, but no permanent	Good concentration of bombing around aiming point but considerable scatter to W, some on Neuss and some in open country. Flares dropped by enemy may have caused this. Few aircraft 17 mls off target.	20%	42%	Improved	–	Very heavy damage including some important industrial incidents. 120 acres devastated. Not much damage in Neuss.
...fective. Blobs not very ...e. Burst of 4000lb I.B. ...e, but no permanent	Only 5 Group Lancasters attacked with Pathfinders. Rest of Main Force 1 hr later. Most Lancasters attacked near aiming point but some near blobs dropped wide. Remainder of Main Force in target area but somewhat scattered.	20%	27%	Improved	Error of judgement by 2 crews.	Cover incomplete but considerable damage seen including some L. Focke-Wulf Works.
...fective. Blobs not very ...e.	Good concentration of bombing near aiming point but some scatter in suburbs to N and W.	20%	39%	Improved	–	–
...nd blobs useful to some ...ome confusion caused by ...ares as Main Force had ...told they were to be used.	Small proportion of Main Force bombed target but majority scattered, mainly to NW between 2 and 8 mls off. Some were confused by flares dropped by the enemy.	10%	21%	Improved	Too few Pathfinder aircraft particularly too few finders.	No cover available. Reports of fires by crews who took photographs of target area suggest this was most successful raid yet on Essen.
...fective but blobs too	Somewhat scattered but falling mainly between aiming point and a point about 5 mls W of it.	(35%)	42%	(None)	Error of judgement by 1 crew. Blobs not large enough.	No. of important incidents of damage in city but no large areas of devastation.

231

Date and Target 1	F 2	Illuminators 3	Ground Markers 4	Marker Flares 5	Weather and Moon 6	Execution of Pathfinder Technique 7	Success Pathfinde 8
		Planned Pathfinder Technique					
19/20 Sept Saarbrücken	–	9 aircraft at Zero hour 7 ➡	7 aircraft 6 x 250lb	–	Moderate Medium	Target not located. Flares scattered. Very few blobs dropped.	Failure
2/3 Oct Krefeld	4	14 aircraft at Zero hour	4 aircraft 12, 10 x 250lb	–	Moderate None	Only 1 finder on time. Most illuminators dropped flares before identifying target with certainty. A few dropped flares in single bundles whilst searching and one of these found and illuminated target. Most blobs not on target.	Partially S
5/6 Oct Aachen	8	9 aircraft at Zero hour	6 aircraft 15 x 250lb	–	Bad None	Only 1 finder reached target owing to various mishaps. Rest of Pathfinders unable to locate target. A number released flares and blobs near Mechelen, 18 mls NW of target in open country.	Wrong Ta
6/7 Oct Osnabruck	8	12 aircraft at Zero hour	–	Last Turning Point & Coast	Moderate None	Dummer See well marked. Flares over Osnabruck always rather scattered and some dropped short.	Successfu
13/14 Oct Kiel	10	12 aircraft at Zero hour 9 ➡	9 aircraft 1 x 4000lb	Last Turning Point	Good None	Selenter See well marked. Few early sticks of flares rather wide but target well illuminated from Zero + 5 mins. All 4000lb I.B. dropped on town but rather scattered.	Successfu
15/16 Oct Cologne	9	11 aircraft at Zero hour	3 aircraft 2 x 4000lb	–	Moderate Medium	Finder flares promptly released but scattered and S of target. Navigation very difficult owing to very short range of Gee and high wind. Illuminators unable to pin-point by finder flares. Some dropped flares in scattered positions.	Failure
9/10 Nov Hamburg	12	18 aircraft, 6 at Zero, 3 at Zero +5, +10, +15, 2 at Zero +20	–	Last Turning Point	Bad None	No aircraft located target. Sudden change of wind, not forecast, blew most aircraft well south of track.	Failure

Attacks on Italy

Date and Target 1	F 2	Illuminators 3	Ground Markers 4	Marker Flares 5	Weather and Moon 6	Execution of Pathfinder Technique 7	Success Pathfinder 8
22/23 Oct Genoa	–	8 aircraft at Zero hour	–	–	Good Bright	Flares released punctually over target which was well illuminated.	Successfu
23/24 Oct Genoa	–	8 aircraft at Zero hour	–	–	Bad Bright	A few Pathfinders claim to have released their flares over Genoa, but there is no evidence whether they did. 1 released flares over Turin.	Failure
24/25 Oct Milan	–	15 aircraft 9 at Zero hour 6 at Zero +10	–	Last Turning Point	Bad Bright	Target not located and most aircraft brought flares back.	Failure
6/7 Nov Genoa	–	14 aircraft	–	Target	Good None	Target well illuminated on time but flares rather to east of aiming point. Marker flares dropped rather east also.	Successful
7/8 Nov Genoa	–	22 aircraft 10 at Zero –1 4 at Zero +5, +10, +15	–	–	Good None	Target well illuminated from Zero hour to Zero + 20 mins. All flares well placed.	Successfu
13/14 Nov Genoa	–	15 aircraft 6 at Zero hour 3 at Zero +4, +8, +12	–	–	Good None	Target well illuminated from Zero hour to Zero + 15 mins. All flares well placed.	Successfu
15/16 Nov Genoa	–	14 aircraft 9 at Zero hour 2 at Zero +5 3 at Zero +12	–	Target	Good Medium	Target well illuminated by accurately placed flares at Zero hour but illumination rapidly became thin. This was owing to cancellation of 156 Squadron.	Successfu
18/19 Nov Turin	6	15 aircraft 1 ➡ 3 at Zero hour 2 at Zero +5, +10, +15, +20, +25, +30	1 aircraft 1 x 4000lb	Target	Good Bright	Finder aircraft late owing to inaccurate forecast winds. Illuminators found and lit up target without them. 4000lb I.B. dropped on target.	Successful
20/21 Nov Turin	–	21 aircraft 9 at Zero 1 at Zero +4, +6, +8, +10, +12, +14, +16, +18, +20, +22, +24, +26	–	–	Good Bright	Target illuminated by well placed flares from Zero hour to Zero + 30 mins with a few gaps owing to slight inaccuracies of timing.	Successful

ce Reports on r Technique	Attack of Main Force 10	Photographs Expected 11	Photographs Obtained 12	Effect on Main Force Results 13	Reason for Failure or Partial Failure 14	P.R.U. Results 15
	Main attack between 2 and 6 mls W and SW of target.	25%	31%	None	Too few Pathfinders and weather.	–
	Attack scattered, but a small proportion in target area.	15%	19%	None	Too few finders. Finders late.	–
	Generally scattered. A few aircraft near Aachen but a considerable number in open country near Mechelen.	5%	7%	Diverted	Weather. Arrival of only 1 finder.	–
See flares very useful. er target effective.	Some of Main Force bombed short but a large proportion were close to aiming point but slightly to the east.	15%	42%	Improved	–	Many heavy incidents but no large areas of devastation
See flares very useful. er target not very effective smoke screen. Bursts of B. distinctive but no t mark made.	Some aircraft on town but majority centred about 4 mls SE in open country.	40%	25%	None	Flares not precise enough for heavily defended tar- get with smoke screen. 4000lb I.Bs ineffective as ground markers.	Scattered damage in town but not on a large scale.
	Scattered, within a small aggregation about 10 mls SW of aiming point.	7.5%	0%	None	Finder flares not well enough placed owing to navigation not being suffi- ciently accurate. Weather.	–
	Widely scattered.	0%	–	None	Weather.	–
	Average	21%	24%			
eful to first aircraft, but late to benefit.	Heavy and well localised attack.	75%+	89%	*	–	Very heavy damage in city.
	Some on Savona. Rest scattered. Possibly a few on Genoa.	0%	0%	None	Weather.	–
	Most bombed on glow of fires on clouds. Probably fires started in Milan in dusk attack.	0%	–	None	Weather.	–
ective but markers over- d by coloured Italian flak.	Heavy attack centred about 1½ miles E of aiming point.	65%+	80%	*	–	Heavy damage but mainly in east part of city.
ective.	Heavy and well placed attack but a small amount of scatter up to 2½ mls E.	65%+	80%	*	–	Heavy damage.
ective.	Heavy and well placed attack.	65%+	89%	*	–	Heavy damage.
ective.	Heavy and well placed attack.	75%+	91%	*	–	Heavy damage.
ective.	Heavy attack but mostly W and SW of aiming point.	*	79%	*	–	Many items of damage but large areas of devastation.
ective.	Heavy attack but rather more scatter than previous night.	*	67%	*	–	Heavy damage includ- ing many industrial items.

The following notes are given to supplement the headings of the columns when these are not self-explanatory.

Column Explanation

2   In this column the number of aircraft detailed as finders is given. These aircraft drop long sticks of flares across the target area at the beginning of the attack.

3   The number of aircraft detailed to illuminate the target by short sticks of flares and their briefed times are given in this column. A figure on the right hand side with an arrow pointing to column 4 indicates that this number of illuminators also acted as ground markers.

4   The number of aircraft dropping ground markers, and the incendiary loads which they carried for this purpose, are given in this column. The total number of 4,000lb incendiary bombs used is indicated by a figure in brackets. These loads were dropped as salvos except when otherwise stated. (4,000lb incendiary is a 4,000lb bomb case containing 2,700lb incendiary mix)

An underline in column 3 or 4 indicates whether the main method of target indication was illumination or ground marking.

5   The places at which coloured marker flares were to be dropped are given in this column.

6   'Good', 'Moderate' and 'Bad' weather is according to official definition. The state of the moon is given below that of the weather.

11, 12   In these columns the % of photographs taken with bombing and showing ground detail which have been plotted within three miles of the aiming point, is given. The expectation figure in column 11 is based on pre-PFF results.

Figures in brackets are based on very scanty data.

+   Based on attacks on Lübeck and Rostock.

*   No estimate possible.

APPENDIX H

IDENTIFICATION MARKERS AND BOMBS

CANDLE, AIRCRAFT, TI, BOMB, TYPE H
Red to yellow, red to green, or yellow to green

Introduction

1. The Type H candles are change colour candles which are similar in construction but contain different flare pellets. Each candle contains pellets to give two different colours and the colours are arranged to show alternately. A candle contains either red and yellow, red and green, or yellow and green flare pellets. Each pellet gives an illumination for a period of 15secs. and the duration of illumination of a candle is approximately $5^{1}/_{2}$ min. During this period the colour of the illumination changes approximately every 15secs.

General description

2. The Type H double length change colour candle is approximately 23.3in long and 1.8in in diameter. It consists of two cylindrical candle cases joined end to end, each case containing 11 flare pellets. The joint is reinforced with a tinplate sleeve about 8in long, and a turn of calico is glued to the outside of the candle. The lower end of the candle case (see *fig. 1*) is protected by a tinplate

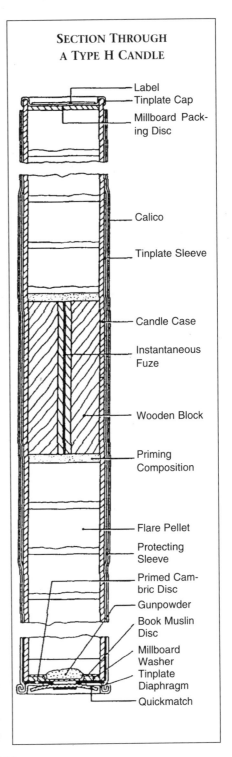

SECTION THROUGH A TYPE H CANDLE

- Label
- Tinplate Cap
- Millboard Packing Disc
- Calico
- Tinplate Sleeve
- Candle Case
- Instantaneous Fuze
- Wooden Block
- Priming Composition
- Flare Pellet
- Protecting Sleeve
- Primed Cambric Disc
- Gunpowder
- Book Muslin Disc
- Millboard Washer
- Tinplate Diaphragm
- Quickmatch

235

diaphragm secured to a protecting sleeve which consists of a tinplate cylinder. This sleeve is to prevent damage to the candle on impact. The top of the candle case is closed by a millboard packing disc and a tinplate cap.

3. Placed loosely under the tinplate diaphragm is a primed cambric disc slit in two places to take a short length of quickmatch, the ends of which project through a hole in the tinplate diaphragm and are secured to its outside edges. The flash from the quick match fires a small quantity of gunpowder priming held in place by a book muslin disc and a millboard washer.

4. The primings ignite the first flare pellet and thereafter the pellets ignite consecutively until the first 11 pellets have burnt. Above the 11th pellet is a small quantity of priming composition which, when ignited by the 11th pellet, fires a length of instantaneous fuze passing through a hole in a cylindrical wooden block. This wooden block is positioned centrally in the candle to strengthen it where the two candle cases abut. Another small quantity of priming composition above the wooden block is ignited by the flash from the instantaneous fuze and ignites the adjacent flare pellet. The remaining flare pellets ignite consecutively, each giving the appropriate illumination.

Identification markings
5. A white label is affixed to the top of the tinplate cap and on the label, in black letters, is stated the colours of the illumination given by the candle (red to yellow, yellow to green, or red to green).

[*Reproduced from the pages of contemporary Air Ministry Publications*]

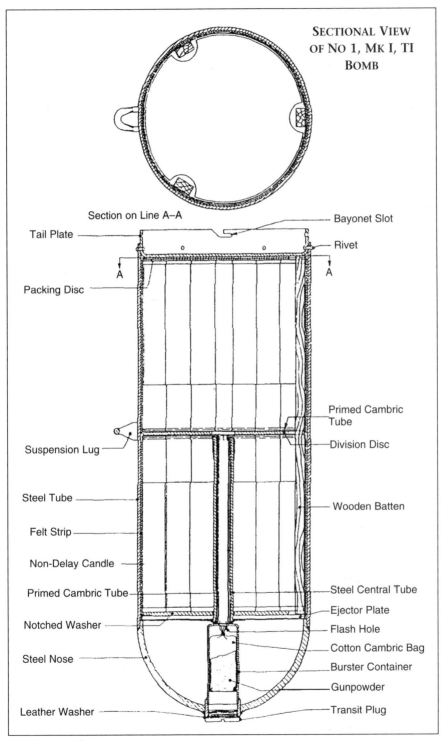

SECTIONAL VIEW OF NO 1, MK I, TI BOMB

Section on Line A–A

Tail Plate

Packing Disc

Suspension Lug

Steel Tube

Felt Strip

Non-Delay Candle

Primed Cambric Tube

Notched Washer

Steel Nose

Leather Washer

Bayonet Slot

Rivet

Primed Cambric Tube

Division Disc

Wooden Batten

Steel Central Tube

Ejector Plate

Flash Hole

Cotton Cambric Bag

Burster Container

Gunpowder

Transit Plug

SECTION THROUGH THE NO 7, MK I, MULTI-FLASH BOMB

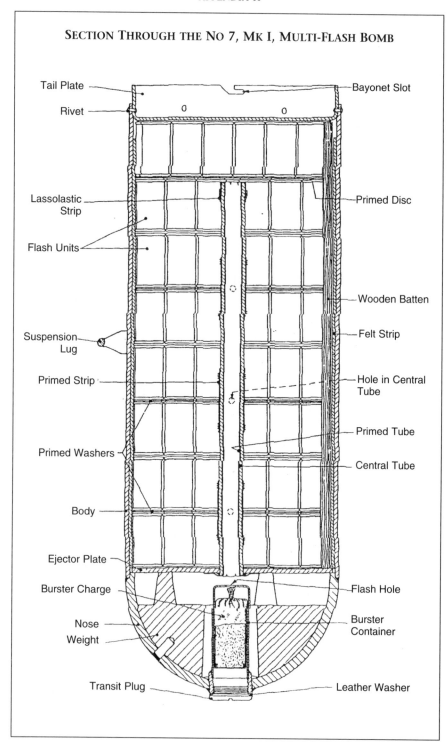

Tail Plate — Bayonet Slot
Rivet —
Lassolastic Strip — Primed Disc
Flash Units —
Wooden Batten
Suspension Lug — Felt Strip
Primed Strip — Hole in Central Tube
Primed Tube
Primed Washers — Central Tube
Body —
Ejector Plate —
Burster Charge — Flash Hole
Nose — Burster Container
Weight —
Transit Plug — Leather Washer

SECTION THROUGH THE NO 8 MK I, SPOTFIRE BOMB

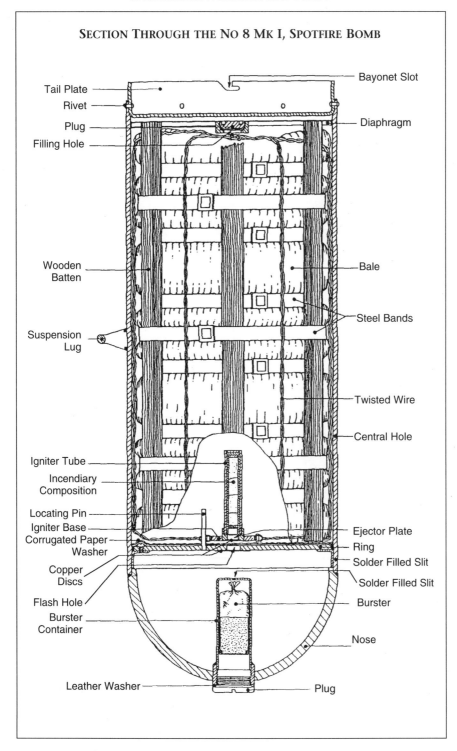

Tail Plate
Rivet
Plug
Filling Hole

Wooden Batten

Suspension Lug

Igniter Tube
Incendiary Composition
Locating Pin
Igniter Base
Corrugated Paper Washer
Copper Discs
Flash Hole
Burster Container
Leather Washer

Bayonet Slot
Diaphragm
Bale
Steel Bands
Twisted Wire
Central Hole
Ejector Plate
Ring
Solder Filled Slit
Solder Filled Slit
Burster
Nose
Plug

BIBLIOGRAPHY

Air Ministry, *Bomber Command*, HMSO 1941

Batt, Reg, *The Radar Army*, Robert Hale 1991

Bennett, Don, *Pathfinder*, Frederick Muller 1958

Bowyer, Michael and Sharp, C. Martin, *Mosquito*, Faber & Faber 1967

Bowyer, Michael, *Military Airfields of East Anglia*, Patrick Stephens 1992

Brookes, Andrew, *Bomber Squadron at War*, Ian Allan 1983

Campbell, James, *Maximum Effort*, Frederick Muller 1957

Campbell, James, *The Bombing of Nuremburg*, Allison and Busby 1973

Cheshire, Leonard, *Bomber Pilot*, Hutchinson 1943

Chorley, W. R. *Royal Air Force Bomber Command Losses 1939–1942*, 3 vols, Midland Counties 1992/94

Falconer, Jonathan, *RAF Bomber Airfields of World War 2*, Ian Allan 1992

Fellowes, P. F. M. *Britain's Wonderful Air Force*, Odhams 1942

Freeman, Roger, *The Mighty Eighth*, Macdonald 1970

Gibson, Guy, *Enemy Coast Ahead*, Michael Joseph 1946

Goulding, J. and Moyes, P. *RAF Bomber Command and its Aircraft 1936–1940*, Ian Allan 1978

Hampton, James, *Selected for Aircrew*, Air Research Publications 1993

Harris, Sir Arthur, *Bomber Offensive*, Collins 1947

Harvey, Maurice, *The Allied Bomber War 1939–1945*, BCA 1992

Hastings, Max, *Bomber Command*, Michael Joseph 1979

Hecks, Karl, *Bombing 1939–1945*, Robert Hale 1990

Hogben, Arthur and MacBean, John, *Bombs Gone*, Patrick Stephens 1990

Irving, David, *The Mare's Nest*, William Kimber 1964

Jackson, A. S. *Pathfinder Bennett*, Terence Dalton 1991

Jackson, Robert, *Storm from the Skies*, Arthur Barker 1974

James, John, *The Paladins*, Macdonald 1990

Jones, R. B. *Most Secret War*, Hamish Hamilton 1978

Lovell, Sir Bernard, *Echoes of War*, Adam Hilger 1991

Mahaddie, Hamish, *Hamish*, Ian Allan 1989

Mason, Francis, *The Avro Lancaster*, Aston Publications 1989

Middlebrook, Martin, *The Berlin Raids*, Viking 1988

Morris, Richard, *Guy Gibson*, Viking 1994

Moyes, Philip, *Bomber Squadrons of the RAF and their Aircraft*, Macdonald and Janes 1964

Musgrave, Gordon, *Pathfinder Force*, Macdonald 1970

Price, Alfred, *Battle over the Reich*, Ian Allan 1976

Renaut, Michael, *Terror by Night*, William Kimber 1982

Richards, Denis, *The Hardest Victory*, Hodder & Stoughton 1994

Rothnie, Niall, *The Baedeker Blitz*, Ian Allan 1992

Royal Aeronautical Society – Manchester Branch, *The Design and Development of the Avro Lancaster*, Finchmark 1991

Saward, Dudley, *Bomber Harris*, Cassell 1984

Spooner, Tony, *Clean Sweep*, Crecy 1994

Terraine, John, *The Right of the Line*, Hodder & Stoughton 1985

Thetford, Owen, *Aircraft of the Royal Air Force from 1918*, Putnam 1970

Williams, Geoffrey, *Flying through Fire*, Alan Sutton 1995

INDEX